Leadership in
Academic Libraries Today

Leadership in Academic Libraries Today

Connecting Theory to Practice

Edited by
Bradford Lee Eden
and
Jody Condit Fagan

ROWMAN & LITTLEFIELD
Lanham • Boulder • New York • Toronto • Plymouth, UK

Published by Rowman & Littlefield
4501 Forbes Boulevard, Suite 200, Lanham, Maryland 20706
www.rowman.com

10 Thornbury Road, Plymouth PL6 7PP, United Kingdom

British Library Cataloguing in Publication Information Available

Library of Congress Cataloging-in-Publication Data

Leadership in academic libraries today : connecting theory to practice / edited by Bradford Lee Eden and Jody Condit Fagan.
pages cm
Includes bibliographical references and index.
ISBN 978-1-4422-3259-4 (cloth : alk. paper) — ISBN 978-1-4422-3260-0 (ebook)
1. Academic libraries—Administration. 2. Academic libraries—Personnel management. 3. Leadership. I. Eden, Bradford Lee, editor of compilation. II. Fagan, Jody Condit, 1976–, editor of compilation.
Z675.U5L37 2014
025.1'977—dc23
2013040884

♾™ The paper used in this publication meets the minimum requirements of American National Standard for Information Sciences Permanence of Paper for Printed Library Materials, ANSI/NISO Z39.48-1992.

Printed in the United States of America

Contents

Introduction

Jody Condit Fagan

Academic librarians live in their research laboratories. Each workday they observe their most commonly studied research subjects—students, faculty, and one another—even as they provide services to support the discovery, delivery, and use of knowledge. Librarians are aware that this environmental immersion skews and limits their perspective when trying to write research questions, design research studies, and interpret results. Nevertheless, upon repeated observations of similar patterns, they are inspired to ponder, investigate, and solve problems.

Although it is not unheard of for academic library practitioners to conduct meticulously designed empirical studies, the bulk of their research is either descriptive or conducted with small samples, or both. The methodology may be considered and described after much of the data has been gathered; the literature review may be written after the results section is nearly complete. These characteristics are only natural in a profession where people work because they love to help people; many would rather spend hours helping freshmen find high-quality sources or developing a finding aid for unique materials than writing a research paper. Librarians are often inspired by their focus on the particulars of the trees; stepping back to see the forest, let alone the ecosystem, may require a concerted effort. Despite what is too often insufficient training or mentoring in research methods, librarians' attempts to connect practice to a larger body of research are laudable.

Librarianship is certainly not the only field experiencing growth amid struggles in an attempt to understand itself better through more systematic research. Social work, education, and sport sciences all feature dedicated, hard-working professionals who may turn to research as a secondary activity. Despite occasional ties to the robust organizational behavior research field (Parry 2011), leadership also falls into this category. Nitin Nohria and Rakesh Khurana note, "Leadership is an elusive construct, riddled with so much ambiguity that it is hard to even define, let alone study systematically" (2010, 5). They acknowledge that most best-selling books on leaders have been written by leadership icons, journalists, and consultants rather than academics (Nohria and Khurana 2010, 5). Leadership researchers do not even agree about the most useful areas to observe. Does one examine the leader, her characteristics, and behaviors (Northouse 2007, 15–90)? Does one examine the interaction between leader influence and organizational culture (Alvesson 2010)? Does one examine followers' thoughts, feelings, and behaviors (Bligh 2010)? Before long, the leadership scholar realizes that the appropriate choice for framing "leadership" investigations depends on how the investigation's results will be used. For pure academics and theorists who want to develop a unified leadership theory or a textbook definition, such a conclusion may be frustrating.

Academic librarians, however, are familiar with selecting a tool based on its purpose. Information types such as newspaper articles, peer-reviewed journals, popular novels, and scholarly monographs all have their places in the world, and the reader's purpose should influence her choice of material. When approaching leadership in academic libraries, therefore, it is important to choose the theoretical leadership frame that best fits the purpose. As Jennifer Platt states, "The development of theory and empirical generalizations is a collective enterprise, and no individual project has to cover all the possible ground in order to make a useful contribution to that process" (Platt 2007, 114).

This book aims to connect leadership theory to library-specific challenges. Its chapters demonstrate the rich variety of approaches one can take to do so. Despite their different views, the benefits of taking the time to investigate existing theories and applying them to the library setting can be seen across the chapters. Such benefits include:

1. The implications of a specific case or individual's perspective can be understood in a larger theoretical context, making observations more illustrative and meaningful.
2. Theories provide a vocabulary and a semantic structure for learning more about specific cases and applications that can then be applied to other cases and applications.
3. Theories focus attention on specific aspects of a situation in a way that reduces the chaos inherent in discussions of abstract concepts.
4. Connecting case studies, surveys, individual analysis, and action research to leadership theories builds a more solid foundation of shared knowledge and understanding, upon which a deeper research agenda, potentially including empirical investigations, could be developed.

In part one, the first three chapters illustrate how creatively combining or expanding existing theories can provide an effective frame for a particular problem. In chapter one, Julie Artman explores the characteristics, behaviors, and expectations of millennials and how transformational leadership can support communication across generations by gazing through the lens of an organic theatre director. Her proposed model of "transformative collaboration" may serve as a possible new leadership style to empower millennial librarians to succeed as leaders or as followers. In chapter two, drawing from path-goal theory, contingency theory, and transformational leadership theories, Susan Parker proposes a new and original leadership model suitable for academic libraries. Her theory of credible optimism incorporates developments in positive psychology (Carroll and Flood 2010) and considers change as a learning process requiring trust between leaders, followers, and library patrons. She illustrates her model using two university library leaders with two very different change agendas at two very different institutions.

In the early 21st century, just as the United States' financial sector demonstrated a need for more ethical leaders, the academic library world has demonstrated a need for leaders who can bring organizations safely through the inevitable transformational changes wrought by technology, connectivity, and the information marketplace. Both Parker and Artman offer new perspectives that may help work toward this goal. Likewise, in chapter three, Deborah Garson and Debra Wallace use Bolman and Deal's four-frame model (2008) to examine two case studies from Harvard in which leaders guided organizations through highly charged change environments. Their chapter illustrates not only how different leadership styles may be appropriate for different situations but how using different frames can help the abstract construct of leadership become visible, illuminating aspects relevant to each situation. The authors discuss how Bolman and Deal's structural and human resource frames, as well as the possibility of combining multiple frames, can inform a leader's selection of strategies for a given situation.

In part two, chapters illustrate how program specifics can influence success. In chapter four, Starr Hoffman explores how mentoring can play a major role in encouraging women and minorities to enter leadership roles in academic libraries. Based on her dissertation research, she provides guidance for mentors and mentees in hopes of stimulating more widespread mentoring of minority and female library leaders. In chapter five, Marta Deyrup focuses specifically on women's leadership roles in a profession historically dominated by women but led by men. She also considers the influence of second wave feminism on female library leaders' perspectives. Based on a survey netting 204 respondents, her observations describe women library administrators' values, experiences, and challenges and perceptions of feminism's effects on academic librarianship.

The three chapters in part three examine how leaders might apply current ideas in the business world to the library setting. In chapter six, Michael Germano presents value co-creation, a concept from the marketing field, as a way to support meaningful learning in library environments. He describes how leadership is essential for fostering organizational culture, changing mind-sets, and implementing programs and services that reflect the ideals of value co-creation. He considers several leadership theories as options for supporting the co-creation dynamic but concludes that a hybrid model of transformational-servant leadership seems to best serve the goal of value co-creation. Dominique Roberts, in chapter seven, explores how Collins's idea of the "hedgehog concept" could be applied to academic libraries and how a leader might guide an organization through identification of defining objectives and measures based on what the library can do for its customers like no other competitor can. These chapters demonstrate how concepts from other disciplines require creative adaptation for the library environment.

In chapter eight, Jason Martin engages with mainstream leadership theories at a broader level, exploring the relationship between organizational culture and leadership in the academic library context. Like leadership, "organizational culture" is an abstract concept, essentially "a pattern of shared basic assumptions that was learned by a group" (Schein 2004, 17). Martin asserts organizational culture is a major force affecting library effectiveness. He also advocates the transformational leadership style as key to fostering cultural change. After reviewing major approaches to organizational culture and their potential application to libraries, Martin presents a research agenda to help the library profession develop a deeper understanding of organizational culture and leadership in academic libraries.

In part four, the two concluding case studies are offered in sequence to contrast how successful leadership can be the result of a formal leader's actions in his positional role or the result of ground-up participatory leadership. Although they focus on different domains, both chapters describe the tension that exists between positional leadership and social constructivism. Kristen Willmott and Andrew Wall's case study in chapter nine of a head librarian's practice of entrepreneurship uses institutional theory to examine how library history and norms influenced his actions and how his actions in turn transformed the library's institutional logic and culture. The lenses of academic restructuring (2000) and academic capitalism (Slaughter and Rhoades 2004) help illustrate, from a top-down view, how actions such as proposing a budget cut, restructuring academic space, and upgrading and integrating technology into library processes created tension between an individual and his social context. By contrast, in chapter ten, Bharat Mehra and Donna Braquet examine a series of events whereby academic library professionals led advocacy efforts to promote social justice. Rather than focusing on formal leaders' activities, they describe how collaborative efforts furthered the adoption and implementation of benefits equality at the University of Tennessee–Knoxville. Whereas Willmott and Wall examined the effects of the entrepreneurial leader's actions on the organization, Mehra and Braquet examined the effects of organizational groups upon academic administrators. They use ideas of participatory leadership (Yukl 2011) and situational leadership (Hersey 1985) and the methods of action research (Greenwood and Levin 1998) to illustrate their experiences with policy development and implementation. They found these perspectives useful in creating action-oriented steps that were effective for navigating academic policies and administrative protocols. Together these chapters demonstrate how leadership is not a two-way street but rather a plaza, where an individual may exert control but the many occupants of the plaza can also take action to effect change.

With the addition of this volume to the literature, academic library practitioners now have a suite of approaches for integrating theory into their research problems. Many statistical techniques (e.g., structural equation modeling, multiple regression) have been developed to test theories; studies that use these techniques can be valuable, but they also require training to be effective. Without discouraging the use of such techniques, this book advocates that theory can also be used to provide frameworks for case studies, surveys, and translations of mainstream theories to the library environment. As Platt reminds us, "Statistical representativeness, important for descriptive purposes, is not a pre-requisite for the testing of theories" (2007, 113). Theory and practice are a dialectic. By allowing the vision and the mind to travel alternatively between the forest and the trees, one begins to build meaningful knowledge about abstract concepts such as leadership.

REFERENCES

Alvesson, Mats. 2010. "Leadership and Organizational Culture." In *The SAGE Handbook of Leadership*, edited by Alan Bryman, David Collinson, Keith Grint, Brad Jackson, and Mary Uhl-Bien, 151–64. Thousand Oaks, CA: Sage.

Bligh, Michelle C. 2010. "Followership and Follower-Centered Approaches." In *The SAGE Handbook of Leadership*, edited by Alan Bryman, David Collinson, Keith Grint, Brad Jackson, and Mary Uhl-Bien, 425–36. Thousand Oaks, CA: Sage.

Bolman, Lee G., and Terrence E. Deal. 2008. *Reframing Organizations: Artistry, Choice, and Leadership*. 4th ed. Jossey-Bass Business & Management Series. San Francisco: Jossey-Bass.

Carroll, Stephen J., and Patrick C. Flood. 2010. *The Persuasive Leader: Lessons from the Arts*. San Francisco: Jossey-Bass.

Greenwood, Davydd, and Morten Levin. 1998. *Introduction to Action Research: Social Research for Social Change*. Thousand Oaks, CA: Sage.

Gumport, Patricia. J. 2000. Academic Restructuring: Organizational Change and Institutional Imperatives. *Higher Education* 39, 67–91.

Hersey, Paul. 1985. *The Situational Leader*. New York: Warner Books.

Nohria, Nitin, and Rakesh Khurana, editors. 2010. *Handbook of Leadership Theory and Practice*. Boston: Harvard Business Press.

Northouse, Peter G. 2007. *Leadership: Theory and Practice*. 4th ed. Thousand Oaks, CA: Sage.

Parry, Ken. 2011. "Leadership and Organization Theory." In *The SAGE Handbook of Leadership*, edited by Alan Bryman, David Collinson, Keith Grint, Brad Jackson, and Mary Uhl-Bien, 53–70. Thousand Oaks, CA: Sage Publications.

Platt, Jennifer. 2007. "Case Study." In *The SAGE Handbook of Social Science Methodology*, edited by William Outhwaite and Stephen P. Turner, 100–18. Los Angeles: Sage.

Schein, Edgar. 2004. *Organizational Culture and Leadership*. San Francisco: Jossey-Bass.

Slaughter, Sheila, and Gary Rhoades. 2004. *Academic Capitalism and the New Economy: Politics, Markets, State and Higher Education*. Baltimore: Johns Hopkins University Press.

Yukl, Gary. 2011. "Contingency Theories of Effective Leadership." In *The Sage Handbook of Leadership*, edited by Alan Bryman, David Collinson, Keith Grint, Brad Jackson, and Mary Uhl-Bien, 286–98. Thousand Oaks, CA: Sage.

Part One

Combining Theory and Practice

Chapter One

Motivating Millennials

The Next Generation of Leaders

Julie Artman

"... leadership does not stifle collaboration, it guides it ... collaboration does not undermine leadership, it enhances it ..."
—Robert Cohen, *Working Together in Theatre*

"... we must work, just work!"
—Anton Chekhov, playwright

The theatre director is not unlike a leader in any organization, including an academic library. The best and most skilled theatre directors cajole, inspire, and always seem to have the heart and mind of each actor in the company. By its nature, theatre is a collaborative art. The director (or leader) brings together the ensemble (or library organization) to create a performance that communicates meaning to an audience, in order to succeed artistically and commercially. The director taps into the creative process and produces her or his best work. The theatre director does not think in terms of a multigenerational cast or design team or company, rather the theatre director observes and responds with flexibility and an adaptable nature, in order to solve problems effectively and efficiently. Creative and successful directors recognize how each individual actor or actress thinks and behaves and how to use this information, respond appropriately, and achieve production objectives and goals. This is an organic and seemingly effortless process on the part of the director. Understanding how to model this leadership style is best explored by way of the transformative and collaborative leader. The transformative and collaborative leader has the skills and abilities to navigate the often unpredictable management of a multigenerational group of librarians, especially millennial librarians under the supervision or leadership of baby-boom ("boomer") or gen-X librarians.

This chapter explores some of the characteristics, workplace behaviors, and expectations of millennials and how these perceptual differences challenge boomer or gen-X leaders. The author will take a closer look at how transformative leadership may strengthen communication and understanding among multigenerational librarians. The author will use the lens of the organic theatre director to provide an alternative model for any library leader to adapt the skills of a collaborative theatre ensemble to the academic library workplace for the purpose of forming a productive and innovative academic library unit. The author proposes the name "transformative collaboration" for this blended leadership style. Finally, the author will consider how millennial librarians may successfully model this leadership style as the next generation of leaders.

TROPHY KIDS IN THE WORKPLACE

Library case studies, literature reviews, and other surveys have described the behaviors and thinking of a multigenerational workforce, including millennials (Smith and Galbraith 2012; Balda and Mora 2011; Myers and Sadaghiani 2010; Kowske, Rasch, and Wiley 2010; Hershatter and Epstein 2010; Deal, Altman, and Rogelberg 2010; Gordon 2010; Penney and Neilson 2010; Young, Hernon, and Powell 2006; Smola and Sutton 2002). Early concerns about millennials entering the workforce centered on a sense of entitlement due to "helicopter" parenting (Alsop 2008, 49–73) and a lack of sustained focus, commitment, and loyalty resulting from being born into a socially networked, Google-powered world of instantaneous gratification (Connaway et al. 2008). Perhaps at the expense of their reputation, millennials are labeled as generation me, trophy kids, or genNet. Large numbers of millennials will continue to enter the workforce until around 2022 (Hershatter and Epstein 2010, 211) and demand attention from library leaders. This generational influx is of special concern as boomer librarians will continue to retire at an increasing rate (Toossi 2005; Horrigan 2004), and millennials will be asked to assume a greater leadership role (Arns and Price 2007). Because millennials are already assuming leadership, management, or supervisory responsibilities in academic libraries (Murray 2011), taking a closer look at workplace behaviors and expectations by millennials is timely.

Notable characteristics detailed for millennials[1] from a comprehensive report by the Pew Research Center (2010) included greater technology and social media use and connection (25) and a greater percentage of them expecting to "switch careers sometime in their work life" (46–47) as compared to gen-Xers or boomers (see figures 1.1 and 1.2). A survey of gen-X academic librarians provided characteristics attributed to effective library leaders, including the ability to acknowledge the work and contributions of others, commitment to development of staff, and support for employees' work/life balance (Young 2007, 154). Interestingly, these same attributes are seen as desirable by millennials, and retention of millennials may additionally include a desire for feedback on request (Young 2007, 164), which may be seen as an opportunity for mentoring and grooming of millennials to lead in the future. As reported by Pew (2010), millennials are accustomed to working collectively, and their "collective interactions" may require "both new collaborative organizations and new expressions of leadership that flex, create, learn, adapt, and serve" (Balda and Mora 2011, 14). The creation of a leadership model that infuses an immediate engagement and achievable yet sustainable organizational goals, and builds on the successes of previous leadership models may be the key to unlock and set free the apprehensions and unrealistic expectations among multigenerational librarians, in order to form a more productive and dynamic academic library team.

TRANSFORMATIVE VERSUS TRANSFORMATIONAL LEADERSHIP

Transformative leaders differ from the more familiar use of transformational leadership in several unique ways. As articulated by Bass and Riggio (2006), transformational leaders exude charisma, and "followers seek to identify with the leader and emulate him or her." Additional behaviors inhabited and exhibited include leadership that "inspires followers with challenge and persuasion, providing both meaning and understanding" and leadership that demonstrates the ability to be "intellectually stimulating, expanding the followers' use of their abilities." Transformational leadership is "individually considerate, providing the follower with support, mentoring, and coaching" (5).

Transformative leadership extends these critical behaviors by emphasizing a style that is predominately an "ethically based leadership model" and wholly "integrates a commitment to values and outcomes by optimizing the long-term interests of stakeholders and society and honoring the moral duties owed by organizations to their stakeholders" (Caldwell et al. 2012, 176). Due to an increasing cynicism toward the trustworthiness of leadership in a time of crisis in today's uncertain marketplace, Caldwell et al. (2012) created a blended leadership style to provide a fresh perspective on the transformational model. This new model presented critical ethical attributes from several leadership models[2] and offered performance indicators, including: passionate commitment, deep personal humility, commitment to the welfare of the organization, continual learning, empowering others, and personal example

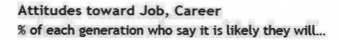

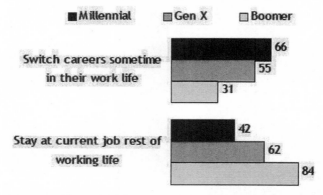

Note: Based on those who are employed full time or part time.

PewResearchCenter

Figure 1.1.   Copyright Pew Research Center, Social & Demographic Trends Project, Millennials: Confident, Connected, and Open to Change. www.pewsocialtrends.org/2010/02/24/millennials-confident-connected-open-to-change/.

(177–81). Transformative leadership seeks to integrate a moral foundation in order to "articulate a clear and compelling set of moral principles . . . creating highly committed team members" (Caldwell et al. 2012, 178). Interestingly, millennials consider service to others a favorable attribute to possess and often volunteer (Pew 2010), which correlates to the transformative leadership model. Leadership that values service and "giving back" to those inside and outside the organization is highly desirable and attractive to millennials. Transformational and transformative leadership are closely linked in attributes, with transformative leaders described in terms of responding to workplace challenges with an immediacy and open communication style that may ultimately support the retention of millennials. Additionally, the transformative leader is a creative force for powerful organizational growth and change (Jones, Harris, and Santana 2008) and leads with an authenticity that can be trusted (Avolio 2010) by millennials seeking transparent communication. Millennials may also be seeking a "rewards remix" that emphasizes flexible work arrangements, or other work-life balance considerations, instead of only monetary incentives (Hewlett, Sherbin, and Sumberg 2009, 72). Millennials may find more in common and feel more energized by an environment that supports organizational growth and promotes positive change, rather

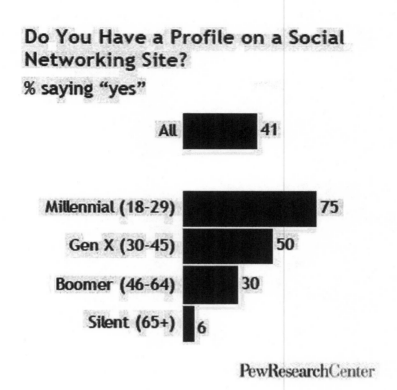

Do You Have a Profile on a Social Networking Site?
% saying "yes"

All — 41

Millennial (18-29) — 75

Gen X (30-45) — 50

Boomer (46-64) — 30

Silent (65+) — 6

PewResearchCenter

Figure 1.2. Copyright Pew Research Center, Social & Demographic Trends Project, Millennials: Confident, Connected, and Open to Change.
www.pewsocialtrends.org/2010/02/24/millennials-confident-connected-open-to-change/.

than organizations embedded in past practices that may no longer serve current needs and expectations.

The rejuvenation of a leadership style that acknowledges and tolerates ambiguity, encourages contextual-relational solutions, and uses creativity to navigate the edge between order and disorder is necessary to challenge other methods that may be unsustainable in a multigenerational and potentially globally connected workplace (Montuori 2010). Certainly, the academic library of the 21st century may be poised to position itself as a contributing partner with the university, in support of educational global connectivity and in order to promote its own successful operational and academic model, whereby leaders and followers become authentic collaborators in order to achieve institutional goals together (Bolman and Gallos 2011). Therefore, transformative collaboration may express a holistic and, more importantly, an organic approach to leadership that mixes well with the workplace behaviors and expectations of millennials or any multigenerational group. According to transformative studies educator Montuori (2010), "Transformative Leadership explores the immensely generative potential in metaphors and exemplars from the arts, which often provide a radically different approach" (8). As a theatre director, the author has observed that these transformative indicators correlate nicely with the theatre director's collaborative leadership style, and the author suggests a symbiotic library leadership model for the management of a multigenerational library and suggests the name of transformative collaboration.

TRANSFORMATIVE COLLABORATION IN THE ARTS

Transformative collaboration leadership skills may best be demonstrated by the organic theatre director, especially when juxtaposed against an auteur[3] leader—one who inhabits the top-down, purely hierarchical structured view of leadership. The theatre director as complete auteur uses a static approach by extreme control of the stage movements of the actors (i.e., blocking) and, in a sense, using the actors as puppets to promote his or her singular vision of the play to an audience. The actor's opinion or will is subservient, to the extent of the auteur director dictating how the actor should say his or her lines of dialogue. Individual creativity is stifled, resulting in clichéd and artificial performances. Additionally, an extension of this dictatorial style overshadows individual creative contributions by designers and theatre technicians. Instead of engagement and synergistic interest among the entire ensemble, the actors and the design/technical teams are subordinate to the director's overarching vision. Whether or not the autocratic director's vision has resulted in success in terms of box office and critical reviews, company morale is diminished, and resentment and disloyalty may breed among the entire acting company. Future healthy collaborations and collective harmonies are threatened.

Robert Cohen has seen his share of tyrannical directors in his more than fifty years as an educator and theatre artist. Cohen (2011) learned through experience as a theatre director and leader that collaboration is critical to "attain artistic heights that none could attain independently" (3) and it is these "dynamic and free-flowing collaborations [that] make theatre art successful—not just for the artists involved, but for their audiences as well" (11). Cohen describes the role of the director as providing guidance. The director will "unite and aim" toward a "shared challenge"—the mission; each member of the team is engaged to their "highest point of creativity" (57). Trust and respect provide anchors for building relationships as the director uses a "collaborative voice" (196). Ultimately, the director is directing or guiding "a person: a perceptive, sensate, emotional human being" (142).

And, the successful director "must sensitively balance the desire to be collaborative, approachable, encouraging, protective, receptive, and sharing, on the one hand, with the clear responsibility to be persuasive, authoritative, decisive, and sometimes driving on the other" (140). The successful director is wholly flexible and adaptable, able to provide more direction when necessary and less when desired. Practical strategies and skills to support a collaborative leadership style from the organic director include: energizing the ensemble; balancing idealism and pragmatism; making choices; defining and reaching goals; mediating conflict; and exhibiting confidence and dependability (Knopf 2006, 17–20). Collaboration helps to "create a sense of engagement in the production" that is "satisfying and motivating for those involved" (Kramer and Crespy 2011, 1034). Additionally, Cohen (2011) equated the collaborative director (or leader) with "an authentic force that proves compelling, captivating, and charismatic"; this leader must "inspire without stultifying, must challenge without inhibiting . . . must lead the charge without draining the energies, the talents, the joy, and the commitment of those that follow them" (57). The collaborative director (or leader) inhabits these transformative traits and thus emerges as a transformative collaborator.

Yet, even as theatre creates a dynamic ensemble, there will always be disruptive, uncooperative, or needy actors that may jeopardize positive collaborations. What tools does the organic theatre director possess in her/his toolkit to counter these unproductive behaviors? And, how may we apply these leadership skills to leading millennial librarians or any multigenerational group who may also present difficulties due to communication and attitudinal missteps? The answers are embedded within the unique relationship and interactions that emerge between the director and the actor during the course of developing the actor's character within the world of the play and as part of the ensemble.

Although the director is leading the ensemble, the inclusive and collaborative director knows that he or she is merely one more member of the group. A "collaboration culture in action" begins with a collaborative philosophy to articulate how interactions are to take place, creating a collaborative climate (Kramer and Crespy 2011, 1027–33). Communicating respect for the actor and providing the actor with a trusting environment to explore character and expose emotional vulnerability within the play's demands are, ultimately, the director's goals. The director coaches the actor in hopes that the actor will "own" the performance, making a seamless connection between the actor and the play. The director must "hear" the actor in order to understand and reciprocate a direction that makes sense to the actor, in order to enhance the performance. The director and actor make many choices during the course of rehearsals. The collaborative director uses personalized direction to fit the needs of the individual actor; specific notes and feedback assist the actor when the need arises and allows the actor to explore, create, and polish the performance. The director and actor are comfortable working through ambiguity. The director nurtures and encourages instinct and impulse, eventually honing each actor/character into the overall demands of the play and production goals. The director and the actor work with intention, whether it is an understanding and agreement with the motivations of the actor's character or the direction of the conceptual forces within the play and production. Consequently, the relationship is a positive synergy, and the best collaborations are less about individual ego and more about the good of the ensemble—with an eye toward communicating the overall purpose or "heart" of the play to the audience.

TRANSFORMATIVE COLLABORATION IN THE ACADEMIC LIBRARY

What do millennial librarians need from academic library leadership in order to succeed? How can library leaders use the voice of collaboration and a transformative nature to engage, excite, motivate, and retain millennials? It may begin with seeing millennial librarians with individual needs, not merely responding to collective stereotypic behaviors. Library leaders may, subsequently, be free to discover, discuss, and reciprocate, within a positive and productive feedback loop, the necessary solutions to achieve organizational goals together. The successful leader views each librarian as an individual, as a collaborative director considers each actor in an ensemble: not as inevitably separated by generational differences, but with an opportunity to begin a conversation and rally around a critical purpose, goal, or mission. And, with any new and developing relationship, listening and truly understanding how to provide an environment that encourages a creative and innovative workplace may produce good faith and good works. The demands of a 21st-century academic library with expanding research programs, innovative services to meet faculty and student expectations, and university administrators dealing with limited budgets will require a flexible and adaptable group of librarians, ready to take on any challenge.

Library leaders may have contributed to the myth of generational apprehensions that truly do not have an impact on the inculcation of millennial librarians into an academic library. Perhaps the profession should look beyond these stereotypic generalizations and closely consider the individual career choice and motivation of each librarian entering the library profession with an underlying connection and purpose to serve (similar to the analytical work of the director and actor to "serve" the play). And, the profession should consider a leadership style that taps into what is desired and demanded by university and library administrators in order to create an innovative and forward-thinking workforce, equipped to embrace 21st-century information and research needs desired and demanded by students and faculty alike.

TRANSFORMATIVE COLLABORATION AND THE NEXTGEN LEADERS

Transformative collaboration may indeed help library leaders embrace and discover a comfort with ambiguity and change within a multigenerational workforce. Using key ethical attributes from transformative leadership, library leaders can be the trustworthy, "good people to work with" and report to as highly desired by millennials (Ng, Schweitzer, and Lyons 2010, 286–288), providing a nurturing environment that meets millennial librarian expectations and retention needs (Chaudhuri and Ghosh 2012; Alsop 2008, 97–114). This author's conversations with millennial librarians echo a positive response to leaders who are accessible, authentic, and transparent, and facilitate, mentor, and encourage independence while maintaining clear direction. Leaders who model these encouraging and engaging behaviors may stem negative reactions or counterproductive outcomes from millennials, as a collaborative director uses these skills or tools to do the same with actors. Transformative collaboration invites librarians to share (Cawthorne 2010), become stakeholders and, more importantly, decision makers in the development of library programs and services that will benefit all users. Millennial librarians can begin their leadership path by chairing committees, overseeing task forces, and seeking other leadership developmental opportunities (De-Long 2009, 455). And, it may indeed be that baby boomers, gen-Xers, and millennials are "more similar than different" and consider "the same leadership practices to be important" (Gentry et al. 2011, 45). No matter the generational uniqueness, librarians are all in this together. Successful library leadership must embrace newer forms of leadership practice, including transformative collaboration. In *Reframing Academic Leadership*, Bolman and Gallos (2011) explore the "dramaturgical image" of the academic institution as a theatre and its leaders as artists:

> . . . always on stage, closely observed by their audience. . . . Their success depends on how well their performance conveys the messages and evokes the responses they intend . . . the leader's role is generative, interpretive, and inspirational. . . . Academic administrators who bring the imagination to envision new possibilities and the skills to convey a compelling picture of the future enable others to feel positive and hopeful about their work, their institutions, and its leadership (110–11).

If library leadership is successful, millennial librarians will become empowered and model transformative collaboration as they themselves grow into innovative and creative leaders, and are encouraged to do so.

NOTES

1. The Pew Research Center report defines millennials as those born after 1980; generation X covers those born from 1965 through 1980; and baby boomers were born post–World War II during 1946 to 1964. Findings in this study were the result of a telephone survey in January 2010 with a nationally representative sample of 2,010 adults and an oversample of 830 respondents, ages 18–29. Data from this 2010 survey were supplemented by other Pew Research Center surveys (and census data), including a survey on changing attitudes toward work (October 2009) and a survey on generational differences (July 2009). Millennials: Confident. Connected. Open to Change. http://www.pewsocialtrends.org/2010/02/24/millennials-confident-connected-open-to-change/. © 2010 Pew Research Center, Social & Demographic Trends Project.

2. The leadership models used to form the authors' transformative model were transformational leadership, charismatic leadership, level 5 leadership, principle-centered leadership, servant leadership, and covenantal leadership.

3. Theatre history is rife with the legendary stories of "Czarist" directors from Max Reinhardt (1873–1943) to Vsevolod Meyerhold (1874–1940) to more modern auteur directors such as Tyrone Guthrie (1900–1971), Harold Clurman (1901–1980), and Joshua Logan (1908–1988). In today's theatre, autocratic directors have given way to collaborators with a unique theatrical vision who leave their singular mark nonetheless, and may suggest a transformative leadership style. These contemporary directors include Daniel Sullivan, George C. Wolfe, and Anne Bogart.

REFERENCES

Alsop, Ron. 2008. *The Trophy Kids Grow Up: How the Millennial Generation Is Shaking Up the Workplace.* San Francisco: Jossey-Bass.

Arns, Jennifer Weil, and Carol Price. 2007. "To Market, to Market: The Supervisory Skills and Managerial Competencies Most Valued by New Library Supervisors." *Library Administration & Management* 21 (1): 13–19. http://journals.tdl.org/llm/index.php/llm/article/view/1657/937.

Avolio, Bruce J. 2010. "Pursuing Authentic Leadership Development." In *Handbook of Leadership Theory and Practice*, edited by Nitin Nohria and Rakesh Khurana, 739–68. Boston: Harvard Business School Publishing Corp.

Balda, Janis Bragan, and Fernando Mora. 2011. "Adapting Leadership Theory and Practice for the Networked, Millennial Generation." *Journal of Leadership Studies* 5 (3): 13–24. doi:10.1002/jls.20229.

Bass, Bernard M., and Ronald E. Riggio. 2006. *Transformational Leadership.* 2nd ed. Mahwah, NJ: Lawrence Erlbaum.

Bolman, Lee G., and Joan V. Gallos. 2011. *Reframing Academic Leadership.* San Francisco: Jossey-Bass.

Caldwell, Cam, Rolf D. Dixon, Larry A. Floyd, Joe Chaudoin, Jonathan Post, and Gaynor Cheokas. 2012. "Transformative Leadership: Achieving Unparalleled Excellence." *Journal of Business Ethics* 109: 175–87. doi:10.1007/s10551-011-1116-2.

Cawthorne, Jon E. 2010. "Leading from the Middle of the Organization: An Examination of Shared Leadership in Academic Libraries." *The Journal of Academic Librarianship* 36 (2): 151–57. doi:10.1016/j.acalib.2010.01.006.

Chaudhuri, Sanghamitra, and Rajashi Ghosh. 2012. "Reverse Mentoring: A Social Exchange Tool for Keeping the Boomers Engaged and Millennials Committed." *Human Resource Development Review* 11 (1): 55–76. doi:10.1177/1534484311417562.

Cohen, Robert. 2011. *Working Together in Theatre: Collaboration and Leadership.* New York: Palgrave Macmillan.

Connaway, Lynn Silipigni, Marie L. Radford, Timothy J. Dickey, Jocelyn De Angelis Williams, and Patrick Confer. 2008. "Sense-Making and Synchronicity: Information-Seeking Behaviors of Millennials and Baby Boomers." *Libri* 58 (2): 123–35. http://www.librijournal.org/pdf/2008-2pp123-135.pdf.

Deal, Jennifer J., David G. Altman, and Steven G. Rogelberg. 2010. "Millennials at Work: What We Know and What We Need to Do (If Anything)." *Journal of Business and Psychology* 25 (2): 191–99. doi:10.1007/s10869-010-9177-2.

DeLong, Kathleen. 2009. "The Engagement of New Library Professionals in Leadership." *The Journal of Academic Librarianship* 35 (5): 445–56. doi:10.1016/j.acalib.2009.06.006.

Gentry, William A., Tracy L. Griggs, Jennifer J. Deal, Scott P. Mondore, and Brennan D. Cox. 2011. "A Comparison of Generational Differences in Endorsement of Leadership Practices with Actual Leadership Skill Level." *Consulting Psychology Journal: Practice and Research* 63 (1): 39–49. doi:10.1037/a0023015.

Gordon, Shannon. 2010. "Once You Get Them, How Do You Keep Them? Millennial Librarians at Work." *New Library World* 111 (9): 391–98. doi:10.1108/03074801011089314.

Hershatter, Andrea, and Molly Epstein. 2010. "Millennials and the World of Work: An Organization and Management Perspective." *Journal of Business and Psychology* 25 (2): 211–23. doi:10.1007/s10869-010-9160-y.

Hewlett, Sylvia Ann, Laura Sherbin, and Karen Sumberg. 2009. "How Gen Y & Boomers Will Reshape Your Agenda." *Harvard Business Review* 87 (7/8): 71–76.

Horrigan, Michael W. 2004. "Employment Projections to 2012: Concepts and Context." *Monthly Labor Review* (February): 3–22.

Jones, Beverly, Marilyn E. Harris, and Matias Santana. 2008. "Mastering Developing New Leadership for Transformative Change." *Journal of Academy of Business and Economics* 8 (2): 66–74.

Knopf, Robert. 2006. *The Director as Collaborator.* Boston: Pearson Education.

Kowske, Brenda J., Rena Rasch, and Jack Wiley. 2010. "Millennials' (Lack of) Attitude Problem: An Empirical Examination of Generational Effects on Work Attitudes." *Journal of Business and Psychology* 25 (2): 265–79. doi:10.1007/s10869-010-9171-8.

Kramer, Michael W., and David A. Crespy. 2011. "Communicating Collaborative Leadership." *The Leadership Quarterly* 22 (5): 1024–37. doi:10.1016/j.leaqua.2011.07.021.

Montuori, Alfonso. 2010. "Transformative Leadership for the 21st Century: Reflections on the Design of a Graduate Leadership Curriculum." *ReVision* 30 (3/4): 4–14.

Murray, Adam. 2011. "Mind the Gap: Technology, Millennial Leadership and the Cross-Generational Workforce." *The Australian Library Journal* 60 (1): 54–65.

Myers, Karen K., and Kamyab Sadaghiani. 2010. "Millennials in the Workplace: A Communication Perspective on Millennials' Organizational Relationships and Performance." *Journal of Business and Psychology* 25 (2): 225–38. doi:10.1007/s10869-010-9172-7.

Ng, Eddy S. W., Linda Schweitzer, and Sean T. Lyons. 2010. "New Generation, Great Expectations: A Field Study of the Millennial Generation." *Journal of Business and Psychology* 25 (2): 281–92. doi:10.1007/s10869-010-9159-4.

Penney, Sherry H., and Patricia Akemi Neilson. 2010. "The View from Generation X: Organizations Need to Change." In *Next Generation Leadership: Insights from Emerging Leaders*, 119–139. New York: Palgrave Macmillan.

Pew Research Center. 2010. *Millennials: Confident. Connected. Open to Change.* http://www.pewsocialtrends.org/2010/02/24/millennials-confident-connected-open-to-change/.

Smith, Sara D., and Quinn Galbraith. 2012. "Motivating Millennials: Improving Practices in Recruiting, Retaining, and Motivating Younger Library Staff." *The Journal of Academic Librarianship* 38 (3): 135–44. doi:10.1016/j.acalib.2012.02.008.

Smola, Karen Wey, and Charlotte D. Sutton. 2002. "Generational Differences: Revisiting Generational Work Values for the New Millennium." *Journal of Organizational Behavior* 23 (4): 363–82. doi:10.1002/job.147.

Toossi, Mitra. 2005. "Labor Force Projections to 2014: Retiring Boomers." *Monthly Labor Review* (November): 25–44.

Young, Arthur P. 2007. "Gen-Xers and Millennials Join the Library Express." In *Making a Difference: Leadership and Academic Libraries*, edited by Peter Hernon and Nancy Rossiter, 143–67. Westport, CT: Libraries Unlimited.

Young, Arthur P., Peter Hernon, and Ronald R. Powell. 2006. "Attributes of Academic Library Leadership: An Exploratory Study of Some Gen-Xers." *The Journal of Academic Librarianship* 32 (5): 489–502. doi:10.1016/j.acalib.2006.05.008.

Chapter Two

Positive Leadership in Libraries

The Rise of the Credible Optimist

Susan E. Parker

Libraries are at the center of a whirlwind of change in higher education. All of higher education is facing the disruptive influence of challenges to sustainable funding models as well as public demands for increased accountability, transparency, and demonstration of value. Libraries in institutions of higher learning must change to address and incorporate additional developments, such as the growing importance of digital scholarship, digital resources, and mobile technologies; new modes of research and publishing; and new ways of teaching. These developments have placed pressure on the traditional and familiar functions of libraries as reliable book repositories and the quiet cathedrals of academe. Indeed, "librarians are enmeshed in a struggle for a workable vision of a future for their institutions" (Weinberger 2012, xi).

A traditional, sentimental view of academic libraries has never accurately reflected their myriad activities, and it has given scant credit to the philosophies, education, and leadership talent required of library leaders. Now as never before, libraries in universities and colleges must demonstrate their value to their institutions' core enterprises. They require knowledgeable and persuasive leaders to succeed. These leaders will enhance the quality of their contributions when they are familiar with different leadership theories. The new model of the credible optimist that is introduced in this chapter will add to that understanding.

Library leaders are responsible for helping to raise awareness among those who use and fund libraries and for helping stakeholders understand how libraries continue to create significant value with continued financial and other institutional support. Library leaders have urged libraries to keep pace with change; they also are responsible for leading in their institutions. The academic library "must chart its future in alignment with the direction of learning" (Curzon 2010, 1). As libraries adopt new roles and develop new partnerships with faculty and students, they will continue to deliver value as they always have. They will use their familiar roles and historical strengths as well: preserving knowledge; providing expertise; providing and organizing content; and providing both cyber and physical infrastructures for learning, research, and collaboration. Library leaders understand the library's traditional role will not disappear but also know libraries will adapt and change in an evolutionary fashion. Growth and change is necessary, but so is wisdom balanced with tradition, lest we "burn the great library at Alexandria" only for future generations to find they must rebuild it (Strong 2010).

The late twentieth and early twenty-first centuries have seen an increase of professional administrators in higher education, as additional expertise is needed to meet the increasing demands and requirements for formalized accountability and evidence of institutional value. The analysis of institutional data has become more frequent, and everything from grant applications and reports to enrollment data and spending records must be made transparent and ready for audit. Even private universities must supply more data to participate in state and federal programs. These demands vastly increase universities' administrative workload.

As units of their institutions, libraries are responsible for adhering to laws and regulations and reporting on their efforts to hire, evaluate, and promote staff; to manage, categorize, and spend funds appropriately; to account accurately for all expenditures; and to provide information to outsiders and insiders who audit all of these activities. An increase in litigation has resulted in greater pressure to conform to policies that limit risk and exposure, further necessitating the use of staff members with expertise in counting and measuring, physically examining furniture and hardware, balancing and opening the financial books of the library, and accounting for all purchases, including books and licenses. The Sarbanes-Oxley Act, a response to corporate fraud symbolized by the failure of Enron, requires the head of any enterprise, including a university, to sign a legally binding statement verifying that the library's financial reports are accurate (Sarbanes-Oxley Act 2002). In universities, the deans and directors of colleges and the library must attest to a similar verification of their unit's budget.

Bolman and Gallos (2011) describe the significant differences between for-profit businesses that develop, produce, and sell products, and nonprofit higher education, which aims to increase knowledge and support the development of personal selfhood. Nevertheless, the effort to commodify education is well underway. Legislators and politicians have called for higher education to operate faster and more nimbly, to behave more like businesses, and to give up arcane and sometimes slow ways of operating (Leveille 2005).

Recent legislation in Minnesota required the University of Minnesota to develop a plan for administrative cost-cutting to qualify for new funding (Killey and Davis 2013), and in California, Governor Jerry Brown has actively insisted the state's universities must reign in rising costs that "threaten affordability and quality" (Siders 2013).

Bad publicity from very public mistakes in higher education administration has also undermined public confidence and spread mistrust and cynicism about institutions. Two examples follow.

The 2012 effort to unseat the University of Virginia's president was done in the name of business efficiency. The business professionals who were appointed as regents of the university convinced themselves the university was not capitalizing on the boon of online education. Labeling the president an "incrementalist" who had not led the university quickly enough in the direction of a market-driven opportunity, they convinced the board to agree to dismiss her. The subsequent revolt by the faculty and the return of the president to office showed the balancing power of the university's model of shared governance. Boards of trustees or regents who are impatient with faculty governance and attempt to override this model will continue to meet internal resistance to corporatizing the governance model for universities (Rice 2012).

At another major cultural institution, the New York Public Library, leaders failed to anticipate the public outcries and protests against their well-thought-out plans for emptying the seven-story book stacks, storing most of the books off-site, and renovating the space gained to incorporate a new public library branch within the iconic white marble building located on Fifth Avenue. In an account detailing this controversy, Paul Goldberger reported, "The board members were startled to discover that they were not being hailed for saving the library. They were being accused of destroying it" (2012, 182).

These are cautionary tales for university and library leaders. They demonstrate a need for strong leaders who can persuasively make the case for change to all stakeholders and who are able to put their personal energy and commitment into efforts to convince librarians and library staff to adopt their optimism about the future. Optimism tempered with pragmatism is essential to keep cynicism from poisoning efforts to solve problems and to keep pessimists from leading institutions into disarray (Horgan 2012). This chapter will review some existing leadership theories in the academic library context, propose a new theory, and illustrate the theory with two case studies.

ACADEMIC LIBRARY ORGANIZATIONS AND LEADERSHIP

There is very little recorded analysis of the operation of libraries as organizations, although there is plenty to read regarding the history and operation of particular libraries. Library history is important, but an examination of the relationship between the history of individual libraries and their organizational cultures is in need of more exploration. Along with a growing interest in leadership studies in general, there has been a parallel interest in applying leadership studies to libraries.

In the past decade, the publication of articles by and for librarians about the leadership and management of libraries and library organizations has grown markedly. There have also been studies attempting to identify library leadership traits. Hopper (2011) presented case studies of two different academic libraries, one with an internally recruited leader and one with an externally recruited leader. This examination revealed that "The element having the greatest impact upon the recruitment of a successor to a departed academic library director is university executive administration's perception of library conditions at the time of and just prior to the director's departure" (Hopper 2011, 236). Hernon and Schwartz's research agenda for managerial leadership in academic libraries outlined topics for study, including organizational transformation, leader actions and accomplishments, and leaders themselves, including their traits and limitations (2008). They also pointed to the need to connect leadership and diversity, investigate talent management, and study leaders' familiarity with different leadership theories (Hernon and Schwartz 2008). In a dynamic environment requiring change management, libraries need leaders who can create a vision, energize stakeholders into taking action, and create an organizational climate where employees from all backgrounds are valued. Such leaders demonstrate positive leadership and understand their impact on others. Emotional intelligence, distributed leadership, and resonant leadership were found to be highly applicable to success among leaders surveyed in a number of studies (Hernon, Giesecke, and Alire 2008).

There are many leadership theories, and new ones seem to appear frequently. They have evolved and multiplied as the study of leadership has grown. These theories share many similarities. There is no shortage of research on leadership effectiveness, but no agreement on criteria for measuring it exists. Leadership theories are organized around a number of variables for measurement or analysis: traits, behaviors, power and influence, processes, and situations (Yukl 2002).

The following discussion focuses on three of the most important leadership theories. They describe leader behaviors that are most effective for leading change in organizations. They are well-known, well-researched, and well-articulated. These three theories—path-goal theory, contingency theory, and transformational leadership theory—are of particular interest to library leaders because they concern themselves with leaders' behaviors and their influence on organizational change. Their emphasis on leader behaviors connects them to the new model introduced in this chapter, the credible optimist.

Path-Goal Theory

The path-goal leadership theory attempts to explain how leaders' behaviors influence their employees' performance and personal satisfaction (Evans 1970; House 1971). It is based on a theory of motivation known as expectancy theory (Vroom 1964). Path-goal leadership theory identifies the work of leaders as delivering the kind of environment in which workers invest in serious effort because it will produce rewards and outcomes that are valuable to the workers and to the organization (Yukl 2002).

Path-goal theory describes how leaders' behaviors help show the way to a stated goal. This model requires leaders to keep employees' motivation at the forefront of planning (Northouse 2004). Path-goal theory presumes formal power relationships and hierarchical organizational structures are the strongest influences on employee behavior (Northouse 2004).

Four major leader behaviors are fundamental to path-goal theory. *Supportive* leaders promote a positive quality of work life and show concern for employees' needs. *Directive* leaders establish rules, specify job duties, and expect employees to follow them (Yukl 2002). *Achievement-oriented* leaders set high and challenging expectations and express confidence in employees' abilities to meet them, encouraging high work quality (Bandura 1991; House and Mitchell 1974). *Participative* leaders solicit and consider employees' opinions in making decisions. Employee effort and satisfaction are optimized when leaders' behaviors best suit the situation, work tasks, and employees' own personality characteristics or behaviors (House and Mitchell 1974). Therefore, leaders should seek to understand which of their behaviors are most effective in particular situations. For example, when tasks are dangerous or highly stressful, supportive leadership may be most effective (House and Mitchell 1974). When employees are confident in their abilities to do a task, especially if the task itself is pleasant, less leader support and encouragement is required (Bandura 1997).

Libraries exist in a fast-changing world. Path-goal theory could be a valuable tool for libraries when there is an urgent message of change or crisis in the environment. For example, a leader who has to recover a library building or collections from a damaging disaster like a flood or an earthquake might set a particular goal of salvaging books or relocating services and assign related tasks to specific teams or individuals. There may be hard deadlines for counting and describing losses; protocols for removing and packing books for repair may be specified by a vendor for protection of workers' health and safety. This is described in accounts of recovery from two different disasters affecting the libraries at Colorado State University and California State University, Northridge (Alire 2000; Curzon 2000, 2006). Different variables are combined with path-goal theory: leader style, work setting, and worker characteristics. The leader provides the most significant motivating factors by aligning employee needs and expectations, even over time (Northouse 2004). A recovery project, then, would have specific item-ized goals, projects, timelines, and work assignments, and the leader would provide supportive behaviors and frequent acknowledgement and encourage-ment for workers (Alire 2003; Curzon 2006).

Some researchers find limitations to path-goal theory. It may be too sim-ple to explain the wide variety of human motivation of leaders and workers, and that variety makes it difficult to test (Yukl 2002). Path-goal theory never-theless remains important to experts who study leadership because it offers a valuable conceptual frame for the interaction of leaders and workers.

Contingency Theory

Fiedler said, "The effectiveness of a group is contingent upon the relation-ship between leadership style and the degree to which the group situation enables the leader to exert influence" (1967, 15). In the contingency leader-ship model, the leader modifies his or her style, the situation, or the tasks to be completed to improve group performance. Determining the appropriate style requires the leader to understand how certain leadership styles promote success in specific situations. It also requires the leader to be self-aware and to switch stylistic approaches thoughtfully and strategically while always focusing on the needs of the workers (Vroom and Yetton 1973; Rossiter 2007).

Like path-goal theory, contingency leadership theory matches the leader's style with situations and with the quality of the relationship between the leader and employees. The difference between the theories is a matter of emphasis (this will be discussed further in a later section). In a stable situa-tion where tasks are well structured, the leader has more control and gives more directive tasks and instruction, and employees expect the leader to define their work. If the situation's uncertainty level increases, tasks and requirements may become unclear. For example, if an event occurs for which there is no protocol, staff members may hesitate to act, or they may adapt by creating a new protocol. Then the leader has less influence, requiring the leader's response to become more flexible in order to sustain employees' effectiveness (Northouse 2004). The leader will accept a decision made on the fly because it keeps the workflow going smoothly. High-stress condi-tions—including crises, deadlines, and demanding, precise work—require a highly engaged leader. This helps reduce employees' anxiety and improve their self-confidence. It also spreads the burden of difficult, unpleasant, or dangerous work (Fiedler 1967; Sorensen and Goethals 2004).

The utility of contingency leadership theory is well supported by research (Yukl 2002). It was the first theory to emphasize the effect of situations on leaders' behavior (Sorensen and Goethals 2004). In addition, it predicts leader effectiveness and suggests not all leaders will be effective in all situations.

Libraries are under enormous pressure to change their traditional workflows and services to better match all the ways they provide content, access, and expertise today. Some library leaders are more likely to emphasize communication and group-building activities primarily when radical or unexpected change is underway. When stakeholders support a leader's sincerity and his or her ability to overcome a crisis, they are more likely to trust change leadership behaviors; providing structure and stability is an important leader function during a period of adjustment (Fiedler 1967). Leaders use their power to focus stakeholders and sustain their goal orientation, keep communication open, and restructure the situation. In a crisis, leaders can modify their style, but they should put significant effort into actively managing their leadership style. This fits the perspective of contingency leadership theory that context matters greatly: certain leader styles are most effective in specific situations (Fiedler 1967; Northouse 2004).

In a study designed to investigate the application of contingency leadership theory in libraries, Mitchell (1989) surveyed 278 academic library department heads who were responsible for a full range of activities, including acquisitions, collection development, circulation, processing, cataloging, and reference. Mitchell found support for the idea that library work teams are influenced by leaders' behaviors and styles to a certain degree but that the nature of library work and work teams and the motivation of individuals in teams are important variables that interact with both the context and the leaders' style (Mitchell 1989).

Transformational Leadership Theory

The development of transformational leadership theory is described in the classic works of Burns (1978), Bennis and Nanus (1985), Bass (1985), and Bass and Avolio (1990). Transformational leadership theory is quite different than path-goal theory or contingency theory because of the focus on the development of trust between leaders and workers.

Transformational leaders help to mobilize followers by appealing to their values (Burns 1978). They state a clear vision, explain what is needed to attain it, express confidence in the ability of their followers to do this, and empower people to achieve it (Yukl 2002). They are role models; their behavior inspires trust. They "give meaning to organizational life" (Northouse 2004, 198). The mutual engagement of transformational leadership motivates leaders and followers to elevate their relationship into one of common cause (Bass and Avolio 1990).

Bass (1985) identified three types of transformational leader behavior: idealized influence, intellectual stimulation, and individualized consideration. A fourth type, inspirational leadership, was added later (Bass and Avolio 1990).

Transformational leaders develop trusting relationships with followers (Bass 1996). By using techniques like the delegation of authority and the development of employees' skills, transformational leaders help to build effective teams. They empower employees by increasing individual and collective confidence, which reduces employees' feelings of dependence upon the leader (Ashkanasy and Daus 2002) and helps to expand employees' skills. Teams like this are effective in dynamic environments.

Transformational leaders arouse courage and stimulate enthusiasm by providing intellectual stimulation, questioning assumptions, and revealing opportunities (Bass 1996). Extreme change requires leaders who have the talent to make good decisions under pressure and the confidence to try new or untested behaviors and methods (Bass 1996). For leaders to be effective, they must be able to put their own self-interest aside and make stakeholders' goals more important. Even so, transformational leadership theory lacks some conceptual clarity. It suggests leadership is based primarily on the traits of leaders or of team members, rather than skills or competency (Northouse 2004). Leaders must have the trust of organizational stakeholders to engage in this kind of creativity. In times of crisis and uncertainty, when people are likely to feel anxious, they may respond strongly to leaders who strengthen their faith in that relief (Bass 1996).

One type of transformational leader, the charismatic leader, is often singled out. Charismatic leaders' personal characteristics include self-confidence, a sense of moral values, and a strong desire to influence others (Conger and Kanungo 1994). By articulating a transformational goal or calling for an inspirational mission, charismatic leaders may "induce renewal and mobilize collective effort to face the stress or crisis" (Bass 1996, 33). Regardless of personal magnetism, those who appear to be well qualified to lead in a crisis will gain followers. Transformational leaders help people gain agency by spurring them to action, which eventually returns an organization to a state of equilibrium and normality.

A prominent example of transformational leadership in libraries includes the long-term leadership of Carla Stoffle at the University of Arizona Libraries. Stoffle exemplifies the transformational leader whose modeled desired behaviors are needed for change. She responded to fiscal crises with strong, well-articulated visions, challenged traditional processes, and enabled others to function in the new environment (Townley 2009).

Beginning in 1993, Stoffle introduced processes that generated massive organizational and workflow changes at the University of Arizona Libraries. She observed: "The economics of our libraries are in fact driving the need for us to change and endangering our role on campus" (Stoffle, Leeder, and Sykes-Casavant 2008, 4). Stoffle's philosophy was to completely reenvision the library's role in higher education's new constrained financial environment and "to aggressively build the library of the future" (7). Stoffle led an effort that flattened the bureaucracy, requiring leadership to "trust and believe" in decision-making teams (Revock 2013). Stoffle instituted radical changes in organizational structure and culture, shifting the library's organization from one that was "focused on processing, managing and storing *things* to a team-based organization focused on *customers* and providing value-added services" (Stoffle and Cuillier 2011, 133). Her guiding vision was to improve service, maintain or reduce costs, gather and analyze data, and use process improvement techniques (Stoffle and Cuillier 2011). A measure of her success is that transformation has been adopted as a way of doing business and new ideas are the province of the functional teams that manage the library (Tedford, Corbett, and Lock 2012). The innovation was not in restructuring the library but rather in the creation of new services and value for the library's stakeholders (Deiss 2004).

The three theories discussed here have some things in common. All depend on a leader's ability to assess a situation and choose a fitting style or behavior to motivate employees. The theories require leaders with emotional resilience and self-regulation; these leaders are goal- and performance-oriented, and they practice relationship building and communication. In each theory, the leader reassures and guides stakeholders by articulating goals, instilling enthusiasm, encouraging flexibility, and establishing trust.

The differences among the theories are based on technique and application. Path-goal theory requires leaders to motivate others through support and inclusion, using the particulars of a situation as well as the characteristics of employees (House and Mitchell 1974). Contingency theory entails the strategic and conscious effort of changing and matching leader styles to fit situations (Fiedler 1967). Transformational leadership theory describes leaders who delegate authority and increase the independence of workers and work groups (Burns 1978). The three theories all benefit from research on leaders' personality characteristics (Judge et al. 2002; Natonakis 2011). Each theory has room to account for employee characteristics and actions that are alternatively independent from and influenced by leaders' behaviors and characteristics and to recognize the mutual influences of leaders and followers.

Among the challenges for any leadership theory are questions of definition. Is leadership a matter of power, or is it one of influence? Formal or informal? How do group dynamics relate? Is leadership something that is essential or constructed? Disciplinary perspectives and methodological approaches also span the field of leadership research. These are just some of the considerations that must be understood when reviewing leadership theories.

Researchers have toiled to no avail, however, in generating a unified or general theory of leadership. No single integrative or holistic model yet exists, although deliberate efforts have been made to build a more complex, interdisciplinary, and adaptive approach into leadership studies (Sorenson, Goethals, and Haber 2011). Progress toward a general theory of leadership has come from the ongoing testing and modification of existing theories. However, leadership research also must generate and test new theories and models to gain ground. New theories are derived from new knowledge and new perspectives. They also provide a way to build on ideas and information from previous theories.

The three theories discussed so far have useful applications in the library setting. Library leaders need to find a way to help employees to act. A leader using path-goal techniques will find ways to increase employee participation in decision making. A leader working with contingency theory will pay attention to the particulars of a situation and modify his or her style to be more directive when a situation is chaotic or time-bound, and more inclusive when there is a need for group cohesiveness. A leader who employs transformational techniques is usually interested in galvanizing a group around a shared vision. Leaders and change agents use a variety of techniques in library settings, but the leader is responsible for developing and marketing a particular vision of where he or she wants to take the organization and motivating people to act on that vision (Alire 2001). Understanding these and other leadership theories helps to build a bigger tool kit that may help a leader to be more versatile.

Leadership theory can become useful by building a deeper theoretical understanding and finding practical applications. From the study of existing leadership theories, new theories should emerge for use in the contemporary environment of change. Studying the behavior of leaders within the context of a new theory is helpful and necessary to advance knowledge and practice for library leaders, and a new theory is proposed in the following pages.

THE CREDIBLE OPTIMIST THEORY: A NEW MODEL FOR LIBRARY LEADERS

Drawing some characteristics and behaviors from the previously explored theories, the credible optimist theory incorporates new developments in positive psychology and the understanding of the fundamental value of happiness (Carroll and Flood 2010). The credible optimist theory is a new and original model, and it is proposed here for leadership in academic libraries. The credible optimist is a leader whose words and actions inspire trust and confidence. Credible optimists are truth-tellers with strong visions and values who motivate employees and influence others around them to work to improve. This places leaders and their stakeholders inside a systemic learning-motivation-change-process loop. Creating a specific change or set of changes becomes a learning process as well as a production process for leaders that includes employees and patrons.

A growing body of research on trust in the workplace helps to inform this theory. While existing leadership theories imply the need to establish trust, the credible optimist theory is based upon a mutual commitment of trust between employees and leaders. A review of recent research on employee-leader trust is available in Kramer (2011). Peck (2003) provided a thorough examination of the phenomenon of employee trust in leaders. Parker (2007) studied innovation and change in a university library and identified employees' trust in leaders as an essential component in employees' decisions to embrace change and try new things.

The movement of positive psychology is an additional influence. Positive psychologists examine and advocate for the benefits of positive experiences and positive relationships. Some have tried to identify leaders' characteristics or traits (Peterson and Seligman 2004; Zaccaro 2007). Other research examined personal enjoyment and engagement to better understand the contribution of positive experiences to a satisfying life (Seligman 1990, 2002, 2004, 2011).

Under stress, credible optimist leaders appear calm, confident, concerned, self-sacrificing, goal-focused, tireless, and actively visible. Like other leaders who are successful in managing change, they have developed a high level of psychological resilience; they "have the ability to absorb high levels of change while displaying minimal dysfunctional behavior" (Conner 2004, 223). They display and depend on emotional intelligence (Hernon, Giesecke, and Alire 2008; Salovey, Mayer, and Caruso 2002). Their authentic behavior and personhood are expressed in public through their genuine motivation, their articulation of values, their optimism, and their self-awareness (Avolio and Gardner 2005). They work within the frameworks of contingency and transformational leadership theories by helping members of the organization focus on necessary tasks, however tedious or difficult, but they also show a new vision of organizational success based on commitment to stakeholders, commitment to making corrections, and commitment to core values (Ulmer and Sellnow 2002). They value the creation and integrity of mutual social experiences (Cunliffe and Eriksen 2011). Their leadership helps others build their own resilience and strength.

Credible optimists are trustworthy in word and deed. Their followers must believe in their sincerity and their ability to lead effectively. They acknowledge the realities of each situation and offer pragmatic acceptance of what is good and what is difficult. They expose themselves to the same risks and hardships as followers. They demonstrate their command of knowledge and experience, but they also seek advice and admit they do not know all there is to know. They give credit to others and often emphasize stakeholders' contributions. Credible optimist leaders who face big changes can draw from the example of others who use their visibility, language, positive outlook, and beliefs to establish a vision and urge people into forward motion to accomplish it.

Some of the most inspirational leadership language and behavior has come from successful political and social leaders who acknowledge the danger, difficulty, and darkness of crisis but who also urge people not to give up the idea of changing the situation. President Franklin Delano Roosevelt encouraged people to have courage and remain optimistic during the Depression, proclaiming "the only thing we have to fear is fear itself" and urging sacrifice and discipline for the common good (Houck 2002, 3, 7). President Barack Obama described his own credible optimist philosophy, recommending that leaders tell people that things will not be easy when they are not; live by example; inspire by example; become inspired by the stories of others; transcend partisanship; respect and be gracious to those with whom you disagree; be warm, inviting, sincere, and optimistic; and emphasize communication (Obama 2006). Martin Luther King's leadership of the civil rights movement was fully launched by his "I Have a Dream" speech at the march on Washington in 1963, in which he expressed a vibrant hope in the possibility of a future free from racism (Hansen 2003). Other credible optimists have exerted powerful leadership presences in organizations. Gene Kranz, the NASA flight director who ensured the safe return of the Apollo 13 astronauts, placed his faith in his flight team's decision-making processes and problem-solving prowess (Useem 1998). Technical manager Tom West recruited and led to success a team of inexperienced computer engineers who responded to his convincing faith in their ability to build a new, high-powered, game-changing computer (Kidder 1981). Basketball coach John Wooden built a legendary winning dynasty by urging his teams to believe in themselves even more than they believed in winning (Wooden and Jamison 2007). Some credible optimists become heroes. Captain "Sully" Sullenberger landed his disabled plane on the Hudson River in 2009, succeeding not because it was a "miracle on the Hudson," as the press called the episode, but because he knew he needed to use his skills to save the lives of his passengers and thousands of people on both sides of the river in New York City and New Jersey (Sullenberger and Zaslow 2009).

Academic libraries face record increases in the cost of storing, licensing, and accessing scholarly information and products. They face an imperative to invest in technology infrastructure to deliver digital content and create high-tech student-friendly environments. There are shortages of trained librarians; future leaders must be identified and receive the mentoring they need. Libraries must reach out to build more collaborations with different parts of the university and with individual faculty members and programs. Libraries are becoming gathering places and can serve as community living rooms, offering different environments and infrastructure features, such as 24/7 spaces. Librarians need to proactively seize opportunities to reposition and embed themselves into the essential fabric of student and faculty activities.

Leaders' actions in times of extreme change have an important effect on an organization's success or failure in weathering crises. Leaders who harness the opportunities that emerge for organizational learning and renewal presented by the need for change are those who will be most successful in leading an organization. This success may be identified in leader behaviors. Shaw asserts, "Leaders must lead, charting the course with acts that are both symbolic and substantive (2003, 27). The credible optimist is a model of behavior and action that can be useful for leaders and organizations.

The manifestation of the credible optimist model may appear in different forms, depending on the leader's personality and behaviors. Some are bold and charismatic, such as U.S. presidents Franklin Delano Roosevelt and John F. Kennedy; some are supportive, like Gene Kranz; some are heroes, like "Sully" Sullenberger; some are inspirational like Martin Luther King, Jr. Some are values-centered, like the two library leaders whose work will be explored next, Lawrence Clark Powell at the University of California, Los Angeles (UCLA) and Evan Ira Farber at Earlham College.

Powell and Farber led two very different libraries in terms of size and purpose, but both offered an enthusiastic and compelling vision for their libraries. Powell did the unexpected at the UCLA Library, building a great and significant collection and a graduate school of library science at a university that was in its early years; Farber flew in the face of accepted professional practices of librarians by insisting college libraries and librarians become central to the teaching of undergraduates by becoming part of the curriculum itself. Both were prominent library leaders whose influence remains today. Their work and its impact are well documented in their own writings, providing a good opportunity to examine their success as credible optimists. Each will be discussed in turn, then the two cases will be analyzed in the context of the credible optimist theory.

LAWRENCE CLARK POWELL: BOOKMAN

Lawrence Clark Powell (1906–2001), who served as university librarian and head of the William Andrews Clark Library at UCLA from 1944 to 1961, self-identified as a bookman and a writer: "I have always been reconciled to the fact that I was a born bibliomaniac, never have I sought a cure, and my dearest friends have been drawn from those likewise suffering from book-madness" (Powell 1991, 10). Having started his career in Jake Zeitlin's rare book shop in Los Angeles, Powell found ample resources to fulfill his great desire to read; he also shaped a personal philosophy that books need to be read, seeing them "as interactive symbols rather than artifacts" (Haslam 2008, 13). Finally, he decided, "it was either go into the book business for myself or become a librarian and renounce all hope of riches and worldly advancement. I chose the latter" (Powell 1987, 17).

Powell was a talented observer of people, and he made an effort to recruit and appoint excellent unit heads, including Robert Vosper, who succeeded Powell as university librarian. Of his determination to hire Vosper in particular, Powell reported, "I was motivated by the need to have librarians who could do what I couldn't do, or could do it better, which was most everything relating to the operation of a library" (Powell 1968a, 116). He recommended recruiting for librarians early in students' careers, helping educate librarians who are already on staff about the need to recruit librarians, and aiding programs that trained librarians who would make a library become "a place of intense intellectual radiation as well as a technical depot" (Powell 1958, 133). At the new UCLA School of Library Science, Powell recruited superlative librarians from other major institutions and bright academics like mathematics PhD Robert Hayes, who would one day be the head of the school. He invited leading library practitioners and great authors like Aldous Huxley, Henry Miller, and Ray Bradbury to lecture.

Not only did Powell appoint excellent people who performed admirably and notably in UCLA positions and elsewhere, in 1959 he became the founding dean of the School of Library Science at UCLA (what is today the Department of Information Studies). Powell formed a strong opinion about librarian professionals' qualifications. He believed librarians should be readers and bookish: "Having a feel for books is just as important as having a feeling for them" (Powell 1968a, 85). He struggled with the challenge of creating a library organization where certain administrative and routine tasks were accomplished, while at the same time recruiting those who loved reading and were "trained by study and seasoned by experience to catalyze books and people" (Powell 1968a, 88). He railed against "Tinkertoy librarians," who love forms and organizational charts more than books or their readers (Powell 1968a, 89).

Powell fought "against non-bookism in library work" (1968a, 89). He asked, "Are we members of a profession, or are we self-glorified housekeepers?" (98). He bemoaned his observation that academic libraries did not have enough superior candidates to appoint as librarians, chiefly because "we are paradoxically not a bookish profession" (1958, 121). He also believed librarians failed too often to learn about the work of the faculty and to support it. The "desperate deficiency is that of more librarians who have knowledge and interests and sympathy of the same kinds as the faculty . . . who can establish intellectual camaraderie with the faculty" (124). While these complaints may sound retrograde in our modern era, they underlie Powell's far more enthusiastic optimism about the work of faculty and his view that librarians should be oriented toward and interested in faculty research efforts rather than in building a library outside of that context.

As a librarian, Powell wrote, "I never wavered in my conviction that this was the place. Fortune and friendship brought me there at the precise time a librarian of my temperament was needed. If it was made for me, I was made for it" (1968b, 67). This identification of his match with UCLA was a powerful driver of his optimism in library collection building, and it was expanded further when Powell met a cultural soul mate in UCLA chancellor Franklin D. Murphy. Murphy arrived at UCLA in 1960 and made funding the growth of the UCLA Library a priority, seeking to raise its caliber and to equal that of UC Berkeley's library (Dundjerski 2011). Murphy believed a high-quality library was the mark of an institution's intellectual quality. With 24,000 volumes at its opening in 1919, the UCLA Library hit the one million mark in 1953, and by 1971, its collection had more than tripled to three million books. It ranked second in collection size among North American research libraries by 1984 and has remained one of the top libraries in the nation, with more than nine million books (Dundjerski 2011; UCLA Library 2012).

Powell always held the ideal library leader would be "a bookman by choice, education, and experience" (1954, 95). The ideal library leader "will regard books as teachers par excellence . . . a bookman-administrator-educator, possessed of a passionate devotion to his stock-in-trade, as well of skill and common sense in managing a complex organization" (94–95). He lived that example, and he found others to assist him in managing his messages during years of great growth for the UCLA Library. Powell revealed some of the political turmoil that he navigated during his campaign to become UCLA librarian and again when starting the UCLA School of Library Science, but he did not dwell on it; he rose above it because of his passionate and foundational belief in books and bookism. He did not always say or do what librarians wished, but he persisted in his pragmatic optimism to inspire and empower librarians and faculty members alike.

Powell's energy drove him to achieve successes for libraries and librarians. He was an unparalleled optimist in his efforts to build two things at UCLA that were not thought to be wise or even possible at the time: a great library and a great school for training librarians. UCLA itself began in 1919 as the University of California's "southern branch" (Dundjerski 2011). Despite the growth of Los Angeles as an economic and population center in the early twentieth century, it was not deemed an important intellectual center, and few believed UCLA would be very important, at least not compared to UC Berkeley. Powell saw differently and thought bigger. In combination with Franklin Murphy, another optimist who believed in the potential of

UCLA, in a relatively short time he was able to secure the funds and the administrative will to build a great research library that would rival Berkeley's. Similarly, the development of a school for training librarians at UCLA was generated from a need for more librarians and to compete with the existing school at Berkeley. The ambitious course on which Powell founded the UCLA Library and the UCLA School of Library Science has been continued by his successors, and the UCLA Library remains among the top ten research libraries in North America.

EVAN IRA FARBER: FACULTY-LIBRARIAN COLLABORATION

Headed for a career in research libraries or teaching at colleges, Evan Farber (1922–2009) viewed the job of head librarian at Earlham College as a chance to do something different. An original fan of the Library College Movement, which had envisioned the roles of instructors and librarians converging into one, Farber noted, "Along with many others I soon recognized the limitation of that idealism, the practical impossibility of sustaining those views in a real academic setting" (1999b, 230). After following the progression of other efforts to resolve the need for teaching students how to use the library, he realized, "Course-related instruction was the most effective one" (1999b, 231). It was based on the idea that students working in small academic libraries could and should develop strong skills in finding information and doing research.

At Earlham in the early 1970s, Farber started to build functional relationships between librarians and faculty at the same time as the bibliographic instruction movement was taking hold, and he developed "increasing optimism about the possibilities of cooperation with the teaching faculty" (1999b, 231). Noting that in Earlham he had found an innovative place (2007), he also developed and delivered a comprehensive, innovative program of course-related bibliographic instruction at Earlham from the 1970s until his retirement in 1994. This program was by no means the norm when he proposed it, but by the time Farber retired, it was well established at Earlham and other small colleges and universities. Farber took the opportunity to emphasize the importance of library-faculty collaboration in colleges by writing a background paper for the comprehensive study of undergraduate education commissioned by the Carnegie Foundation for the Advancement of Teaching. That report, *College: The Undergraduate Experience in America*, appeared in 1987, recommending that parents and prospective students ask and find satisfactory answers to a number of questions, including "Are those who direct the library also considered teachers?" (Boyer 1987, 292). This study appears to have influenced accrediting associations first, followed by other educators and librarians (Farber 1999a), as evidenced by the teaching experience and duties written into job advertisements for librarians and by the wholesale adoption of this idea by the Association of College and Research Libraries (ACRL).

An essential part of Farber's optimism was to take chances on good ideas. He was also pragmatic, which led him to preach that the library "is not the heart of the college. What is? The teaching learning process" (1980, 51). He also counseled college librarians to view the college library as a training ground, a gateway to knowledge and to learning, and a support to the teaching and learning process. The writings of academics who work with librarians show the influence of this opinion, but it was hardly a mainstream idea and certainly not uniformly popular with librarians when Farber began to promote it (Weiskel 1988; Wilkinson 1997). Farber worked tirelessly to insert librarians into the teaching and learning hub of the college: the classroom itself. This was not at all popular among college instructors at the time. Nevertheless, his optimism about the positive effect of library skills teaching within the curriculum—and the results it achieved—was such that Farber succeeded in reshaping educational methods at Earlham College and elsewhere. A hallmark of coursework at Earlham College in the 1970s and 1980s was that a librarian taught at least one meeting of each course on research skills and tools relevant to the course and its required assignments. The meeting was attended by the instructor and led by the librarian, and it was timed to coincide with each class's major research or writing assignment. Students were each assigned an academic advisor, and librarians were included among faculty as advisors. Librarians were on duty nearly every hour the library was open, and they were available to guide students further in developing their skills in finding and using information (Farber 1999a; 2007).

Faculty-librarian collaboration and assignment-based instruction were fundamental to the success of any instruction from Earlham College librarians. This perspective was Farber's particular manifestation of credible optimism, a perspective perhaps befitting the smaller college library setting. The practice's influence at Earlham and elsewhere began to spread into professional practice and to larger institutional settings, beginning with the Bibliographic Instruction Section (BIS) in ACRL in 1977 and early Library Information Exchange (LOEX) conferences. From these beginnings, the practice is now included by national and regional LOEX conferences and ACRL's Instruction Section and Institute for Information Literacy and Immersion programs for instruction librarians (Kirk 1999; Whyte 2001).

Farber warned against the pitfalls of college libraries emulating university libraries. Faculty and librarians themselves are usually trained in university libraries, and they may succumb to the temptation to assess the staff, resources, and activities of a college library in terms more appropriate for a university library. This dangerous "university-library syndrome" takes away from the unique mission of college libraries (Farber 1974). It also does not take into account Farber's view that college libraries should be funded to purchase and to license *access* to materials and to larger libraries rather than to amass comprehensive collections of their own, like a university library (Farber 1974). Farber's optimism was grounded in the realistic notion that the purpose of a college library is to support teaching. It was also about scaling college library funding and collecting to that particular purpose rather than trying to compete with university libraries. By casting the small college library as a unique and distinct feature of the teaching and learning experience to be had there, Farber used credible optimist tactics and communication to elevate the college library to the status of a valuable and active teaching and learning accessory.

Farber identified the success of the bibliographic instruction movement and the effect of the development of electronic resources as key components in the greater "recognition of the educational role of librarians" (1999a, 215). He minimized the importance of his own role by giving much credit to many others and by winning many librarians and faculty members to his philosophy and practice. The widespread growth and adoption of what is now known as the information literacy movement started with Farber's small-scale, optimistic collaborations between librarians and faculty members.

Farber lectured frequently throughout his career. He served college libraries well as president of ACRL (1978–1979). ACRL honored him by naming him the College and Research Librarian of the Year in 1980, and he received the Miriam Dudley Instruction Librarian Award in 1987. He has inspired several generations of college students to become librarians.

CREDIBLE OPTIMISTS IN LIBRARY LEADERSHIP: TWO DIFFERENT KINDS OF SUCCESS

Identifying two particular library leaders as examples of this new theory demonstrates how credible optimism incorporates elements of the leadership theories that were discussed at the beginning of this chapter. Credible optimism builds on the components of other leadership theories. Components of the credible optimist theory are evident in both leaders' clear focus on the work of librarians as a result of their understanding of the research of faculty members (Powell) and their teaching (Farber). Each leader made clear statements of goals and objectives for the library and the work of librarians. For Powell, the goal was understanding that the purpose of collecting was to build an urgently needed, great library at a young institution; for Farber, the goal was believing that teaching is all—and that librarians should build teaching about research into teachers' instructional goals. Librarians working for either leader had clear expectations. These leaders rewarded librarians' performance with praise and opportunities to do more.

The two examples of Powell and Farber give a sense of how a library leader can be successful as a credible optimist, and they are examples of people who moved their libraries forward based on their strong principles when the path for academic libraries was not always clear. Neither Powell nor Farber followed strictly traditional pathways, and as a result, they learned fundamentals that evolved into strong beliefs. These beliefs in turn served as the foundation of their philosophies of librarianship. They both believed it was necessary to cultivate relationships and collaborate with faculty members and to provide the material and human resources necessary to the teaching, learning, and research enterprises. They situated the library squarely in the middle of the teaching and learning process. Their writings and recollections repeat many examples of their use of personal persuasiveness, intellect, honesty, pragmatism, optimism, and even charm to achieve the small wins that led to the trust their faculty and staff members placed in them (Weick 1984). These small wins led to opportunities to tackle bigger problems.

Both Powell and Farber displayed significant emotional intelligence and relied on it for success. They communicated their intentions to stakeholders, and they made sincere and significant efforts to understand the needs of others. They used their positive outlook to spread enthusiasm and rapport. The appropriate use of emotional cues and support from leaders helps to facilitate problem solving and promote decision making (Lopes and Salovey 2008). Powell and Farber both exhibited some of the positive behaviors and skills that enhanced their credibility. Researchers attribute some of these same behaviors, such as sensitivity to context, the ability to communicate a compelling vision, and taking risks like guiding an organization through uncharted territory or articulating a different philosophy, to charismatic leaders (Riggio and Riggio 2008). Their compelling and authentic communication is what helped others see Powell and Farber as credible.

The credible optimist theory aligns with threads that are emerging from the growing movement of positive psychology, a modern descendant of existential psychology. Many suggest that happiness is an urgent need for our own and our collective existence (Pinker 2011; Carroll and Flood 2010). This mind-set has been applied to the library workplace as well, in the form of the optimism of leaders discussed here.

THE FUTURE FOR OPTIMISTS IN LIBRARIES

There is an imperative need at this time for effective change leadership in academic libraries (Hopper 2011). As these examples of two great library leaders show, there is ample opportunity for progress in libraries and librarianship in even these uncertain times. There is a wealth of research on leadership traits and styles that library leaders should consider; there is a great number and variety among theories of leadership from which library leaders may choose. More research on leadership itself, especially on leadership in and for libraries, is greatly needed.

In a cynical world, it is difficult to find someone who wants to be placed in the position of being so responsible and be required to have a firm command of details that are somewhat peripheral to library work even as those very details influence the future of libraries. That person needs to possess characteristics and behaviors particular to the situation. That person also needs the confidence that he or she will succeed and the ability to convey that positivity in a realistic fashion.

Adopting the skills and the style of the credible optimist is a way for academic library leaders to succeed in keeping their libraries thriving where they belong: in the mainstream of the creation, delivery, and preservation of knowledge and firmly embedded in the processes of teaching, learning, and research. In fact, the credible optimist library leader is one who will be able to demonstrate the value and vitality the library contributes to the institution and its larger goals.

All leadership requires optimism and faith on the part of the person responsible for moving people and their organization forward. Certain characteristics and skills are also needed, as is the maturity and vision to know when to apply them effectively. Optimists must be able to understand the environment in which they operate, and they succeed when their message is well tailored to local needs and sensibilities.

In offering this leadership model and examples of two very different library leaders who practiced as credible optimists in very different academic settings, this chapter aims to show that optimism need not exist without the balancing influence of common sense. Tempered with pragmatism, knowledge, and experience, optimism is a welcome and necessary tool for leading change and evolution in library organizations.

REFERENCES

Alire, Camila A. 2000. "What Do You Do When It Happens to You? Managing a Major Library Disaster." In *Library Disaster Planning and Recovery Handbook*, ed. Camila A. Alire, 3–31. New York: Neal-Schuman.
———. 2001. "Diversity and Leadership: The Color of Leadership." *Journal of Library Administration* 32 (3/4): 95–109. doi:10.1300/j111v32n03_07.
———. 2003. "The Silver Lining: Recovering from the Shambles of a Disaster." *Journal of Library Administration* 38: 101–7. doi:10/1300j111v38no1_12.
Ashkanasy, Neal M., and Catherine S. Daus. 2002. "Emotion in the Workplace: The New Challenge for Managers." *Academy of Management Executive* 16: 76–86. http://www.jstor.org/stable/4165815.

Avolio, Bruce J., and William L. Gardner. 2005. "Authentic Leadership Development: Getting to the Root of Positive Forms of Leadership." *Leadership Quarterly* 16 (3): 315–38. doi:10.1016/j.leaqua.2005.03.001.

Bandura, Albert. 1991. "Social Cognitive Theory of Self-Regulation." *Organizational Behavior and Human Decision Processes* 50: 248–87. http://dx.doi.org/10.1016/0749-5978(91)90022-L.

———. 1997. *Self-Efficacy: The Exercise of Control*. New York: W. H. Freeman.

Bass, Bernard M. 1985. *Leadership and Performance beyond Expectations*. New York: Free Press.

———. 1996. *A New Paradigm of Leadership: An Inquiry into Transformational Leadership*. Alexandria, VA: U.S. Army Research Institute for Behavioral and Social Sciences.

Bass, Bernard M., and Bruce J. Avolio. 1990. *Multifactor Leadership Questionnaire*. Palo Alto, CA: Consulting Psychologists Press.

Bennis, Warren G., and Burt Nanus. 1985. *Leaders: The Strategies for Taking Charge*. New York: Harper & Row.

Bolman, Lee G., and Joan V. Gallos. 2011. *Reframing Academic Leadership*. San Francisco: Jossey-Bass.

Boyer, Ernest L. 1987. *College: The Undergraduate Experience in America*. New York: Harper & Row.

Burns, James MacGregor. 1978. *Leadership*. New York: Harper & Row.

Carroll, Stephen J., and Patrick C. Flood. 2010. *The Persuasive Leader: Lessons from the Arts*. San Francisco: Jossey-Bass.

Conger, Jay A., and Rabindra N. Kanungo. 1994. "Charismatic Leadership in Organizations: Perceived Behavioral Attributes and Their Measurement." *Journal of Organizational Behavior* 15: 439–52. doi:10.1002/job.4030150508.

Conner, Daryl R. 2004. *Leading at the Edge of Chaos: How to Create the Nimble Organization*. New York: John Wiley & Sons.

Cunliffe, Ann L., and Matthew Eriksen. 2011. "Relational Leadership." *Human Relations* 64 (11): 1425–49. doi:10.1177/0018726711418388.

Curzon, Susan C. 2000. "When Disaster Strikes: The Fall and Rise of a Library." *American Libraries* (April): 64–69.

———. 2006. "Coming Back from Major Disaster: Month One." *Public Library Quarterly* 25 (3/4): 17–29. doi:10.1300/j118v25n03_03.

———. 2010. "'Ain't What It Used to Be': The Future of Academic Libraries." Companion website with materials to be used with *Academic Librarianship*, ed. Camila A. Alire and G. Edward Evans. New York: Neal-Schuman. http://www.neal-schuman.com/academic (accessed March 11, 2013).

Deiss, Kathryn J. 2004. "Innovation and Strategy: Risk and Choice in Shaping User-Centered Libraries." *Library Trends* 53 (1): 17–32. http://liaisonprograms.pbworks.com/f/deiss.pdf (accessed March 13, 2013).

Dundjerski, Marina. 2011. *UCLA: The First Century*. Los Angeles and London: Third Millennium Publishing Limited in Conjunction with the UCLA History Project/UCLA Alumni Association.

Evans, Martin. G. 1970. "The Effects of Supervisory Behavior on the Path-Goal Relationship." *Organizational Behavior and Human Performance* 5: 277–98. doi: 10.1016/0030-5073(70)90021-8.

Farber, Evan Ira. 1974. "College Libraries and the University-Library Syndrome." In *The Academic Library: Essays in Honor of Guy R. Lyle*, ed. Evan Ira Farber and Ruth Walling, 12–23. Metuchen, NJ: Scarecrow Press.

———. 1980. "The Library as a Minimal Resource Base." Talk given at a conference on "Issues and Trends in Intercultural Education in the Independent Colleges," Wingspread Conference Center, Racine, Wisconsin, December 9, 1980. Reprinted in David Gansz, ed., 2007, *College Libraries and the Teaching/Learning Process: Selections from the Writings of Evan Ira Farber*, 51–55. Richmond, IN: Earlham College Press.

———. 1999a. "College Libraries and the Teaching/Learning Process: A 25-Year Reflection." *The Journal of Academic Librarianship* 25 (3): 171–77. Reprinted in David Gansz, ed.,

2007, *College Libraries and the Teaching/Learning Process: Selections from the Writings of Evan Ira Farber*, 203–19. Richmond, IN: Earlham College Press.

———. 1999b. "Faculty-Librarian Cooperation: A Personal Retrospective." *Reference Services Review* 27 (1): 229–34. Reprinted in David Gansz, ed., 2007, *College Libraries and the Teaching/Learning Process: Selections from the Writings of Evan Ira Farber*, 194–202. Richmond, IN: Earlham College Press.

———. 2007. "Librarian-Faculty Communication Techniques." In *College Libraries and the Teaching/Learning Process: Selections from the Writings of Evan Ira Farber,* ed. David Gansz, 41–50. Richmond, IN: Earlham College Press. Reprinted from a talk given at the Southeastern Conference on Approaches to Bibliographic Instruction, The College of Charleston, Charleston, South Carolina, March 17, 1978, and published in Cerise Oberman-Soroka, ed., 1978, *Proceedings from Southeastern Conference on Approaches to Bibliographic Instruction*, 70–87. Charleston, SC: The College of Charleston.

Fiedler, Fred Edward. 1967. *A Theory of Leader Effectiveness.* New York: McGraw-Hill.

Goldberger, Paul. 2012. "Firestorm on Fifth Avenue." *Vanity Fair*, December, 180–88. http://www.vanityfair.com/culture/2012/12/new-york-public-library-remodel-controversy.

Grint, Keith. 2011. "A History of Leadership." In *The SAGE Handbook of Leadership*, ed. Alan Bryman, David Collinson, Keith Grint, Brad Jackson, and Mary Uhl-Bien, 3–14. Thousand Oaks, CA: Sage.

Hansen, Drew D. 2003. *The Dream: Martin Luther King, Jr. and the Speech That Inspired a Nation.* New York: CCCO/HarperCollins.

Haslam, Gerald. 2008. *Lawrence Clark Powell: California Classic. A Speech Given at the Library Associates' Dinner for the Powell Society, UCLA Library, September 21, 2006.* Los Angeles: UCLA Library.

Hernon, Peter, and Candy Schwartz. 2008. "Leadership: Developing a Research Agenda for Academic Libraries." *Library & Information Science Research* 30: 243–48. doi:10.1016/j.lisr.2008.08.001.

Hernon, Peter, Joan Giesecke, and Camila A. Alire. 2008. *Academic Librarians as Emotionally Intelligent Leaders.* Westport, CT: Libraries Unlimited.

Hopper, Rosita E. 2011. "Is the Devil You Know Better than the Devil You Don't Know? Issues in Academic Library Leadership Recruitment." Paper presented at the 15th ACRL Conference, Philadelphia, PA, March 20–April 2.

Horgan, John. 2012. "Why Being Optimistic Is a Moral Duty." *Chronicle of Higher Education*, February 26. http://chronicle.com/article/Why-Being-Optimistic-Is-a/130895 (accessed March 11, 2013).

Houck, Davis W. 2002. *FDR and Fear Itself: The First Inaugural Address.* College Station: Texas A & M University Press.

House, Robert J. 1971. "A Path-Goal Theory of Leader Effectiveness." *Administrative Science Quarterly* 16: 321–28. http://knowledge.wharton.upenn.edu/papers/674.pdf (accessed March 11, 2013).

House, Robert J., and Terence R. Mitchell. 1974. "Path-Goal Theory of Leadership." *Journal of Contemporary Business* 3 (Fall): 81–98.

Judge, Timothy A., Joyce E. Bono, Remus Ilies, and Megan W. Gerhardt. 2002. "Personality and Leadership: A Qualitative and Quantitative Review." *Journal of Applied Psychology* 87 (4): 765–80. doi:10.1037/0021-9010.87.4.765.

Kidder, Tracy. 1981. *The Soul of a New Machine.* New York: Avon Books.

Killey, Danielle, and Don Davis. 2013. *Capitol Chatter: A Forum News Service Blog.* "Legislative Notebook: Senator's Message to U is to Be Accountable." http://www.capitolchat.areavoices.com/2013/04/18/legislative-note-book-senators-message-to-u-is-to-be-accountable (accessed April 22, 2013).

Kirk, Thomas G., Jr. 1999. "Course-Related Bibliographic Instruction in the 1990s." *Reference Services Review* 27 (3): 235–41. doi:10.1108/00907329910283160.

Kramer, Roderick M. 2011. "Trust and Distrust in the Leadership Process: A Review and Assessment of Theory and Evidence." In *The SAGE Handbook of Leadership*, ed. Alan Bryman, David Collinson, Keith Grint, Brad Jackson, and Mary Uhl-Bien, 136–50. Thousand Oaks, CA: Sage.

Leveille, David E. 2005. *An Emerging View on Accountability in American Higher Education.* CSHE Research and Occasional Paper Services, CSHE.8.05. Berkeley: University of California, Berkeley Center for Studies on Higher Education. http://www.cshe.berkeley.edu/publications/docs/ROP.Leveille.8.05.pdf.

Lopes, Peter N., and Paulo Salovey. 2008. "Emotional Intelligence and Leadership: Implications for Leader Development." In *Leadership at the Crossroads: Volume 1: Leadership and Psychology,* ed. Crystal L. Hoyt, George R. Goethals, and Donelson R. Forsyth, 78–98. Westport, CT: Praeger.

Mitchell, Eugene S. 1989. "The Library Leadership Project: A Test of Leadership Effectiveness in Academic Libraries." In *Advances in Library Administration and Organization,* ed. Gerald B. McCabe and Bernard Kreissman, 8: 25–38. Greenwich, CT: JAI Press.

Natonakis, John. 2011. "Predictors of Leadership: The Usual Suspects and the Suspect Traits." In *The SAGE Handbook of Leadership,* ed. Alan Bryman, David Collinson, Keith Grint, Brad Jackson, and Mary Uhl-Bien, 269–85. Thousand Oaks, CA: Sage.

Northouse, Peter G. 2004. *Leadership: Theory and Practice.* 3rd ed. Thousand Oaks, CA: Sage.

Obama, Barack. 2006. *The Audacity of Hope: Thoughts on Reclaiming the American Dream.* New York: Crown.

Parker, Susan E. 2007. *Organizational Learning, Innovation, and Employees' Mental Models of Change Following a Disaster: A Case Study of the Morgan Library at Colorado State University.* PhD diss., Capella University.

Peck, Deborah L. 2003. *Trust in Leaders from an Employee Perspective: A Multiple Case Study.* PhD diss., Capella University.

Peterson, Christopher, and Martin E. P. Seligman. 2004. *Character Strengths and Virtues.* Oxford: Oxford University Press.

Pinker, Stephen. 2011. *The Better Angels of Our Nature: Why Violence Has Declined.* New York: Viking.

Powell, Lawrence Clark. 1954. *The Alchemy of Books: And Other Essays and Addresses on Books & Writers.* Los Angeles: Ward Ritchie Press.

———. 1958. *A Passion for Books.* Cleveland: World Publishing.

———. 1968a. *Bookman's Progress: The Selected Writings of Lawrence Clark Powell with an Introduction by William Targ.* Los Angeles: Ward Ritchie Press.

———. 1968b. *Fortune & Friendship.* New York: R. R. Bowker.

———. 1987. *"Next to Mother's Milk" . . . An Englehard Lecture on the Book.* Library of Congress Center for the Book. Viewpoint Series, No. 17. Washington, D.C.: Library of Congress.

———. 1991, *Islands of Books.* Los Angeles: Dawson's Book Shop. First published in 1951.

Revock, Ryan. 2013. "Committee Searches for New Dean of University Libraries." *Arizona Daily Wildcat,* February 5. http://www.wildcat.arizona.edu/article/2013/02/committee-searches-for-new-dean-of-university-libraries (accessed March 11, 2013).

Rice, Andrew. 2012. "How Not to Fire a President: The Attack on Teresa Sullivan, and the School That Rose to Her Defense." *New York Times Magazine,* September 10: 55–67.

Riggio, Ronald E., and Heidi R. Riggio. 2008. "Social Psychology and Charismatic Leadership." In *Leadership at the Crossroads: Volume 1: Leadership and Psychology,* ed. Crystal L. Hoyt, George R. Goethals, and Donelson R. Forsyth, 30–44. Westport, CT: Praeger.

Rossiter, Nancy. 2007. "Leadership Effectiveness." In *Making a Difference: Leadership and Academic Libraries,* ed. Peter Hernon and Nancy Rossiter, 111–24. Westport, CT: Libraries Unlimited.

Salovey, Peter, John D. Mayer, and David Caruso. 2002. "The Positive Psychology of Emotional Intelligence." In *The Handbook of Positive Psychology,* ed. Charles Richard Snyder and Shane J. Lopez, 159–71. New York: Oxford University Press.

Sarbanes-Oxley Act 2002. Pub.L. 107–204, 116 *Stat.* 745. http://www.gpo.gov/fdsys/pkg/PLAW-107publ204/pdf/PLAW-107publ204.pdf.

Seligman, Martin. 1990. *Learned Optimism: How to Change Your Mind and Your Life.* New York: Free Press.

————. 2002. *Authentic Happiness: Using the New Positive Psychology to Realize Your Potential for Lasting Fulfillment.* New York: Free Press.

————. 2004. "Can Happiness Be Taught?" *Daedalus* 133 (Spring): 80–87. http://www.mitpressjournals.org/doi/pdf/10.1162/001152604323049424.

————. 2011. *Flourish: A Visionary New Understanding of Happiness and Well-Being.* Oxford: Oxford University Press.

Shaw, Ruth G. 2003. "Be . . . Know . . . Do . . . A Leadership Model That Works." *Executive Speeches* 18 (3): 24–27.

Siders, David. 2013. "Jerry Brown Pressing for Efficiencies at California's Universities." *Sacramento Bee*, January 13. http://www.sacbee.com/2013/01/13/4110838/jerry-brown-pressing-for-efficiencies.html.

Sorensen, Georgia J., and George R. Goethals. 2004. "Leadership Theories Overview." In *Encyclopedia of Leadership 2*, ed. George R. Goethals, Georgia J. Sorensen, and James MacGregor Burns, 867–74. Thousand Oaks, CA: Sage.

Sorensen, Georgia J., George R. Goethals, and Paige Haber. 2011. "The Enduring and Elusive Quest for a General Theory of Leadership: Initial Efforts and New Horizons." In *The SAGE Handbook of Leadership*, ed. Alan Bryman, David Collinson, Keith Grint, Brad Jackson, and Mary Uhl-Bien, 29–36. Thousand Oaks, CA: Sage.

Stoffle, Carla J. and Cheryl Cuillier. 2011. "From Surviving to Thriving." *Journal of Library Administration* 51: 130–55. doi: 10.1080/01930826.2011.531645.

Stoffle, Carla J., Kim Leeder, and Gabrielle Sykes-Casavant. 2008. "Bridging the Gap: Wherever You Are, the Library." *Journal of Library Administration* 48 (1): 3–30. doi:10.1080/01930820802028948.

Strong, Gary E. 2010. "Restructuring at UCLA Library." *ARL Research Library Issues* 272: 16–22. http://publications.arl.org/rli272.

Sullenberger, Chesley "Sully," with Jeffrey Zaslow. 2009. *Highest Duty: My Search for What Really Matters.* New York: HarperCollins.

Tedford, Rosalind, Lauren Corbettt, and Mary Beth Lock. 2012. "How Transformational Leadership Translates into Recognized Excellence in Academic Libraries." *WakeSpace Digital Archive*, Wake Forest University. http://hdl.handle.net/10339/37358.

Townley, Charles T. 2009. "The Innovation Challenge: Transformational Leadership in Technological University Libraries." Paper presented at the 30th International Association of Scientific and Technological Libraries Conference, Katholieke Universiteit Leuven, Belgium, June 1–4. http://iatul.org/doclibrary/public/Conf_Proceedings/2009/Townley-text.pdf.

UCLA Library. 2012. *Progress Report, 2011–2012.* Los Angeles: UCLA Library. http://www.library.ucla.edu/pdf/UCLA_Library_2011-12_progress-report.pdf.

Ulmer, R. R., and Sellnow, T. L. 2002. "Crisis Management and the Discourse of Renewal: Understanding the Potential for Positive Outcomes of Crisis." *Public Relations Review* 28: 316–65. doi: 10.1016/S0363-8111(02)00165-0.

Useem, Michael. 1998. *The Leadership Moment: Nine True Stories of Triumph and Disaster and Their Lessons for Us All.* New York: Times Books.

Vroom, Victor H. 1964. *Work and Motivation.* New York: John Wiley.

Vroom, Victor H., and Philip W. Yetton. 1973. *Leadership and Decision Making.* Pittsburgh: University of Pittsburgh Press.

Weick, Karl E. 1984. "Small Sins: Redefining the Scale of Social Problems." *American Psychologist* 39 (1): 40–49. doi: 10.1037/0003-066x.39.1.40.

Weinberger, David. 2012. *Too Big To Know: Rethinking Knowledge Now That the Facts Aren't the Facts, Experts Are Everywhere, and the Smartest Person in the Room Is the Room.* New York: Basic Books.

Weiskel, Timothy C. 1988. "The Electronic Library: Changing the Character of Research." *Change* 20 (November/December): 43–44. http://www.jstor.org/stable/40164628.

Whyte, Susan B. 2001. "From BI to IL: The ACRL Institute for Information Literacy." *OLA Quarterly* 7.2 (Summer): 14–15.

Wilkinson, James. 1997. "Homesteading on the Electronic Frontier: Technology, Libraries, and Learning." In *Gateways to Knowledge: The Role of Academic Libraries in Teaching, Learning, and Research*, ed. Lawrence Dowler, 191–95. Cambridge, MA: MIT Press.

Wooden, John, and Steve Jamison. 2007. *The Essential Wooden: A Lifetime of Lessons on Leaders and Leadership*. New York: McGraw-Hill.

Yukl, Gary. 2002. *Leadership in Organizations*. 5th ed. Upper Saddle River, NJ: Prentice Hall.

Zaccaro, Steve J. 2007. "Trait-Based Perspectives of Leadership." *American Psychologist* 62 (1): 6–16. doi: 10.1037/0003-066X.62.1.6.

Chapter Three

Leadership Capabilities in the Midst of Transition at the Harvard Library

Deborah S. Garson and Debra Wallace

The field of academic librarianship is experiencing unprecedented change—a perfect storm unleashed by a combination of university administrative mandates for efficiency driven by cost constraints, expanding faculty and student expectations for access to unique resources delivered via a growing range of technologies, and an explosion of data and information in a highly connected digital world. For some, the tsunami-like wave of change is an overwhelming challenge. For others, it is an opportunity to exercise leadership capabilities,[1] reposition resources and expertise, and develop strategies that leverage the significant value academic librarians and libraries contribute to the pursuit of scholarship.

The libraries at Harvard University are in the midst of significant repositioning: a mandate from the president to create the Harvard Library as part of the One Harvard effort and a call for open scholarship by Harvard faculty provide a backdrop for the additional change agendas at each Harvard school (Harvard University 2009).

In this chapter, case studies from the Harvard Graduate School of Education and Harvard Business School illustrate how reframing—a leadership capability used to look at a context from multiple perspectives—was deployed to achieve a sustainable library transformation. Set within the macrocosm of evolving information, higher-education, and academic-library landscapes and the microcosm of Harvard University and two of its professional schools, these cases present leadership structural and cultural frames. The reflection and subsequent discussion of these cases provide two lenses through which to study leadership capabilities that may be adapted to other libraries managing complex change environments.

NEW PERSPECTIVES ON LEADERSHIP

Leaders are no longer characterized by the adage "born to lead." Rather, leadership is characterized as learning, applying, and refining capabilities that successfully change and sustainably grow organizations (Hannah and Avolio 2010). Many organizations continue to adhere to a top-down management model where a hierarchical structure offers the organization the ease of centralized decision making and "the-buck-stops-here" style of management accountability. In theory and often in practice, centralized authority (i.e., a command-and-control model) enables management to distinguish between performance and functions. However, the rise of a global economy and rapid information technology advances have forced organizations, including institutions of higher education, to reexamine traditional leadership models. In many cases, organizations are moving away from a single, centralized management role to a new, distributed leadership model characterized by team-building, visioning, and modeling a culture of learning (Bolman and Gallos 2011; Kouzes and Posner 2007).

In the past, library administrators have relied on two bodies of literature to acquire professional knowledge about leadership: organizational behavior within business management, and library administration within library and information science. Each field has addressed leadership from its distinct perspectives, research findings, and teaching models.

Within the organizational behavior literature, theorists and practitioners are advocating leadership models characterized by flexibility, agility, innovation, and team-based structures (Ancona et al. 2007; Edmondson 2011; Ibarra and Hunter 2007; Nohria et al. 2010; Robbins and Judge 2012; Thomas and Ely 1996). Contemporary approaches to leadership define leaders as communicators who inspire through words, ideas, and collaborative behaviors (Groysberg and Slind 2012). In an environment of rapid organizational change, leadership is required to identify, communicate, and implement a vision of the library's role and function. Change leadership means aligning resources and inspiring staff to go through the necessary transition processes demanded of an organization in these situations. As Barrett states, it is a time for leaders to "break open some of the rigid conventions" and take a leap of faith into the messiness of leading with engagement, passion, and imagination (2012, xv). Leaders with vision, charisma, and sensitivity to employee needs are the most successful in times of change.

Change is a major cause of stress for an organization's employees. Historically, management has adhered to change initiatives based on theories and practices that subscribe to the concept that individuals resist change. The field of leadership offers a different and more holistic perspective on what has been defined as employee resistance to change. "People don't resist change," Heifetz said (2009, 325). "Nobody gives back a winning lottery ticket. People resist loss." Successful leaders understand employees can be motivated by and successful in a changing work environment and believe in enhancing employee engagement by aligning individual and organizational goals. Such leaders create work environments where employees feel empowered and connected to the change process. A key to the success of organizational change is sustaining an inclusive environment, another responsibility of leadership. Employees become active participants if they believe the change will create opportunities for themselves as well as the organization. They are motivated by and participate in an environment replete with new tasks, functions, and goals.

THE EVOLVING ACADEMIC LIBRARY ENVIRONMENT

Current external and internal factors challenge all organizations; however, academic libraries face additional distinctive challenges. As noted above, change drivers affect both the macro and micro environments, which set the context for this look at leadership capabilities (see figure 3.1).

The academic library environment has been written about and discussed at great length (Association of College and Research Libraries 2010; Hernon 2010; Hinchcliffe 2011; Staley and Malenfant 2010; Sullivan 1999). Often situated in a unique position within their institution, the library is accountable to a diverse group of stakeholders: faculty, students, researchers, administrators, and in some cases consortiums—especially when a legal agreement

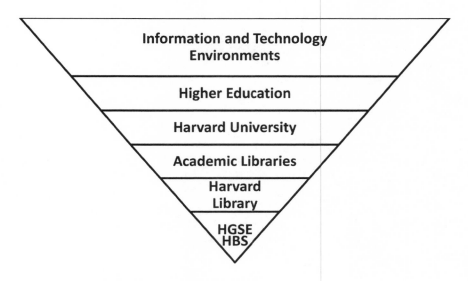

Figure 3.1.   Change Environments: Macro to Micro

among consortium members is in place. Governing bodies, reporting structures, and dependence on information technology departments are no longer standard. Leadership requirements are complex and layered within the higher education institution.

The pace and volume of change within the information technology and higher education landscapes, coupled with the dawn of a new century, are among the many catalysts behind the predictions about the 21st-century academic library by library and information science scholars, libraries, and their professional associations. Library leaders' change management programs are based on a diverse set of inputs, including evidence-based decisions from a multidisciplinary literature, organizational mandates, and intuition.

In the introduction to their call for developing a research agenda to explore academic library leadership, Hernon and Schwartz provide a daunting list of elements influencing the highly charged change environment surrounding academic libraries: "complex organizations, competitive environment, constrained resources, re-engineering and outsourcing, change management, culture of assessment, the extraordinary pace at which information and knowledge is being digitized, convergence and collaboration, and myriad issues associated with information management and services and with the information lifecycle" (2008, 243). Expectations that the library must provide value in new ways across the university, from faculty teaching effectiveness and research impact to enhanced student achievement and learning outcomes to increased economic efficiencies, cause library leaders to innovate across multiple dimensions simultaneously.

A recent environmental scan by the Association of College and Research Libraries (ACRL) provided a comprehensive look at current and emerging trends affecting academic libraries (ACRL 2013). In addition to the changing nature of higher education, new approaches to scholarly communication, and rapid advances in technology, the study notes key shifts in library practice to radical collaboration, assessment, and accountability (ACRL 2013). The long list of challenges and opportunities that require new skills and mind-sets is topped by implications for new information products and services, organizational designs, customer engagement, tools, and assessment approaches. ACRL's website is brimming with white papers, professional development opportunities, and policy statements detailing approaches to reposition traditional libraries.

Likewise, the Association of Research Libraries (ARL) provides extensive resources, including the organization's own strategic plan, to manage an aggressive change agenda. "Scenario 2030: A User's Guide" (ARL 2010) is one example of adapting a business-management strategic-planning technique to ask the question, "How do we transform our organization(s) to create differential value for future users (individuals, institutions, and beyond), given the external dynamics redefining the research environment over the next 20 years?" (12). The resulting 2x2 matrix,[2] comprised of the modalities of research enterprises (aggregated to diffused) versus individual researchers (constrained to unconstrained), yielded four diverse scenarios to guide planning: research entrepreneurs, reuse and recycle, disciplines in charge, and global followers. The study also identified common themes across scenarios—elements that are necessary today and in the future, such as the need for diverse and novel revenue sources, engaging in the full research cycle including content stewardship, and creating cooperative capabilities. These relatively near-term future state themes support Gibson's notion that "The future is here. It's just not evenly distributed yet!" (Kennedy 2012).

Management strategies for library leaders to develop action plans leading toward the future are outlined in theory and in practice. McKnight (2010) identified the importance of managing change, positioning it as a constant as opposed to an event and highlighting the proactive stance leaders must adopt, quoting Sapp and Gilmour (2003, 14): "Change happens. Transformation, however, is planned" (McKnight 2010, xvii). Haycock et al. outlined the importance of building the capabilities of strategic thinking as well as strategic planning:

> Organizations—whether for-profit or not—are competing in an unpredictable and volatile marketplace that demands a greater capacity for innovation and diverse strategic thinking in order to create and sustain advantage. Libraries face competition for the time and attention of the customer or the user. They also face a somewhat unknown future given the changes in resources and technologies and a crowded information marketplace (2012, 13).

Combining creative, synthetic thinking with logical and systematic planning based on informed decision-making results in strategic innovation.

Scholars have also outlined approaches for shaping an organization's culture and its structure. Neal and Jaggars (2010, 55) said an increasing number of academic libraries are adopting new models based on 2.0 thinking. Key characteristics of these new models include: decentralization, distribution, advocacy, complexity, informality, innovation, and collaboration. In order to do so, however, academic librarians "must redefine the physical, expertise, and intellectual infrastructure while promoting and understanding the geography, psychology and economics of innovation" (Neal and Jaggars 2010, 66).

Whether academic library leaders revitalize, reinvent, reconceive, or reposition, the result must be transformational. The game-changing nature of the next-generation academic library with library at web-scale, working with big data in the cloud, or serving up resources to users no matter their personal device preference makes even library 2.0 sound passé (Kwanya et al. 2012). While the literature shows library leaders and scholars are excellent at identifying possible scenarios and applying business management strategies to new situations, it remains to be seen whether individual academic libraries and the industry as a whole can reshape the culture, implement an adaptive organizational structure, and develop the capabilities required to achieve the inspirational vision statements found in strategic plans.

ADAPTING LEADERSHIP MODELS TO CHANGE ENVIRONMENTS

Leadership theory and practice is a body of knowledge based in the fields of organizational behavior and management. As stated earlier, leaders are not born but develop through a combination of education and experience. Leadership as a field of study has developed models based on theories and practices effective in the work environment. A model can guide a leader's actions to achieve successful organizational change and offer effective practices to employ in a change environment. It can inform a leader's decision making and goal setting based on proven and workable theories of organizational behavior. A leadership model can also offer leaders an opportunity to reflect on their individual beliefs and assumptions about management, which can influence success. Leaders may believe their perceptions and beliefs are based on how things work or how things should work, but too often these perceptions and beliefs negate clear, rational decision making. A leadership model applies behavioral knowledge based on proven theory and practice to create and advance an organization's mission. By understanding the causes and effects of individual and group behavior, a leader can shape employees as drivers of organizational effectiveness.

The organizational behavior literature for best practices positions academic library managers to be effective, proactive, and consequential leaders (Avolio, Walumbwa, and Weber 2009; Dyer, Gregersen, and Christensen 2009; Garvin, Edmondson, and Gino 2008; Thomas and Ely 1996). Understanding the organizational behavior literature is the intellectual foundation from which library leaders can develop, build, and demonstrate leadership capabilities. It can guide academic library leaders to achieve goals and objectives, and it can identify new emerging leadership models that are innovative and often outside the higher education institution's reliance on traditional leadership practices. Organizational behavior scholars have quickly responded to and incorporated changing political and demographic environments into innovative leadership theories and practices (Ancona et al. 2007; Dyer et al. 2011; Edmondson 2011; Groysberg and Slind 2012; Ibarra and Hunter 2007; Kegan and Lahey 2010). In a growing global economy, recognizing the education marketplace's diversity and the necessity of new approaches to workplace leadership is critical (Bell 2013; Kanter 2010). In today's environment, a key attribute of effective library leaders is a willing-ness to explore and engage with curiosity, a readiness to learn and adapt, and above all a questioning as to the relevance and applicability of established and new models to the organization (Gwyer 2010).

Traditionally, library management and leadership models have relied on the classics of business theory and practice, as well as established "brick-and-mortar" institutional practices, which are falling short in the new dynam-ic higher education environment (Bush 2003; Doyle and Smith 2001). Neal (in Gilstrap 2009) viewed academic libraries' adherence to the established hierarchical organizational model as a hindrance in a change environment. Despite their guise of leadership, these models situate and perpetuate the academic library as a "slow, linear, and disconnected" organization (Gilstrap 2009, 67). Neal advocated for library science researchers to study academic libraries as complex systems requiring innovative leadership specific to the institution's organization and mission. This research perspective and agenda, Neal believed, would produce the "strong theoretical framework" for the type of leadership required within today's fast-paced change environment of the higher education academic library (Gilstrap 2009, 67). Academic librar-ies require leadership capable of anticipating, addressing, and leading change. Researching and studying models applicable to academic library leadership requires reinterpreting or reframing existing organizational-be-havior leadership models and existing library leadership models to develop a new library leadership framework. Researchers and practitioners such as Bush, Bell, and Gilstrap advocate for a body of leadership literature that addresses the distinct leadership capabilities required in an academic envi-ronment, separate and distinct from the traditional models and practices of the broader field of organizational behavior.

Library leadership is just beginning to develop its own theories and prac-tices from discipline-based research. While the field has come to recognize the need for discipline-specific theory and practice, it is in its infancy and as such must continue to use some existing leadership literature from the broad-er literature of organizational behavior. However, adopting existing theories and practices for the academic library must be done with a critical eye toward the discipline's desired outcomes. What the for-profit business world looks to achieve is usually not what higher education sets out to achieve within its educational organization and mission (Bolman and Gallos 2011). As library leadership research and study evolves, organizational behavior literature can continue to inform and offer a foundation in which to adapt and build a new set of theories and practices, albeit with a critical eye to ongoing evaluation and assessment of the theory's application (Ancona et al. 2007; Dyer, Gre-gersen, and Christensen 2011; Edmondson 2011; Groysberg and Slind 2012; Ibarra and Hunter 2007; Kegan and Lahey 2010). Gilstrap's article analyzing library leadership theories advocated for the development and existence of an

informed academic library leadership to avoid "stumbling" upon inappropri-
ate organizational behavior theories (Gilstrap 2009, 65).

The field of library and information science (LIS) has begun to address
library leadership with emerging studies from Hernon and Schwartz (2008,
2011), Sullivan (1998, 1999), Fagan (2012), and Weiner (2003). Library
leaders are sometimes at a disadvantage in the highly charged and fast-paced
environment of higher education. The leadership required in libraries necessitates its own foundational literature on academic libraries as organizations
within a larger nonprofit institutional setting. Gilstrap's analysis of academic
library leadership research (2009) noted the lack of studies specific to theories, such as contingency and situational, in the library science literature.
Gilstrap acknowledged the existence and growth of leadership and organizational theories in the LIS field, but he also noted a continuing "disconnect
between theory and application" in academic libraries (2009, 66). He advocated for complexity theory as a means to integrate "disparate theories of
organizational behavior and leadership practice" (2009, 72). With the proliferation of leadership theories from various perspectives and fields and these
theories' increasing complexity, a library leader has an increasingly difficult
task in choosing a theory, resolving possible disparities between the theory
and the practice, and implementing best practices to fit the situation at hand.

Many disciplines have recognized a problematic relationship between
theory and practice, and have identified a lack of discourse between theoretical and practical communities. The field of leadership is not exempt from this
debate. The lack of connectedness between theory and practice presents challenges for both the researcher and the practitioner.

In addition to considering which disciplines can inform and advance library leadership study, it is critical to acknowledge and use emerging library
science research on leadership. Traditionally, the field of librarianship has
not prioritized leadership in its learning and teaching pedagogy. Graduate
education and professional development have focused on developing expertise specific to functions, such as reference services and information management, while historically few opportunities existed for library leadership development in either a graduate program or a professional development opportunity. Today's library and information science researchers and practitioners
are very concerned about the growing need for the study and practice of
leadership based on the rapidly changing organizational behavior of libraries
and the evolving needs of its users and institutions. In an article on library
leadership skills, Bell (2013) predicted a lack of leadership in 2020 unless the
profession makes a commitment to learning about "leadership through research studies" (3).

EMERGING LIBRARY LEADERSHIP CAPABILITIES

Changing leadership needs are evidenced in library director position requirements, which have shifted from emphasizing professional research and library science qualifications to management and leadership capabilities. Library leadership positions are being filled with MBAs as well as the traditional MLSs and PhDs. The library and information science field is just
beginning to define degree program and professional development needs
based on these new capabilities, as evidenced by the January 2013 announcement of a new library school with a new online degree (Masters of Management in Library and Information Science—MMLIS) offered in partnership
with the University of Southern California Libraries and the USC Marshall
School of Business (Marshall 2013). Within this evolving environment,
many academic libraries have undergone a change in organizational culture
from a traditional management focus on the institution (i.e., "it's all about the
library") to a broader focus on library users. This user-centric perspective
necessitates a shift in a library's culture. Library directors are moving from a
traditional role of managing functions and tasks in a hierarchical structure to
leading an organization by actively shaping the culture through a discourse
of goals, mission, and outcomes based on user needs. To be successful, this
approach must be dynamic, robust, and closely integrated with the teaching,
learning, and research functions of the institution and aspirations of its users
(Bolman and Gallos 2011).

Obviously, situational factors influence the range of leadership capabilities needed in any given organization. Certainly, library leaders acknowledge that libraries are in a state of constant change in the digital world—
change ranging from incremental stages of moving from print to digital media to rapid changes created by personalized, mobile access to information.
Transitions are occurring more frequently and rapidly than ever before. Corporate takeovers, institutional consolidation and closings, centralization of
functions, and global expansion are a few examples of rapid transition drivers in today's world. The academic library is not exempt from the effects of
these transitions (Budd 2012).

Organizational transitions, whether large or small, require strong, creative
leadership. For academic libraries, a clear vision communicated to all stakeholders about where the changes will lead and how the larger community of
the university, academic librarians, faculty, and students will benefit is
needed. With the emergence of technical advances in information discovery,
data analysis, and open access, librarians require a broader range of capabilities to influence this process. Leading this new workforce of both specialized and generalist professionals to meet the demands of its communities
requires a shift in focus from management to leadership capabilities and the

ability to assess situations from new perspectives. Bolman and Deal's four-frame model is one approach for leaders to consider.

THE FOUR-FRAME MODEL

Combining their interests in organizational design and behavior, symbolism, and change with an analysis of effective leadership capabilities in practice across a wide range of public and private enterprises, Bolman and Deal (1984) developed a four-frame model for managing organizations. Grounded in a blend of social science and managerial wisdom, the frames provide multiple perspectives from which a leader can view a management challenge or opportunity and take appropriate action (Bolman and Deal 2008).

The authors posited that managers often fail because they are clueless. They fail because they do not understand the organizational context, which is complex and ambiguous. They view the organization, an opportunity, or a challenge through a single lens and make decisions based on "faulty thinking rooted in inadequate ideas" (2008, 21). They see only a small slice of their environment. By using multiple frames, leaders have "a filter for sorting essence from trivia, maps that aid navigation, and tools for solving problems and getting things done" (2008, 21). Each frame is described briefly in terms of its purpose and focus, characteristics or assumptions, strategies, challenges, and success criteria.

Structural Frame

The structural frame focuses on designing a social architecture that enables people to succeed by doing their best and avoids misdirecting an organization's energy and resources. Two dimensions are primary influencers of organizational design decisions: allocating work or the division of labor (differentiation) and creating mechanisms for coordinating among distributed responsibilities (integration). If people are put in the right roles with effective integration across functions, both the collective goals and individual differences can be accommodated. The design goal is not to create an inflexible structure but to assess the unique circumstances that will enable the organization to respond to internal and external factors. In addition to the broader organization structure, this frame includes approaches for organizing groups and teams—from hierarchical to networked; centralized to distributed—the key is to find a structure that enables effective group performance. Restructuring is a natural extension of this frame because of the constantly changing environments of most organizations. Success relies on the organization's ability to reconceptualize its goals and strategies; understand its existing structures and processes; align the new structure to changes in goals, technology, and the environment; and experiment, keeping what works and discarding what does not.

Human Resource Frame

Through the human resource frame, leaders focus on aligning people's and the organization's needs, finding a balance in this complex codependency and addressing a longstanding organizational dilemma between downsizing (or employing a different workforce structure) and investing in its people to increase motivation and skills, resulting in high performance. Understanding human behavior and addressing conflict between personalities and management practices is necessary for effective human resources management. With a comprehensive human resource strategy to enable the organization to hire and keep the right people, invest in learning, empower employees by keeping them informed and encouraging autonomy, fostering teams, and offering meaningful work, the organization outlines its long-term commitment to effective human resources practices. A key challenge with using this frame is understanding interpersonal and group dynamics. Developing the capabilities that enable groups and teams to effectively operate at both the task (i.e., what we are going to do) and process (i.e., how we are going to do it) levels is a critical leadership role.

Political Frame

The current view of politics and politicians, which Bolman and Deal (2008) contend is universally despised and seen as an unavoidable evil, tends to position the political frame in a negative light (189); however, this frame's focus is on making decisions and allocating scarce resources—key management responsibilities. Knowing that organizations are coalitions of individuals and interest groups with differences in values, beliefs, interests, information, and perceptions of reality and that conflicts arise because not enough resources exist to meet the diverse needs, leaders are placed in the center of conflict resolution on a day-to-day basis. They need specialized political capabilities to resolve these conflicts (e.g., set the agenda, a strategy for achieving a vision; map the political landscape; establish strategic networks and coalitions; and negotiate win-win approaches). At the same time, they need to address the inevitable ethical dilemma of whether to implement an open, transparent strategy or to wield managerial power. In the end, organizational change and performance rely on constructive politicians.

Symbolic Frame

Creating meaning by making sense of a chaotic or ambiguous environment is central to the symbolic frame, which is based on ideas from multiple disciplines (e.g., sociology, political science, neuroscience, anthropology). The frame assumes that intent and expression are more important than the result or product, that people experience life differently from each other, that people create symbols to address confusion, and that culture brings people together to enable an organization's success. Meaning, belief, and faith are elements from which to explore organizational symbols—the myths, vision, stories, heroes and heroines, and rituals. This frame also explores an organization's culture as a product (i.e., wisdom accumulated from experience) or a process that is renewed and re-created. Used to shape a more effective organization, culture is built over time and defines "the way we do things around here." The organizational process is depicted as theater, where activities such as meetings, strategic planning, evaluation, and collective bargaining are examples of events to express opportunities, discuss issues, and create meaning.

REFRAMING AN ORGANIZATION: TWO CASE STUDIES

In the fourth edition of their 1984 work, Bolman and Deal (2008) emphasize the need for *reframing*—a leadership capability used to look at a context from multiple perspectives, to potentially break existing frames, and create new mental models that enable effective management within the constantly changing environment of any organization. Reframing helps a leader examine a given situation from a variety of perspectives and generate new options, not just rely on a single approach for every situation. The authors emphasized reframing "cannot guarantee that every new strategy will be successful. Each lens offers distinctive advantages, but each has its blind spots and shortcomings" (2008, 339). As academic library leaders are aware, organizations are complex, full of surprises, often deceptive, and ambiguous, and therefore "formidably difficult to comprehend and manage" (Bolman and Deal 2008, 41). Bolman and Deal discussed a blend of management and leadership capabilities; outlined assumptions, characteristics, strategies, and challenges; and described experiences with the four frames in modern organizations across private and public sectors. This discussion gives academic library leaders another tool to assess a situation and judge which frame or combination of frames will yield the best result.

The following case studies are examples of reframing—experimenting with multiple perspectives to manage change. Presented with numerous, significant change drivers (i.e., the perfect storm outlined in the chapter introduction), Knowledge and Library Services at the Harvard Business School experimented with a structural frame, and Gutman Library at the Harvard Graduate School of Education applied various approaches from a human-relations frame. How each frame was applied, the leadership capabilities in play that enabled a positive outcome, and a discussion of the blind spots and shortcomings are described within the context of each related yet unique situation. The cases are prefaced by a brief overview of the multiyear process underway to create a new model for Harvard libraries.

Harvard Library Transition

Since the creation of Harvard's libraries in 1638, change has been a constant. In 2009, the university undertook perhaps the most significant review of the more than 90 libraries that comprise the system. Based on the findings of this multiyear process, Provost Alan Garber announced a new library organization in September 2011.[3] Key to the transition was the development of a hybrid organizational model that included a centralized or shared services management structure combined with defined roles and responsibilities for the various school and faculty libraries. The Harvard Library transition will continue to be a significant change driver for the foreseeable future. With this backdrop and the other change environment drivers noted in figure 3.1, the Harvard Graduate School of Education and the Harvard Business School libraries are faced with a complex change management environment that offers opportunities to experiment with approaches that lead to achieving individual and collective missions and objectives.

The following case studies illustrate what was done with reframing approaches in each and how leadership capabilities were leveraged to create further opportunities for repositioning the libraries, successfully engaging in the broader Harvard Library transition, and identifying new opportunities to add value to their respective communities.

Case Study #1: Knowledge and Library Services, Harvard Business School

Coined a "delicate experiment" by future Harvard president A. Lawrence Lowell, Harvard Business School (HBS) was established in 1908 (Cruikshank and Chandler 1987). Since inception, HBS has pioneered the case method, established a library with extensive historical and contemporary collections, launched a publishing business, built a forty-acre residential campus, and continued to develop the discipline of business management through faculty research, curriculum development, and alumni engagement. The school's flagship two-year MBA program includes about 1,800 students, and its executive education program enrolls 10,000 participants annually. More than 200 faculty teach across the school's programs and conduct research around the globe, contributing to HBS's case collection, academic journals, books, and other forms of scholarly communication. About 800 staff facilitate the school's programs, both on campus and at seven global research centers.

Nitin Nohria became the tenth dean of Harvard Business School in July 2010. Since then, he has outlined an aggressive program for continuing the school's leadership in the field and practice of business management education. Beginning with innovation in the MBA program, the dean's priorities also include a recommitment to intellectual ambition, a broader global strategy, a more inclusive community, and proactive engagement in intra-Harvard University collaboration.

Knowledge and Library Services

An initial gift of $1,000 established a small collection to support the fledgling school, but it was Dean Gay's vision (1908–1919) of a business library that could parallel the Harvard Law and Medical libraries combined with Dean Donham's interest (1919–1942) in business history that fueled aggressive collecting efforts to obtain both published materials and unpublished business records. The "few books and pamphlets in one alcove of Gore Hall" grew exponentially into a collection that required a building of its own (Altman 1981, 171). Baker Library, named after George F. Baker, who funded the initial HBS campus, was dedicated in 1927 and underwent a major renovation between 2003 and 2005.

Starting with the appointment of a superintendent of the school's Reading Room in 1910, the workforce has grown to nearly eighty. A combination of librarians, researchers, archivists, conservators, journalists, information architects, search engineers, taxonomists, and business operations staff in permanent positions is supplemented with term employees, interns, contractors, and consultants. Similarly, services have expanded from collecting and research support to include information-product development, online publishing, enterprise content management, data management, and curriculum and course development. While the Baker Library building remains the campus's iconic symbol, the new range of services and responsibilities prompted renaming the group Knowledge and Library Services (KLS) in 2008.

Today, with nearly 50,000 physical visits to the reading rooms annually, 500,000 hits on the library's public website (see http://www.library.hbs.edu), 3.5 million hits on the library's publication about HBS faculty research (*Working Knowledge*—see http://hbswk.hbs.edu), and continued growth in print, manuscript, and digital collections, KLS sits at an inflection point—an opportunity to chart a course that will support the school's mission into the next century.

The Change Environment

In addition to the change environment enveloping academic research librar-ies, KLS faced significant internal changes. A new dean with an aggressive innovation mandate, a new executive director with an education background, a new organizational model for the Harvard Library, and five open positions presented opportunities and challenges for managing change at both the macro and micro levels. It would be disingenuous to suggest change was anything new to KLS, which has a long tradition of experimentation and repositioning led by senior library administrators and encouraged by the various faculty and administrative governance bodies that advised library leaders on KLS's priorities and directions.

Under the leadership of Mary Lee Kennedy (executive director 2004–2011), KLS had analyzed its current state, outlined a future state through scenario planning, and implemented a series of strategic shifts. As a result, significant changes were implemented, including:

- A balanced scorecard approach was developed to assess performance.
- The knowledge and information asset group was formed to develop stan-dards and practices for enterprise-wide information lifecycle management.
- New internal processes and tools, such as project management, practice areas and annual roadmaps to organize services and track progress against plans, key performance indicators for information product evaluation, and a key customer liaison program, were implemented to increase effective-ness.
- A network of primary data resource providers in India and China was established to support global research.

At the beginning of fiscal year 2012, KLS was well-positioned to contribute to the new dean's priorities and implement the transition to the new Harvard Library structure mandated by Harvard's president. Just as KLS's strategic plan (FY 2008–2011) reached its end date, a new executive director was named. Given the amount of change confronting the library organization, the new executive director took the opportunity to look at KLS with a different perspective.

Reframing through a Structural Perspective

KLS's new executive director combined strategies from Dean Nohria's ap-proach as new dean (e.g., listen, articulate, mobilize and plan, execute and engage, and evaluate and extend) and former HBS professor Michael Wat-kins's management transition advice outlined in *The First 90 Days: Critical Success Strategies for New Leaders at All Levels* (2003). Along with members of KLS's management team, a two-phase strategy for charting KLS's course for the next three years was developed:

Strategy Reflection (August–December 2011). Take stock; understand what is working or not working; update mission and vision; identify realistic priorities for moving forward; prepare a budget proposal for FY13 (July 2012–June 2011).

Strategy Implementation (February–September 2012). Implement new organizational and leadership structures; develop priority goals and deliverables for FY13; implement funded priorities; begin culture shift.

Guiding principles provided continuity across project components. These included:

- Build on distinctive capabilities, core strengths, and the foundation in place. Continue the strategic shifts.
- Remain aligned with the school's mission and priorities with a focus on where KLS can continue to grow and extend its value.
- Keep the approach, language, tools, and processes simple.
- Leverage the faculty's work and ground decisions in evidence. Be informed leaders.
- Engage staff. Be inclusive at all levels. Create buy-in through ownership of ideas and shared responsibility. Validate understandings, assumptions, and directions.
- Promote authentic, systematic, and regular communication. Manage expectations.
- Involve senior HBS management. Create buy-in for FY13 budget implementation.

To begin the strategy reflection component, KLS engaged a consultant from HOW Management—someone who had worked on an earlier organization redesign, was knowledgeable about KLS's business, and had considerable experience with change management environments. He was instrumental in helping design the approach, manage the process, and complete deliverables. Over a four-month period, KLS worked through a series of steps that look linear but in practice were iterative (see figure 3.2).

Using KLS's existing project management process, the leadership team created a project charter, established a core project team, and developed a project plan that outlined the key tasks, milestones, and communication approach. Although the process resembled a standard project management approach, steps were shaped to meet organizational needs, adopting the motto attributed to an anonymous Spanish poet, "We build the road as we travel." As illustrated in figure 3.2, staff engagement (x-axis) increased not only at the visioning stage but throughout the project. At the same time, the commu-

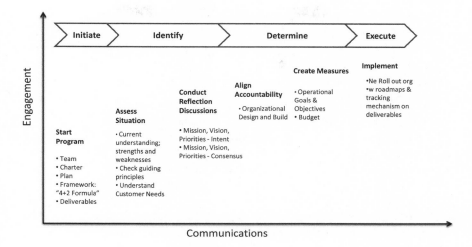

Figure 3.2.   KLS Strategy Reflection Approach

nication level (y-axis) significantly increased across KLS participant and stakeholder groups.

Start Program

To frame the process, the project team used the 4+2 formula for sustained business success (Nohria, Joyce, and Roberson 2013). In a ten-year study of 160 organizations, the authors investigated the management practices that differentiated companies dramatically outperforming their peers. Their findings identified four common practices plus an additional four practices of which at least two were present in successful organizations. The common elements included:

- a well-defined and clearly communicated **strategy**;
- operational excellence—**execution** that consistently meets customers' expectations;
- a **culture** of high performance and high values—inspiration, empowerment, and reward within a challenging and satisfying work environment; and
- a **structure** that simplifies working in and with the organization—(i.e., reduced bureaucracy).

In addition to these four practices, the project team identified two practices that aligned with the school's priorities and the Harvard Library Transition's objectives:

- superior **talent** at all levels (given the number of specialized capabilities found within KLS and the number of open positions we had to work with) and
- driving **innovation**—turning out innovative products and services and anticipating disruptive events rather than reacting when it's too late.

Assess Situation

As part of the executive director's orientation plan, she conducted interviews with thirty key KLS customers, including members of the dean's management group (senior associate deans), senior faculty, and the school's senior administrators. Key findings showed that KLS's primary users:

- did not know the full range of available services (what work was undertaken for the rest of the faculty, student bodies, and administrative groups) from KLS. A more comprehensive communication approach was needed with an increase in frequency and variety of channels.
- did not understand staff verbal or written communications. "Can you put that in plain English?" was a common request.
- knew KLS had a lot of people who provided great service but found the organization complicated. Users needed guidance on how to get to the right place.
- never thought about the library as anything but a traditional academic research library. Users requested help in understanding the possibilities to experiment, trying new approaches, and integrating information sources and tools in new ways.

Conduct Reflective Discussions

Through a series of meetings, workshops, and informal discussions, the project team engaged in reflective conversations with staff and among themselves. Five key questions aligned with project deliverables (see table 3.1).

Staff engagement was critical to developing an achievable mission, vision, and set of priorities. About 75 percent of the staff volunteered to participate in multiple sessions, culminating in an all-staff meeting, where the mission, vision, and priority statements were ratified—a key step for creating buy-in and ownership for the three-year vision.

Align Accountability

With goals defined, the project team assessed the internal structures needed to achieve them. The organizational design was approached in terms of a reporting structure, working group descriptions, individual role and job outlines, performance measures, and integrating mechanisms. The school's

Table 3.1.   Reflective Conversation Topics

Question	Deliverable
Why do we exist? What's our purpose?	Mission
What are going to do? What's the future state we want to achieve?	Vision
How are we going to get there?	Priorities
What is the work to be done?	Goals/roadmaps of tasks and deliverables
What results will we measure?	Objectives and budgets

chief human resources officer also helped think creatively about leveraging full time equivalents, filling open positions, and promoting staff from within. As a result:

- The organization was flattened, pushing responsibility for budget management and achieving priorities to group directors.
- Two new groups to lead future-facing priorities were formed (digital content program and an information products and innovation program), and a new group to provide administration and communication support was created.
- Two virtual groupings across the organizational design were formed: customer services (research, teaching, learning, knowledge dissemination, and information management services) and organizational capabilities (collections, technology infrastructure, business management, Harvard Library Shared Services integration, and management).
- Two new integrating mechanisms were implemented: a customer experience program to work across the four customer-facing service groups to ensure consistency and excellence in service delivery and a new leadership structure that broadened the engagement of managers through a series of targeted meetings (e.g., leadership exchange, customer service management, organizational capabilities, strategy management, and budget review).

Create Measures

The strategy reflection project laid the groundwork for preparing KLS's FY13 budget proposal, which was needed to fund the new priorities. In other words, without appropriate funding, the resources necessary to deliver the proposed vision would not be available. As the budget submission was prepared (a combination of operating budget and special project funding requests), KLS was also engaged in the school's information technology project prioritization process. Given KLS's future dependency on a robust information technology infrastructure, the operational goals were heavily reliant on successful project proposals.

In early May 2012, KLS learned the majority of the budget requests had been approved, but only one of the four technology projects would be included in FY13. Knowing the funding levels, goals could be finalized along with the tasks and deliverables necessary to move toward achieving KLS's vision. Leadership team members were assigned as "priority owners" and held another series of workshops where staff volunteered to work on a priority of interest to them. Workshop output was amalgamated to form the FY13 Plan—a road map of the cross-KLS work focused on achieving priorities. This road map, combined with ongoing work related to providing KLS services, gave staff an outline of their FY13 work and related professional development needs, two components of the yearly performance review and planning process.

Implement

At this time, KLS is nearing the end of FY13 and already experiencing another wave of change that requires adjustments to priorities. Transactional statistics have increased across services, the dean announced a new initiative to explore online learning, the school received a major gift to build a new executive education building that will house a satellite library service point, Special Collections obtained a significant collection of contemporary business records, and the Harvard Library has undergone senior leadership changes. The organization's emphasis on implementing the two inward-facing priorities—a flexible organization and a culture of collaborative innovation—will help KLS keep pace with the constantly evolving environment.

Internal Assessment of Approach and Lessons Learned

Given that the original future course aligned with the school's priorities was maintained, KLS's enduring goals, developed nearly five years prior to the strategy reflection work, still resonate. The focused reflection that included a commitment to build on successes and ensure broad engagement of staff and senior decision makers has been successful. Financial support and the resources necessary to move forward on KLS's vision are in place—almost 90 percent of KLS's FY14 budget was approved. The strategy reflection provided an opportunity to pause and think strategically about positioning services and expertise. KLS's values were confirmed, and services were validated with a wide range of stakeholders. Key to the project's success was the ability to:

- engage staff and HBS senior administrators so KLS leaders had buy-in during budget decisions, which in turn facilitated implementing KLS operational goals;
- conduct targeted outreach to KLS partners and customers, which was an opportunity not only to get valuable feedback, but to educate them about the wide range of value we could contribute to achieving their goals;
- develop a leadership culture with accountabilities and shared responsibilities that were not organized by department but by priorities, which enabled the cross-department teaming needed to do increasingly complex work;
- begin to shift culture and improve employee engagement, a process that was in and of itself transformative in that we modeled the behavior we hoped to see to shape a new culture of risk taking and learning through small- and big-scale innovation; and,
- leverage the school's planning process, allowing KLS to act on planning, show immediate gains, and position the organization to deliver on commitments, given that leadership was now in sync with the school's decision-making cycle.

Strategy Reflection to Strategy Implementation to Strategy Evaluation

KLS is still in the early days of implementing the new priorities identified during the strategy reflection phase. Like Baker's pioneering librarians, the staff continues to seek ways to add value and to contribute significantly to the school's mission. While the eight priorities identified were not presented in ranked order, shaping a new culture is key. Without a collaborative culture that fosters trust, recognizes performance, values innovation, and enhances our capabilities, KLS cannot achieve its other seven priorities. While many of the building blocks are in place, KLS must deliver on its brand promise in concrete ways valued by the HBS community and related stakeholders.

Baker Library, both as an iconic symbol of the campus and a trusted brand promise, is well recognized by its stakeholders, and KLS's new tag line *Baker 2.0: Informed Leaders Start Here* is beginning to resonate. As FY13 draws to a close, FY14 planning has begun, starting with an evaluation of the existing priorities: what has been accomplished, what has diminished in importance because of new factors, and what has not succeeded. The cycle of listening, planning, executing, evaluating, and extending continues to iterate.

Discussion

Working at HBS is inspiring for any leader, no matter the teaching unit, program, or department. With the HBS mission "to educate leaders who make a difference in the world," KLS is surrounded by faculty, students, and

staff who are exploring the components of effective leadership (see http://
www.hbs.edu/about/academic-programs/Pages/default.aspx). As is often the
case with "shoemaker's children," the richness of opportunity afforded by an
environment that encourages learning and experimentation, drawing on the
knowledge of thought-leaders, and accessing the extensive resources held
within the library collections and produced by Harvard Business Press could
easily be missed.

Former Baker Library directors have been recognized for their innovative
approaches to collection development, early adoption of information technologies, expansion from traditional library services to Web design, scholarly
publishing and enterprise-wide information management services, and excellence in facility renovation and space planning. Continuing this history of
innovation was a key leadership challenge; building on previous successes
while repositioning the library's priorities demanded a more flexible organization, broader and deeper staff engagement, and delivery of concrete value
through products and services aligned with user needs.

The structural frame provided a lens for the executive director to first
make sense of the turbulent change environment and avoid "the curse of
cluelessness" (Bolman and Deal 2008, 7). Understanding the new dean's
thinking, KLS staff's opinions on challenges and opportunities and the users'
needs contributed to articulating key drivers and priorities that needed to be
considered. The strategy reflection phase broadened staff engagement, created a new level of shared understanding, and highlighted the importance of
transparency. In the strategy implementation phase, when a new organizational design was developed, the need for greater clarity concerning roles and
responsibilities was key. To achieve the strategic shifts outlined in the
2008–2011 strategic plan, new groups had been established to provide more
nontraditional services. Unfortunately, the staff was clearly confused about
performance expectations and how their distinctive knowledge and skills
would be most effectively used. Ambiguity had increased to a point of dis-
traction. Possible next steps to address the situation are found within the
structural frame's six underlying assumptions (i.e., appropriate division of
labor and analysis of structural deficiencies) (Bolman and Deal 2008, 47). In
2013, KLS has undertaken a workforce planning project to clarify roles and
responsibilities of the two new groups formed during the Strategy Implementation Phase (digital content program and the information products group).
As with the initial work, staff engagement and continuous communication
are key components of the organizational redesign project.

KLS's change management approach resulted in a new statement of vision, mission, and priorities; an understanding of how existing structures and
processes work; a redesigned organization based on its change environment;
and a shift in culture to embrace experimentation, reflection, and learning.
When these outputs are compared to the basic principles of successful struc-

tural changes (see Bolman and Deal 2008, 96–97), KLS's approach bodes well for weathering the perfect storm and transforming the organization into a sustainable model of an academic research library for the new century.

Case Study #2: Monroe C. Gutman Library, Harvard Graduate School of Education

The following case study offers a view of academic library management and leadership during a time of change. The case study uses Bolman and Deal's human resource framework, which places a high value on individuals in the workplace, as a lens on change management and leadership (2008). Why study the relationship between the individual employee and leader, and why is understanding a leader's relationship to employees important for success? Employees contribute to organizational goals, and their contributions relate to fit and satisfaction within the job and the organization.

In this framework, theory and practice are based on the idea that people are more important than the organization. Bolman and Deal directly relate organizational success and effectiveness to employee growth and development (2008). This is opposite to the early organizational behavior theories and practices that were based on the concept of shaping employees to fit the needs of the organization. Instead, when operating in the human resources frame, leaders focus on the employee or the workplace "family" (Bolman and Deal 2008, 402). This frame emphasizes support, empowerment, staff development, and responsiveness to employee needs to achieve organizational success, which proved successful in a small academic library.

In this case study, three factors quickly combined to pose a significant challenge to the organizational culture of an academic library. Separately, each factor was challenging to the library's organization, operations, and maintenance of its culture; while the three combined for another example of a perfect storm of change and upheaval. The three factors were: the Harvard Graduate School of Education (HGSE) expanded its academic programs and initiated a major library building renovation; the university reorganized and centralized its campus-wide library system; and the faculty librarian of thirty years announced his retirement, effective June 2013.

Monroe C. Gutman Library is the library of record for HGSE, one of many Harvard University libraries serving a professional school. Today, the building houses a conference center, café, classrooms, offices, and information technology services as well as the library. The library's mission is to support the teaching, learning, and research of the School of Education. In theory and practice the library's mission is user-centric and requires flexibility and adaptability, which drives the library's administrative and organizational policies and practices. The library has a long history of resourcefulness and commitment to responding to and anticipating changing user needs. Library staff are innovative, and entrepreneurial, and work collaboratively in a culture defined by high standards of service to users.

HGSE Expanded Programs and Library Renovations

On the academic front, in 2010 the school launched a three-year practice-based Doctor of Education Leadership Program that combines courses from the fields of education, business, and public policy, thus offering doctoral students a cross-discipline degree with courses taught among the professional schools of HGSE, the Harvard Business School, and the Harvard Kennedy School. In addition, in 2012 the school was granted a new inter-faculty PhD program in education in conjunction with the Harvard Faculty of Arts and Sciences. This program will enroll its first doctoral students in fall 2014. These changes in the school's academic program and physical space have affected students' and faculty's access to library resources and changed how the school's librarians interact with students and faculty to serve their information needs.

Library Centralization

Since its inception, Monroe C. Gutman Library functioned in the university's decentralized library system of more than 90 libraries. Within this decentralized environment, the library staff were a full participants in collaborative initiatives across libraries through committees, work groups, and task forces involving public service, information technology, access, and collections. Professionals and staff participated in cross-unit committees, projects, and informal networks with other Harvard librarians. With the transition to a centralized library organization, Gutman Library required leadership to guide and motivate the staff to develop and accept a new model and emerging culture for the new library system and how local services would be delivered.

Faculty Librarian's Retirement

The library is administered by a faculty librarian who reports directly to the dean of administration. Since assuming the position in 1983, the librarian has led the organization through continuous growth and change to meet the school's evolving programs and needs. The faculty librarian is a member of the faculty of the Graduate School of Education and in addition serves as director of the master's program in Special Studies. In 2012, the faculty librarian announced his retirement, effective June 2013. This announcement was not anticipated, and staff were initially concerned about the loss of a longtime leader and advocate who had a direct role in the current library reorganization. The transition to a new, as yet unknown librarian was also viewed with uncertainty and fears.

Reframing Organizational Culture

Several key elements of the human resource framework were employed during this period of change. Certainly the emphasis on leadership practices over management functions was an important strategy. Three elements of effective change management were employed: staff participation; communication; and integrating employee needs with organizational goals and objectives. These elements have been identified as important to effective leadership as well as change management (Ancona et al. 2007; Bolman and Deal 2008; Ibarra and Hunter 2007; Robbins and Judge 2012).

In reframing workplace culture, a leader's knowledge and understanding of the "organizational DNA" is a key attribute to gain employee participation. Initially, the relocation of Gutman Library staff to the library system's new centralized reporting structure was problematic. Centralization goals and objectives were not clearly aligned with individual employee needs, and the relocated staff were separated from their former positions and colleagues, diminishing employee buy-in. Employee empowerment is a central concept in the human resource frame and cannot be achieved without leadership engagement with employees. The faculty librarian communicated at meetings with staff his belief in "the turbulence of the present to build on and bring closure to the past" (Heifetz, Grashow, and Linsky 2009, 54) to move staff from a sense of disengagement to one of participation. He spoke openly and frequently with relocated and local staff about their concerns and the uncertainty of the transition's processes and procedures. He acknowledged the necessity of adapting and creating new processes and procedures that aligned with transition goals and objectives and brought staff into the process of how to solve the problems and issues that were being raised. For example, the relocation of the library's catalogers to another physical location left local staff with a sense of not knowing how to resolve local cataloging questions from users and staff. The library's strong reputation of a high level of service had been built upon in-house availability of staff expertise to answer user and staff questions, ranging from purchase of materials to cataloging processes to ready reference. Meetings held to address this change focused not on what had been in the past, but what could be accomplished going forward within the new system of reorganized local and relocated services. A solution was reached whereby cataloging questions were triaged and prioritized by local staff who worked with relocated cataloging staff to chart to whom cataloging questions would be addressed using phone and e-mail. Additionally, the faculty librarian ensured continuing connections between relocated staff and local staff by maintaining the relocated staff members' offices at Gutman Library and communicating that relocated staff were still considered part of the Gutman 'family.' The family metaphor used by Bolman and Deal (2008,

402) defines this type of leadership as developing and supporting staff as valued participants in and contributors to the organization.

In the absence of university-wide library committees and work groups, the librarian also encouraged staff to engage in and rely on their relationships inside and outside the library to understand the evolving status of the centralization process. Based on his own experiences, the librarian viewed library colleagues as a resource for professional development within the Harvard Library. At the same time, the faculty librarian increased the number of staff meetings. The initial decision was met with resistance from staff who did not view additional meetings as necessary or productive given the challenges of established and emerging day-to-day transition and renovation responsibilities. Quickly, however, the staff came to value the meetings' informality and the opportunity to engage and explore what was happening as explained and communicated by the faculty librarian. The meetings focused on informing the staff of the latest plans and listening to their comments and concerns. Through trial and error, the faculty librarian framed the conversations from a position of inquiry rather than one of directives (Ancona et al. 2007; Sullivan 2004), thereby continuing to build trust and buy-in in the change environment. The librarian began to reduce the sense of a hierarchical- or organizational-driven agenda by creating an informal format with open questions and answers, which added to the shared sense of commitment and participation in the change.

Recognizing the tumultuousness of the multiple changes occurring, not least of which was his upcoming retirement and the resulting leadership transition, the librarian quickly moved to a participatory leadership approach by involving his library leadership team made up of department heads in this process of communicating with and engaging staff as participants in the transition process. The librarian discussed this approach with the department heads who were involved, and they helped in assigning, mentoring, and supporting leadership among library staff to enable full participation in the transition process. This approach focused on anticipating transition issues and engaging in problem solving with relevant staff. Previously, problem solving was often done by reacting to unexpected issues to achieve resolution and stability in the workplace. In the present model, the librarian applied participatory or distributed leadership that incorporated four elements: sensemaking; relating; visioning; and innovating (Ancona et al. 2007). Additionally, the local teams were given new responsibilities in their areas of work pertaining to reference, public services, and collection services, as part of the new staff participation. Team leaders were newly accountable for the integration and alignment of local functioning and relocated services. The librarian expressed that he was able to shift his energy to focus on the larger challenges of the university-wide library organizational changes underway by using a participatory leadership approach.

Given the often fragmented and incomplete state of transition communications by the university, the faculty librarian used a well-developed formal and informal communication process to inform his staff. He continually discussed the transition's documented strategic plan with the department heads at regular library management staff meetings and also communicated directly with individual staff on an informal basis. The importance of fitting the strategic plan with staff needs and benefitting both is a characteristic of human resources leadership that generated less resistance to change among the library's staff.

As stated earlier, the human resources frame requires strategic and open communications by a leader who develops and uses relationships and information resources that contribute to balancing employee needs and organizational goals (Bolman and Deal 2008; Ibarra and Hunter 2007; Krackhardt and Hanson 1993). The importance of established strategic networks is critical to effective leadership and is essential to leading in times of change (Ibarra and Hunter 2007; Krackhardt and Hanson 1993). The value of the faculty librarian's networking was visible through outcomes such as retaining key library staff during the transition process and providing a comfortable new office layout for professional library staff during the building renovation.

Change requires leadership to motivate employees to give up old meanings and to understand, accept, and effectively transition to the organization's new culture and mission. As noted by Bolman and Deal, a leader must have established trust to motivate and engage staff during change (2008). Employees must believe leadership decisions and actions support their interests, as well as the organization's mission. With centralization came the possibility of staff reductions, a difficult and emotional issue that challenged the librarian to reinforce and reframe employee trust in the organizational goals and objectives; as Robbins and Judge acknowledged, "Downsizing or centralizing tests the highest levels of trust" (2012, 57). At a time of employee job uncertainty, the faculty librarian adopted an iterative and interactive process of building deeper trust through continuous communication. The librarian listened to employee concerns with personal warmth and openness. Acknowledging employee anxiety about potential layoffs, the librarian openly expressed his and the school's commitment to staff retention. In meetings the librarian requested staff input for justifying positions, rewrote dated job descriptions, and created new positions aligned with the school and the Harvard Library missions. This created a supportive climate for library employees, allowing them to continue to be productive in a time of uncertainty. It also addressed and required alignment of employees' individual goals with that of the local organization, Gutman Library, and the broader organization, Harvard Library.

To move through this cultural shift and organizational transition, the library's family-focused workforce required application of the human resource frame. The librarian functioned as a leader and catalyst who supported and empowered employees, as characterized by Bolman and Deal (2008). This strategic adoption of support and empowerment generated staff belief in the centralized library system concept (referred to by the university president as "One Harvard") and a willingness to engage in and contribute to the new organizational structure and mission.

Employee concerns, such as "why me? why now? and what for?," are initiators and opportunities for ongoing conversations around change. In this case, concerned employees were transformed into change agents through employee and leadership engagement throughout the process, from decision making to visioning. Influential leadership capabilities were used to build employee participation based on why, how, and when. As Robbins and Judge state, it is the "ability to influence a group toward the achievement of goals" rather than the "use of authority . . . to obtain compliance" that distinguishes an effective leader (2012, 135). In each situation—whether organizational transition, facility renovation, or retirement announcement—the faculty librarian guided as "head of the family" with influence rather than managing using positional authority (Robbins and Judge 2012).

WEATHERING THE STORM AND TAKING THE HELM

Recognizing the perfect storm (e.g., evolving information technology, innovation in higher education course platforms, expanding user expectations and evolving information seeking behaviors, and market globalization), academic librarians are reexamining the definition, theory, and practice of library leadership in their organizations—how to not just cope but to excel and not just address issues but turn challenges into opportunities. Redefining the "why, when, and how" to provide effective leadership, rather than simply "managing" or providing administrative oversight, is the critical discussion that must take place in the library profession and the higher education field. As organizations, academic libraries are uniquely situated within their parent institutions. Libraries are often defined as the heart of the university (Faust 2012), but are considered low-hanging fruit when efficiencies need to be found in times of budget challenges. Because of this, the academic library requires innovative leadership in addition to competent management more than ever before.

The natural tendency is to turn to a handbook on leadership models to find an appropriate solution, or a description of leadership style, strategies, and outcomes. What should library leadership look like? Instead, these case studies highlight the need to look at leadership through the lens of actions taken rather than a prescribed framework. Given the complex change environment, the question remains: Do leaders in academic libraries require distinctive capabilities? Are library leaders different from other leaders in changing environments?

Library science literature offers a wide range of theories, practices, and models of leadership for professional development and organizational initiatives. How-to manuals, workshops, professional development programs, academies of library leadership, and graduate education courses all attempt to address what has been viewed as a critical need for leadership development. The response, however, has highlighted the lack of an explicit definition of the difference between "management" and "leadership" and the possibility of the academic library profession requiring unique leadership capabilities in today's changing environment. The wide range of leadership nomenclature speaks to the profession's lack of clarity and understanding about the differentiation of leaders and managers. Phrases such as "managing leaders" and "managerial leadership" indicate the profession's perspective that the two roles are similar—or even interchangeable, in the view of many academic librarians.

A recent ACRL leadership institute titled "Library Leadership in a Digital Age" highlighted the emerging challenges facing library leadership.[4] Institute participants brought more questions than answers to the table. Leadership capabilities were categorized by skill, knowledge, or ability (Sullivan 2013) and included managing change; leading versus presiding; embracing tension; understanding purpose and mission; identifying and posing questions; integrating diverse and dissimilar pieces; and identifying and adapting new capabilities (Sullivan 2013). The capabilities identified by institute participants reflect the current change environment library leaders find themselves facing within their academic organizations. These newly articulated capabilities are not explicitly defined or developed in the prevailing business models of leadership. Leadership models based on principles and practices of management have and continue to offer a proscribed approach to academic library leadership (Verzosa 2003). The classic management-based models use industrial age theory and practice to try to solve the unique leadership challenges facing academic libraries. The change environment of academic libraries has created a proliferation of library leadership models. With reliance on the corporate model, the library leadership models have neglected the importance of "fit": specifically, how does an individual select an appropriate leadership model? These leadership models may well be constructed with sound theory and best practices for managing in the for-profit world. Taking a page from the business textbook models rather than tailoring theory and practice to the academic library environment can result in the library's failure to thrive. It is important that leaders recognize and employ library leadership literature that explicitly engages with the academic library's distinct organizational structure in theory and practice. Additionally, the emerging literature is lacking in addressing diversity and globalization as a key component of library leadership.

To address academic library leadership capabilities, it is critical for the profession to establish an intellectual home where there is debate, exploration, and consensus building. As Hernon and Rossiter' stated, "leadership in academic libraries is not a fad" (2007, 251). Academic library leadership is an iterative process, not an image to be put forth or a position held on an organizational chart. It is dynamic, involving managing and shaping change that is layered, complex, unique, and critical to the everyday and long-term success of the institution. Success in one organization, particularly one that does not have the same cultural or institutional values and practices, is not a blueprint for organizational success in another—even from library to library, as the cases show. The profession must examine its own unique characteristics of leadership through times of stability and change to develop new capabilities of successful leadership.

To determine the capabilities of effective academic library leadership, leaders must continue to pose questions: What's the definition of library leadership? What does an effective library leader look like? How can professional schools, associations, networks, workplaces, and literature come together in the conversation? What can library leaders learn from their own university and college leaders? Are there transferable capabilities within the higher education environment, or are libraries more impacted by rapid evolution of the digital world?

Academic libraries require leadership that addresses the organizational opportunities and challenges of today's world, not yesterday's practices or models. Successfully implementing sustainable, strategic shifts in order to remain relevant to the academy will be determined by a library's ability to move from practicing static management to implementing a culture of dynamic change leadership. What does that leader look like?

Developing the capabilities that academic library leaders need begins with analyzing the gaps—a systematic review of what works and what's not working. What capabilities enable successful leadership? Discovering this knowledge requires a research agenda to address library leadership development and continuing education set within the context of the change environments, with an exploration and examination based on the interests and perspective of the academic library; however, this work cannot be accomplished in a library vacuum. All stakeholders need to sit at the table. The proliferation of academic library leadership attention (e.g., articles, institutes, books, workshops, blogs, etc.) is a barometer of the sea change needed to fill the growing crisis of management devoid of leadership.

In the authors' opinion, the literature on academic library leadership has yet to study the many examples of transitions that reposition academic libraries within their macro and micro environments. Additionally, the academic library literature has yet to identify what constitutes the leadership capabilities needed to enable the next generation of librarians to add value to their communities. Through case studies, which Sullivan (2010) suggests is an effective way to learn, this study of leadership capabilities used in two highly charged change environments shows that reframing enables leaders to assess opportunities and challenges from various perspectives. This chapter contributes to the ongoing discussion of capabilities required to lead effective change.

NOTES

1. For the purposes of this chapter, *capability* is defined as "a collection of cross-functional elements that come together to create the potential for taking effective action. These elements include attributes, skills, knowledge, systems, and structures. Capabilities represent tangible and intangible components that are needed to enable performance" (Saint-Onge and Armstrong 2004, 231).

2. The 2x2 matrix is a tool used for representing a complex situation in order to make a decision or solve a problem. Elements are grouped according to common variables along high-low axes in an effort to identify possible solutions and/or priorities. See examples in Covey et al. 1994; Lowy and Hood 2004; Porter, Chandler, and Doriot 1980.

3. For more information about the process and outcomes, see the Harvard Library website at http://lib.harvard.edu/about-us and an overview of the Harvard Library at http://isites.harvard.edu/icb/icb.do?keyword=k77982&pageid=icb.page399556.

4. Jointly sponsored by Harvard Graduate School of Education and Association of College and Research Libraries.

REFERENCES

Altman, Elizabeth C. 1981. "A History of Baker Library at the Harvard University Graduate School of Business Administration," 169–96. Harvard University. Harvard Library Bulletin. Cambridge, Mass., Harvard University Library. Volume XXIX, Number 2 (April 1981)." Harvard University Library. Accessed January 12, 2013. http://nrs.harvard.edu/urn-3:FHCL:139076?n=14133.

Ancona, Deborah, Thomas W. Malone, Wanda J. Orlikowski, and Peter M. Senge. 2007. "In Praise of the Incomplete Leader." *Harvard Business Review* 85 (2): 92–100.

Association of College and Research Libraries. 2010. *Value of Academic Libraries: A Comprehensive Research Review and Report.* Chicago: American Library Association.

———. 2013. *Environmental Scan 2013.* Chicago: American Library Association.

Association of Research Libraries. 2010. *The ARL 2030 Scenarios: A User's Guide for Research Libraries.* Association of Research Libraries.

Avolio, Bruce J., Fred O. Walumbwa, and Todd J. Weber. 2009. "Leadership: Current Theories, Research, and Future Directions." *Annual Review of Psychology* 60 (1): 421–49.

Barrett, Frank. 2012. *Yes to the Mess: Surprising Leadership Lessons from Jazz.* Boston: Harvard Business Press.

Bell, Steven. 2013. "Skills for Leading Libraries of the Future/Leading from the Library." *Library Journal*, March 27, accessed July 22, 2013. http://lj.libraryjournal.com.ezp-prod1.hul.harvard.edu/category/leading-from-the-library.

Bolman, Lee G., and Terrence E. Deal. 1984. *Modern Approaches to Understanding and Managing Organizations.* 1st ed. San Francisco: Jossey-Bass.

———. 2008. *Reframing Organizations: Artistry, Choice, and Leadership.* 4th ed. San Francisco: Jossey-Bass.

Bolman, Lee G., and Joan V. Gallos. 2011. *Reframing Academic Leadership.* 1st ed. Jossey-Bass Higher and Adult Education Series. San Francisco: Jossey-Bass.

Budd, John. 2012. *The Changing Academic Library: Operations, Culture, Environments.* Chicago: Association of College and Research Libraries.

Bush, Tony. 2003. *Theories of Educational Leadership and Management.* London: Sage.

Covey, Stephen R., A. Roger Merrill, and Rebecca R. Merrill. 1994. *First Things First: To Live, to Love, to Learn, to Leave a Legacy.* New York: Simon & Schuster.

Cruikshank, Jeffrey L., and Alfred D. Chandler. 1987. *A Delicate Experiment: The Harvard Business School, 1908-1945.* Boston: Harvard Business School Press.

Doyle, Michele E., and Mark K. Smith. 2001. "Classical Models of Managerial Leadership: Trait, Behavioural, Contingency and Transformational Theory." In "Classical Leadership," the Encyclopedia of Informal Education. http://ww.infed.org/leadership/traditional_leadership.htm.

Dyer, Jeffrey H., Hal B. Gregersen, and Clayton M. Christensen. 2009. "The Innovator's DNA." *Harvard Business Review* 87 (12): 60–67.

———. 2011. "Innovative Teams." *Leadership Excellence* 28 (9): 5.

Edmondson, Amy C. 2011. "Strategies for Learning from Failure." *Harvard Business Review* 89 (4): 48–55.

Fagan, Jody Condit. 2012. "The Effectiveness of Academic Library Deans and Directors." *Library Leadership & Management* 26 (1): 1–19.

Faust, Drew. 2012. "Changes Will Position Library for 21st Century and Beyond." Harvard University. Harvard Library. *President Faust's Reflections on the Future of the Harvard Library, February 8, 2012.* http://isites.harvard.edu/icb/icb.do?keyword=k77982&pageid=icb.page492663.

Garvin, David A., Amy C. Edmondson, and Francesca Gino. 2008. "Is Yours a Learning Organization?" *Harvard Business Review* 86 (3): 109–16.

Gilstrap, Donald L. 2009. "A Complex Systems Framework for Research on Leadership and Organizational Dynamics in Academic Libraries." *Portal: Libraries and the Academy* 9 (1): 57–77.

Groysberg, Boris, and Michael Slind. 2012. "Leadership Is a Conversation." *Harvard Business Review* 90 (6): 76–84.

Gwyer, Roisin. 2010. "Leading in Difficult Times: What Can We Learn from the Literature?" *New Review of Information Networking* 15 (1): 4–15.

Hannah, Sean T., and Bruce J. Avolio. 2010. "Ready or Not: How Do We Accelerate the Developmental Readiness of Leaders?" *Journal of Organizational Behavior* 31 (8): 1181–87.

Harvard University. 2009. *Report of the Task Force on University Libraries.*

Haycock, Ken, Anne Cheadle, and Karla Spence Bluestone. 2012. "Strategic Thinking: Lessons for Leadership from the Literature." *Library Leadership & Management (Online)* 26 (3/4): 1–23.

Heifetz, Ronald A., Alexander Grashow, and Martin Linsky. 2009. *The Practice of Adaptive Leadership: Tools and Tactics for Changing Your Organization and the World.* Boston: Harvard Business Press.

Hernon, Peter. 2010. *Shaping the Future: Advancing the Understanding of Leadership.* Santa Barbara, CA: Libraries Unlimited.

———. 2011. "Becoming a University Library Director." *Library & Information Science Research* 33 (4): 276–83.

Hernon, Peter, and Nancy Rossiter, eds. 2007. *Making a Difference: Leadership and Academic Libraries.* Westport, CT: Libraries Unlimited.

Hernon, Peter, and Candy Schwartz. 2008. "Leadership: Developing a Research Agenda for Academic Libraries." *Library & Information Science Research* 30 (4): 243–49.

———. 2011. "The Preparation of Leaders in Library and Information Science." *Library & Information Science Research* 33 (4): 259.

Hinchcliffe, Lisa. 2011. "Understanding, Demonstrating, and Communicating Value: The Leadership and Management Challenge." Presentation at the 77th IFLA General Conference and Assembly, San Juan, Puerto Rico, August 16.

Ibarra, Herminia, and Mark Hunter. 2007. "How Leaders Create and Use Networks." *Harvard Business Review* 85 (1): 40–47.

Jordan, Mary Wilkins. 2011. "Developing Leadership Competencies in Librarians." Paper presented at International Federation of Library Associations (IFLA), San Juan, Puerto Rico, May 25, 2011.

Kanter, Rosabeth. M. 2010. "Leadership in a Globalizing World." In *Handbook of Leadership Theory and Practice*, edited by Nitin Nohria and R. Khurana, 569–610. Boston: Harvard Business School Publishing.

Kegan, R., and Lisa Lahey. 2010. "Adult Development and Organizational Leadership." In *Handbook of Leadership Theory and Practice*, edited by Nitin Nohria and R. Khurana, 769–87. Boston: Harvard Business School Publishing.

Kennedy, Pagan. 2012. "Rewiring Reality." *The New York Times*, January 15, 1.

Kouzes, James M., and Barry Z. Posner. 2007. *The Leadership Challenge*. 4th ed. San Francisco: Jossey-Bass.

Krackhardt, David, and Jeffrey R. Hanson. 1993. "Informal Networks: The Company behind the Charts." *Harvard Business Review* 71 (4): 104–11.

Kwanya, Tom, Christine Stilwell, and Peter G. Underwood. 2012. "Intelligent Libraries and Apomediators: Distinguishing between Library 3.0 and Library 2.0." *Journal of Librarianship and Information Science* 0 (0): 1–11, accessed August 6, 2013, doi: 10.1177/0961000611435256.

Lowy, Alex, and Phil Hood. 2004. *The Power of the 2x2 Matrix: Using 2x2 Thinking to Solve Business Problems and Make Better Decisions*. 1st ed. Jossey-Bass Business & Management Series. San Francisco: Jossey-Bass.

"Marshall Announces New Master of Management of Library and Information Science." 2013. News at Marshall. University of Southern California School of Business, February 14. http://www.marshall.usc.edu/news/releases/2013/marshall-announces-new-master-management-library-and-information-science.

McKnight, Sue, ed. 2010. *Envisioning Future Academic Library Services: Initiatives, Ideas and Challenges*. London: Facet.

Neal, James G., and Damon E. Jaggars. 2010. "Web 2.0: Redefining and Extending the Service Commitment of the Academic Library." In *Envisioning Future Academic Library Services: Initiatives, Ideas and Challenges*, edited by Sue McKnight, 55–68. London: Facet.

Nohria, Nitin, William Joyce, and Bruce Roberson. 2013. "4+2 +Sustained Business Source." HBS Working Knowledge. HBS Working Knowledge, Accessed January 12, 2013. http://hbswk.hbs.edu/item/3578.html.

Nohria, Nitin, Rakesh Khurana, Noam Wasserman, Bharat Anand, Walter A. Friedman, Robin Ely, Jay Lorsch, et al., eds. 2010. *Handbook of Leadership Theory and Practice: An HBS Centennial Colloquium on Advancing Leadership*. Boston: Harvard Business Press.

Porter, Michael E., Alfred D. Chandler, and Georges F. Doriot. 1980. *Competitive Strategy: Techniques for Analyzing Industries and Competitors*. New York: Free Press.

Robbins, Stephen P., and Tim Judge. 2012. *Essentials of Organizational Behavior*. 11th ed. Upper Saddle River, NJ: Pearson Prentice Hall.

Saint-Onge, Hubert, and Charles Armstrong. 2004. *The Conductive Organization Building beyond Sustainability*. Amsterdam: Elsevier.

Sapp, Gregg, and Ron Gilmour. 2003. "A Brief History of the Future of Academic Libraries: Predictions and Speculations from the Literature of the Profession, 1975 to 2000–Part Two, 1990 to 2000—." *Portal: Libraries & the Academy* 3 (1): 14.

Staley, David J., and Kara Malenfant. 2010. *Futures Thinking for Academic Librarians: Higher Education in 2025*. Chicago: Association of College and Research Libraries.

Sullivan, Maureen. 1998. "Leadership through the Lens of Learning." *College & Research Libraries News* 59 (9): 673–74.

———. 1999. "Reflections on Academic Libraries as Self-Organizing Systems: Ways Leaders can Support Staff." *College & Research Libraries News* 60 (5): 393–94.

———. 2004. "The Promise of Appreciative Inquiry in Library Organizations." *Library Trends* 53 (1): 218–29.

————. 2010. "Case Studies Method: An Overview." In *Shaping the Future: Advancing the Understanding of Leadership*, edited by Peter Hernon, 115–34. Santa Barbara, CA: Libraries Unlimited.

————. 2013. "Future Competencies for Librarians" Library Leadership in a Digital Age (LLDA), Cambridge MA, March 22–24, 2013.

Thomas, David A., and Robin J. Ely. 1996. "Making Differences Matter: A New Paradigm for Managing Diversity." *Harvard Business Review* 74 (5): 79–90.

Verzosa, Fe A. M. 2003. "Leadership Literature on Academic Librarianship: A Bibliographical Essay." Unpublished manuscript. http://hdl.handle.net/10760/11312.

Watkins, Michael. 2003. *The First 90 Days: Critical Success Strategies for New Leaders at All Levels; First Ninety Days*. Boston: Harvard Business School Press.

Weiner, Sharon Gray. 2003. "Leadership of Academic Libraries: A Literature Review." *Education Libraries* 26 (2): 5–18.

Part Two

Women and Minorities in Leadership Roles

Chapter Four

Leadership in Academic Libraries Today—Connecting Theory to Practice

Mentoring Diverse Leaders in Academic Libraries

Starr Hoffman

One of the reasons that women and minorities have struggled to succeed in library leadership is the typically homogenous organizational culture across libraries. Although librarianship has traditionally been and remains a profession full of women, women have not yet reached representative numbers in administrative positions, particularly in academic libraries (Moran, Leonard, and Zellers 2009). Minorities continue to be underrepresented in librarianship overall, particularly in administrative positions (Johnson 2007; Neely and Peterson 2007; Wheeler 2000). Library literature has promoted mentoring to encourage and better prepare women and minorities for leadership positions. Is this position supported by theory and research? If so, can mentoring opportunities be realistically increased? This chapter will investigate how mentoring relates to research and theory about library leadership, and how mentoring opportunities may be expanded for women and minorities.

Lumby and Morrison (2010) discussed the lack of leadership theory that directly addresses disadvantages faced by those who don't fit the typical leader profile where "whiteness" and "maleness" are associated with power. They look to feminist and critical race theory to point out how non-white, non-male, and other nonconformist individuals have difficulty attaining and being effective in positions of power. In academic institutions, where change can be particularly slow, such nonconformity may still be viewed with suspicion. Lumby and Morrison (2010) searched for more inclusive theories of leadership in education. Their foundation was built on transformative leadership as the ideal style, because it best addresses the need to consider the various needs and frameworks of different communities and institutions.

The idea of transformational leadership was developed by Burns (1978) and Bass (1985, 1990). Transformational leaders change their followers' expectations and grow their perspective in order to achieve new, more aspirational goals. Collard (2007) expands this theory to show that transformational leaders have a duty to question the typical way of doing things and to be particularly sensitive to varied cultural perspectives. He explains that in order to effectively lead change, transformational leaders "need to unfreeze established traditions and contest unexamined assumptions" (Collard 2007, 751). Minorities and women bring a fresh perspective to long-stagnant library leadership. Thus, if they can overcome barriers to attaining leadership positions, they are suited to be particularly transformative.

LITERATURE REVIEW

Gender and Mentoring

Mentoring has been a key strategy in librarianship's efforts to achieve gender and ethnic parity in leadership positions (Cargill 1989). Historically, a disproportionately large number of men have held positions of authority in libraries as managers, directors, and deans (Fennell 1978; Kirkland 1997; Moran, Leonard, and Zellers 2009; Moran 1983). In the 1970s, the American Library Association focused on mentoring and other methods of advancing women into positions of library leadership. The numbers of women in positions of library leadership began to increase accordingly, although slowly (Cargill 1989; McNeer 1988; Turock 2001). This can be clearly seen in the number of female deans of the Association of Research Libraries (ARL), which rose from none in 1958 to one in 1966, four in the mid-1970s, 12 in 1981, 32 in 1989, 63 in 2009, and 68 in 2010 (Karr 1984; Kyrillidou and Bland 2010; Myers and Kaufman 1991; Parsons 1976). Deyrup (2004) determined that gender parity has in fact been reached, showing that women outnumber men in administrative library positions. Moran, Leonard, and Zellers (2009) disagree, stating that although women do outnumber men in administrative positions, these numbers are still not proportionate to the percentage of female academic librarians overall. The situation is remarkably better in research libraries (where 64 percent of librarians are women and 61 percent of library deans are women) versus selective liberal arts institutions (where 70 percent of librarians are women and 51 percent of library deans are women). Work remains to be done to ensure that women are fully represented in positions of library leadership.

Mentoring was found to be particularly effective in advancing women to positions of library leadership (Fennell 1978; Moran, Leonard, and Zellers

2009; Turock 2001). Effective methods of mentoring included formal programs sponsored by organizations (in which mentors and mentees are selected by organizers) and informal mentor relationships that naturally developed between individuals. Turock said one of the chief benefits of mentoring is that it enables women to "bypass the hierarchy, to get inside information, to short-circuit cumbersome procedures, and to cut red tape" (Turock 2003, 495). Kirkland's (1997) research described how mentoring helps remove barriers to advancing into a leadership position by counteracting the "deprivation behavior" many female academic librarians face. These behaviors included women being denied the opportunity for professional responsibilities, purposeful delays in or denial of communication, lack of recognition or approval, and using women against each other (Kirkland 1997). Respondents to Kirkland's survey described mentoring and networks of female library leaders as the best ways to encourage women's advancement in library leadership. Kirkland's second survey identified mentoring as the most important factor in helping female academic library administrators to reach their positions (Kirkland 1997). She concluded that mentoring is a key strategy for continuing the journey toward gender parity in academic library administration.

Ethnic Diversity and Mentoring

The situation for ethnic parity is much graver. The percentage of white academic librarians has remained at 85 percent for several years (ALA 2012; ALA Office for Research and Statistics and ALA Office for Diversity 2012; Davis and Hall 2007; Kyrillidou and Morris 2011; Kyrillidou and Young 2006). This underrepresentation is even more pronounced in positions of authority. Only 9 percent of research library managers are minorities, and just 5 percent of research library deans are minorities (Hernon, Powell, and Young 2003; Hipps 2006; Wheeler 2000). Ethnic minorities are employed at a higher rate in lower-paying, non-credentialed positions as library assistants (Davis and Hall 2007). Public and school libraries tend to have a more diverse workforce than do academic libraries (Davis and Hall 2007).

The homogenous nature of librarianship does not reflect the demographic makeup of the constituents that these libraries serve. Current census data indicates that about 38 percent of the population is nonwhite, with projections indicating further increases (Humes, Jones, and Ramirez 2011). Minorities also represent 37 percent of students enrolled in higher education (NCES 2012). This shows how dramatically unbalanced the underrepresentation of minorities is in academic libraries, particularly in leadership positions. In an increasingly diverse and globalized context, academic libraries will do themselves and their constituents a great disservice if they do not address this mismatch (Alire 2001). It is imperative that minorities are recruited and retained into academic librarianship, and in particular that academic library leadership becomes more diverse (Alire 2001; Davis and Hall 2007; Neely and Peterson 2007; Turock 2003).

Similar to the way it has supported women's entry into leadership, mentoring has encouraged ethnic minorities to attain positions in library administration (Bonnette 2004; Mavrinac 2005; Turock 2001). Early mentoring initiatives focused merely on recruiting minorities into librarianship (Wheeler 2000); however, recent studies have shown that recruitment is not enough, that retention and promotion into leadership are the true keys to creating a sustainably diverse profession (Epps 2008; Johnson 2007; Neely and Peterson 2007; Wheeler 2000). One of the telling and distressing consequences of the inhospitable nature of librarianship toward minorities is that although recruitment into the profession has increased, early retirement and career changes keep numbers of minority librarians and those promoted to leadership positions low (Wheeler 2000).

Although much literature exists urging support for mentoring as a strategy to retain and promote librarians from underrepresented groups, there is little empirical research about the outcomes of formal or informal mentoring for these librarians. Damasco and Hodges (2012) mention this gap in their survey of the tenure and promotion of academic librarians from minority groups. In order of highest frequency, their respondent ethnicities were reported as: Black or African American (41.7 percent), Asian (21.7 percent), Hispanic or Latino (16.7 percent), Multiracial/multiethnic (16.7 percent), American Indian/Alaskan Native (1.7 percent), and Native Hawaiian or Pacific Islander (1.7 percent). Over half had worked as degreed librarians for nine years or longer, 50 percent held subject masters in various fields, and 6.7 percent held doctorates.

Damasco and Hodges (2012) asked nonwhite academic librarians about several methods of preparing for promotion or tenure, including mentoring, and asked how important and effective these methods were. Formal mentoring was perceived as important by 70.7 percent of respondents, but not effective (only 30.0 percent rated it as effective or very effective). Informal mentoring was viewed as both important (88.3 percent) and effective (56.7 percent). In part, this finding may be due to the fact that more respondents experienced informal mentoring than mentoring; 36.7 percent chose "not applicable" for formal mentoring versus 16.7 percent for informal mentoring. Damasco and Hodges (2012) mentioned that the selective nature of leadership training programs (many of which include formal mentoring) lead to few opportunities for most minority librarians, which may account for the lower participation in formal mentoring.

Comments from respondents indicate the range of opinion on the value of mentoring from a "vital role" to a negative experience (Damasco and Hodges 2012, 295). One librarian said, "These programs imply that the problem is with the librarians of color, that librarians of color need to be taught to assimilate" (Damasco and Hodges 2012, 295). The authors concluded that simply creating formal mentoring or other leadership programs for minority librarians was not enough, that regular evaluation of their effectiveness and relevance should be performed.

SUMMARY OF RELEVANT RESEARCH RESULTS

Seven hundred forty-nine academic library deans responded to a survey about their experiences preparing for deanship, including informal and formal mentoring (Hoffman 2012). The research questions relevant to the current chapter were:

- What value do current academic library deans place on mentoring?
- Does this vary by gender?
- Does perceived value of mentoring vary by minority status?

The majority of the respondents were female ($n = 462$, 61.7 percent). Respondents were ethnically homogenous, with the majority being White, non-Hispanic ($n = 674$, 90.0 percent). The largest minority group was Black, non-Hispanic ($n = 29$, 3.9 percent). The percentages of minority-status respondents are representative of the population (Hoffman 2012). Full frequencies and percentages for the sample are presented in table 4.1.

Hoffman reported limitations of potentially influential variables outside her control, including the selection criteria of the search committees and administrators that hired the deans and the deans' motivations for seeking their positions. The instrument in this study was a self-report measure, thus the objective effectiveness of deans participating in the study cannot be determined. The study's scope was limited to the deans' perception of importance of mentoring to their preparation for academic leadership, not how mentoring experiences relate to their effectiveness as academic leaders.

In general, academic library deans in this study viewed the value of formal mentoring as moderately beneficial with regard to academic leadership, and informal mentoring as beneficial (Hoffman 2012). Respondents' perceived value of formal mentoring did not differ by gender; however, female respondents placed greater value on informal mentoring than did male respondents. Minorities viewed both formal and informal mentoring as more beneficial than did nonminorities. The difference in perceived value was found to be statistically significant.

Since Hoffman's study indicated respondents' overall higher perceived value for informal mentoring over formal mentoring, this suggests that librarianship's push for formal mentoring programs may not be as valuable as

Table 4.1.   Frequencies and Percentages of Respondents (n=749)

Ethnicity	f	N%
American Indian or Alaska native	7	0.9
Asian or Pacific Islander	10	1.3
Black, non-Hispanic	29	3.9
Hispanic	17	2.3
White, non-Hispanic	674	90.0
Race/ethnicity unknown	4	0.5
Other	8	1.1

finding ways to foster informal mentoring. Mentoring relationships, particularly for women seeking positions of library leadership, should be encouraged to grow naturally. It may be that what the profession needs is more encouragement and institutional support for experienced library leaders to reach out to new or potential library leaders.

Hoffman's research also indicates that formal mentoring programs designed to encourage underrepresented groups in library leadership are important and effective. One such program is ARL's Leadership and Career Development Program (LCDP), which enrolls mid-career academic librarians from underrepresented groups in an 18-month fellowship that includes a formal mentoring relationship with an established library leader (ARL 2012; Neely 2009; Wittkopf 1999). A related program is the Association of College and Research Libraries' (ACRL) Spectrum Scholar Mentor Program, which provides scholarships and assigns mentors for library science students of color (ACRL 2012). Programs such as these should be given continued support. Additional support is found in higher education literature, which indicates mentoring's value for connecting minority faculty and administrators, particularly those who are both women and minorities (Smith and Crawford 2007; Turner 2002).

Hoffman suggests future research should seek to connect objective measures of leader effectiveness with mentoring experiences, in order to judge how mentors may affect leadership ability. This corresponds with Fagan's (2012) recommendation to use Heck, Johnsrud, and Rosser's (2000) and Rosser, Johnsrud, and Heck's (2003) surveys to measure the leadership effectiveness of library deans. This effectiveness data could be compared with experiences of informal and formal mentoring, to see which methods of mentoring produce more effective leaders.

Furthermore, qualitative studies on the mentoring of library deans at non-research institutions would add to the literature provided by Hernon, Powell, and Young (2003) about mentoring of leaders at large research institutions.

Asking deans in greater detail about specific aspects such as what mentoring activities were most helpful could provide guidance for ways to improve both formal and informal mentoring. In addition, it would be helpful to ask female and minority academic library deans about their motivation for pursuing leadership, barriers they faced, and what helped them reach and succeed in their positions. Finally, studying female and minority academic librarians near the end of their career who did not become administrators could be valuable. Asking these librarians if their flat career trajectory was a personal choice or due to insurmountable barriers would greatly increase understanding on this topic.

OVERCOMING BARRIERS TO INCREASE MENTORING

Research has shown that informal mentoring is widely viewed as beneficial. Particularly women and minorities who are new library deans or who desire such positions should seek out formal mentor programs or informal mentor relationships. Moving forward in any field requires initiative and networking; librarianship is no different.

Institutions and professional organizations should find ways to increase current mentoring programs and further encourage members to find opportunities to act as informal mentors. Considering the attention to mentoring in library literature and the positive benefits from mentoring that research has shown, it is unfortunate that many librarians still lack these opportunities. Those who are established or retired library deans who are minorities or women would benefit the profession greatly by seeking ways to mentor newer deans and academic librarians.

Formal mentoring programs for minorities should be further publicized and potentially expanded. The low participation rate in formal mentor programs indicates that while these programs are judged effective by minorities, too few are being served. In this author's study of academic library deans, only 15.6 percent of minority deans experienced formal mentoring (Hoffman 2012). Such a small percentage will not increase minority leadership as dramatically and quickly as is needed.

Barriers to increasing formal mentoring opportunities include the time and cost of institutional organization. If programs such as the ARL's Leadership and Career Development Program were expanded to include more participants, would increased costs be passed directly to the participants? How would more mentors and organizers be located for the program? An individual's ability to participate in such programs is not only limited, but also is not typically under their control because of selective admission.

Particularly because of these organizational costs, the most feasible way to expand mentoring opportunities is to do so on an informal basis. One of the greatest barriers to informal mentoring is a lack of initiative, particularly among potential mentees. Shollen et al. (2008) describe how junior female and minority faculty (or librarians) in particular may not seek out mentoring due to not wanting to take up another faculty member's valuable time, or fear of showing weakness. Mentees may also assume that interested mentors will take the initiative to start a relationship, that it is not a mentee's place to request it.

Successful, ongoing mentoring relationships also require a great deal of initiative from the mentor; the implied secondary barrier here is lack of time. Mentoring can be an involved process. Work-life balance is already tenuous for many who have risen to positions of leadership; adding a regular meeting with an eager mentee isn't easy to add to a packed schedule. One reason mentoring may fall to a lower priority is the lack of professional acknowledgment for this activity. Annual performance and tenure review committees don't typically recognize mentoring as a professional activity on par with publication, presentation, and association involvement (Nies and Wolverton 2000; Shollen et al. 2008). Library leaders who believe in the power of mentorship and the importance of preparing a new generation of leaders must fight in their institutions and professional organizations to create recognition for this activity and its contribution to the professional community. Many higher education institutions have missions that state their support for diversity. If these institutions truly seek to support diversity, they should encourage mentoring and other professional development practices that would increase the potential for successful female and minority administrators (both in libraries and across the institution). Professional associations and individual institutions should also work to find solutions to these obstacles, and enable and encourage current library leaders to reach out to up-and-coming leaders. Until institutions and associations create a system where mentoring is seen as a valuable investment in their future, there will continue to be a shortage of mentors.

Another barrier is a lack of understanding among newer librarians about what mentoring is, how helpful it can be, and how to seek such a relationship. There is a misconception that mentoring relationships are almost apprenticeships, where a mentor formally approaches an individual and asks to be their mentor, and afterward there are weekly meetings in which the mentor produces wise counsel and the mentee takes notes. In reality, these relationships are usually less formally defined, not strictly scheduled, and may occur with multiple mentors, mentees, or both. Most importantly, mentoring relationships do not have to be formally acknowledged or labeled in order to be valuable. A common misconception is that a potential mentee should wait, hoping to be discovered by a mentor. If this notion persists, informal mentoring in librarianship is unlikely to increase any time soon.

The value of mentoring should be impressed upon library students throughout their coursework. Assignments should be created that require speaking with professional librarians, and specifically connected in the coursework as a potential bridge to a future mentoring relationship. Leadership and/or management courses in library curricula should specifically address the benefits of mentoring relationships. Such emphasis should be included in professional organizations as well, particularly in groups made up of new members and/or new librarians. Mentoring is too beneficial to career development to not let new librarians know about it. New librarians aren't as immersed in the literature of the profession, and often aren't starting out by looking for advice on how to advance their careers. The profession must make it a point to let them know, early and often, about mentoring's value.

One way to encourage informal mentoring would be to create organizational events promoting such relationships and making meeting potential mentors and mentees easier. For instance, a meet and greet could be organized where potential mentors and mentees mingle, with the goal of each mentor identifying at least one mentee match. Another way would be to organize an event similar to a "speed date," where mentors and mentees each have five minutes to discuss their interests and backgrounds, and are later matched by organizers. A monthly mentoring lunch hour could provide a convenient getaway time for participants and provide discussion questions to spark meaningful conversations.

GUIDANCE FOR MENTEES

Librarians (or library students) interested in mentor relationships should look for individuals whom they feel have a valuable perspective to offer. These individuals may be experienced library leaders, but it may also be beneficial to consider people outside of the library. For a young librarian seeking to learn more about how to effectively lead an academic library, cultivating a relationship with a vice-provost or other higher education leader outside the library could be just as valuable as one with a current library administrator. Brown (2005) stated the importance of mentee initiative; mentoring opportunities may not be obvious, and may be something that require work on the part of the mentee to set up. Mentor candidates could be identified at committee meetings, university functions, or through professional associations.

Penny and Galliard (2006) stressed the importance of setting realistic expectations and goals for a mentoring relationship. As busy as professionals are, there is typically time to carve out one hour a month. Penny and Galliard mention that even a brief check-in by phone or e-mail to say hello can be a valuable means of growing the mentoring relationship over time. When a traditional one-on-one in-person mentoring relationship isn't possible, remote technologies or newer mentoring models may be productive (Mullen 2009; Sorcinelli and Yun 2007). Virtual meetings are possible by using a tool such as Skype. Research shows that peer mentoring and group mentoring can be beneficial, and is typically easier and less intimidating for new librarians (Smith et al. 2001). In addition, peer mentoring relationships may be easier to arrange on a regularly recurring basis.

Mullen (2009) suggest group-oriented mentoring for academic faculty, particularly those in the same department. This would be a great strategy to apply to a library setting. She suggests several ways for organizing these groups, for instance as support groups that share faculty needs and concerns, or writing groups that collaborate on research (Mullen 2009). She emphasizes that mentoring doesn't need to start at the institutional level or by an established campus leader; mentoring can start in a single department when a faculty member (or a librarian) works to make it happen. Even group mentoring doesn't have to start with a mentor; it can start with a mentee who seeks like-minded colleagues.

GUIDANCE FOR MENTORS

Penny and Galliard (2006) state that it is important for mentors to keep their mentees' goals in mind. Mentors should ask mentees about their career goals, what they perceive as barriers, and what communities appear closed to them. Honestly sharing both positive and negative experiences can be helpful. Above all, mentors should foster trust, maintain confidentiality, and treat mentees with respect (Shollen et al. 2008). Mentors should focus on building their mentees' network, increasing their professional development, and expanding their opportunities.

Mentors should particularly keep in mind when mentoring minority librarians to encourage them to maintain their personal perspective, rather than advising them how to conform to mainline librarian culture. This danger is revealed in Damasco and Hodges, where respondents' comment that mentoring programs "imply that the problem is with the librarians of color, that librarians of color need to be taught to assimilate" (2012, 295). Meaningful change through transformational leadership will only become possible when library leaders embrace their diverse backgrounds and utilize them as strengths.

For additional guidance on mentoring, see the list at the end of this chapter titled "Mentoring Resources."

CONCLUSION

While the literature shows that both formal and informal mentoring are viewed as valuable experiences by library leaders, such experiences are not available to all. One has to wonder if the percentage of minority and female library deans would be greater and thus more representative if mentoring were more widespread. Minorities are dramatically underrepresented in academic librarianship overall and in administrative positions in particular. Existing academic library mentor programs should continue to be developed and promoted, and more mentoring opportunities must be created, if parity is to be reached in librarianship and library leadership. Without an influx of more diverse library leaders and innovative ideas, academic librarianship risks making little meaningful change and becoming irrelevant to an increasingly diverse student and faculty population.

MENTORING RESOURCES

Johnson, W. Brad. 2007. *On Being a Mentor: A Guide for Higher Education Faculty*. Mahwah, NJ: Lawrence Erlbaum Associates. Includes case studies and provides guidelines grounded in mentoring research. There are chapters devoted to mentoring across gender and across race.

Lee, Marta K. 2011. *Mentoring in the Library: Building for the Future*. Chicago: American Library Association. This book provides the basics of developing a strong mentoring movement in a library. Specific chapters cover starting a mentoring program, mentoring students and interns, and mentoring librarians for promotion.

Smallwood, Carol, and Rebecca Tolley-Stokes, eds. 2012. *Mentoring in Librarianship: Essays on Working with Adults and Students to Further the Profession*. Jefferson, NC: McFarland and Co. This is another basic guide to mentoring at different levels from students to librarians. There are a variety of perspectives from the essay authors. Standout information includes ideas on using technology to effectively mentor at a distance.

Sullivan, Maureen, and Robert D. Stueart. 2010. *Developing Library Leaders: A How-To-Do-It Manual for Coaching, Team Building, and Mentoring Library Staff*. New York: Neal-Schuman Publishers. A guide for library leaders to coach and mentor at all levels of their organization. Includes a self-assessment tool that measures readiness to become a mentor.

REFERENCES

Alire, Camila A. 2001. "Diversity and Leadership: The Color of Leadership." *Journal of Library Administration* 32 (3/4): 95–109. doi:10.1300/J111v32n03_07.

ALA (American Library Association). 2012. *Member Demographic Study*. http://www.ala.org/research/initiatives/membershipsurveys.

ALA (American Library Association) Office for Research and Statistics and ALA Office for Diversity. 2012. *Diversity Counts 2012 Tables*. http://www.ala.org/offices/sites/ala.org.offices/files/content/diversity/diversitycounts/diversitycountstables2012.pdf.

ACRL (Association of College and Research Libraries). 2012. *The ACRL Dr. E. J. Josey Spectrum Scholar Mentor Program*. http://www.ala.org/acrl/membership/mentoring/josey-mentoring/mentorprogram.

ARL (Association of Research Libraries). 2012. *Leadership and Career Development Program (LCDP)*. http://www.arl.org/diversity/lcdp/index.shtml.

Bass, Bernard M. 1985. *Leadership and Performance beyond Expectation*. New York: Free Press.

———. 1990. *Bass & Stogdill's Handbook of Leadership: Theory, Research, and Managerial Applications*, 3rd ed. New York: Free Press.

Bonnette, Ashley E. 2004. "Mentoring Minority Librarians up the Career Ladder." *Library Administration and Management* 18 (3): 134–40.

Brown, Terri Moore. 2005. "Mentorship and the Female College President." *Sex Roles* 52 (9/10): 659–66. doi: 10.1007/s11199-005-3733-7.

Burns, James M. 1978. *Leadership*. New York: Harper Collins.

Cargill, Jennifer. 1989. "Developing Library Leaders: Role of Mentorship." *Library Administration and Management* 3 (4): 12–15.

Collard, John. 2007. "Constructing Theory for Leadership in Intercultural Contexts." *Journal of Educational Administration* 45 (6): 740–55. doi: 10.1108/09578230710829919.

Damasco, Ione T., and Dracine Hodges. 2012. "Tenure and Promotion Experiences of Academic Librarians of Color." *College & Research Libraries* 73 (3): 279–301. http://crl.acrl.org/content/73/3/279.full.pdf+html.

Davis, Denise M., and Tracie D. Hall. 2007. *Diversity Counts*. Chicago: American Library Association, Office for Research and Statistics and Office for Diversity.

Deyrup, Marta M. 2004. "Is the Revolution Over? Gender, Economic and Professional Parity in Academic Library Leadership Positions." *College & Research Libraries* 65 (3): 242–50. http://crl.acrl.org/content/65/3/242.full.pdf+html.

Epps, Sharon K. 2008. "African American Women Leaders in Academic Research Libraries." *portal: Libraries and the Academy* 8 (3): 255–72. doi: 10.1353/pla.0.0001.

Fagan, J. 2012. "The Effectiveness of Academic Library Deans and Directors: A Literature Review. *Library Leadership & Management* 26 (1).

Fennell, J. C. 1978. "A Career Profile of Women Directors of the Largest Academic Libraries in the United States: An Analysis and Description of Determinants." PhD diss., Florida State University. ProQuest (UMI No. 7909754).

Heck, R. H., Johnsrud, L. K., and Rosser, V. J. 2000. "Administrative Effectiveness in Higher Education: Improving Assessment Procedures. *Research in Higher Education* 41 (6): 663–84.

Hernon, Peter, Ronald R. Powell, and Arthur P. Young. 2003. *The Next Library Leadership: Attributes of Academic and Public Library Directors*. Westport, CT: Libraries Unlimited.

Hipps, Kaylyn. 2006. "Diversity in the US ARL Library Workforce." *ARL Bimonthly Report* 246, (June 2006): 1–2. http://www.arl.org/bm~doc/arlbr246diversitywkfc.pdf.

Hoffman, Starr. 2012. "The Preparation of Academic Library Administrators." PhD diss., University of North Texas, Denton.

Humes, Karen R., Nicholas A. Jones, and Roberto R. Ramirez. 2011. *Overview of Race and Hispanic Origin: 2010* (2010 Census Briefs: C2010BR-02). http://www.census.gov/prod/cen2010/briefs/c2010br-02.pdf.

Johnson, Peggy. 2007. "Retaining and Advancing Librarians of Color." *College & Research Libraries* 68 (5): 405–17. http://crl.acrl.org/content/68/5/405.full.pdf.

Karr, Ronald D. 1984. "The Changing Profile of University Library Directors, 1966-1981." *College & Research Libraries* 45 (4): 282–86. http://crl.acrl.org/content/45/4/282.full.pdf+html.

Kirkland, Janice J. 1997. "The Missing Women Library Directors: Deprivation versus Mentoring." *College & Research Libraries* 58 (4): 375–83. http://crl.acrl.org/content/58/4/375.full.pdf.

Kyrillidou, Martha, and Les Bland, eds. 2010. *ARL Annual Salary Survey 2009 - 2010*. Washington, DC: Association of College and Research Libraries.

Kyrillidou, Martha, and Shaneka Morris, eds. 2011. *ARL Statistics 2008 - 2009*. Washington, DC: Association of College and Research Libraries.

Kyrillidou, Martha, and Mark Young, eds. 2006. *ARL Statistics 2004 - 2005*. Washington, DC: Association of College and Research Libraries.

Lumby, Jacky, and Marlene Morrison. 2010. "Leadership and Diversity: Theory and Research." *School Leadership & Management* 30 (1): 3–17. doi: 10.1080/13632430903509717.

Mavrinac, Mary Ann. 2005. "Transformational Leadership: Peer Mentoring as a Values-Based Learning Process." *Portal: Libraries and the Academy* 5 (3): 391–405. doi: 10.1353/pla.2005.0037.

McNeer, Elizabeth J. 1988. "Mentoring Influence in the Careers of Women ARL Directors." *Journal of Library Administration* 9 (2): 23–22. doi:10.1300/J111V09N02_04.

Moran, Barbara B. 1983. "Career Patterns of Academic Library Administrators." *College & Research Libraries* 44 (5): 334–44. https://www.ideals.illinois.edu/bitstream/handle/2142/40574/crl_44_05_334_opt.pdf?sequence=2.

Moran, Barbara B., Elisabeth Leonard, and Jessica Zellers. 2009. "Women Administrators in Academic Libraries: Three Decades of Change." *Library Trends* 58 (2): 215–28. doi: 10.1353/lib.0.0088.

Mullen, Carol A. 2009. "Mentoring and Faculty Development." *The Department Chair* (Winter 2009): 18–21.

Myers, Marcia J., and Paula T. Kaufman. 1991. "ARL Directors: Two Decades of Changes." *College & Research Libraries* 52 (3): 241–54. http://crl.acrl.org/content/52/3/241.full.pdf+html.

NCES (National Center for Educational Statistics). 2012. *The Condition of Education 2012*. http://nces.ed.gov/pubs2012/2012045.pdf.

Neely, Teresa Y. 2009. "Assessing Diversity Initiatives: The ARL Leadership and Career Development Program." *Journal of Library Administration* 49 (8): 811–35. doi: 10.1080/01930820903396830.

Neely, Teresa Y., and Lorna Peterson. 2007. *Achieving Racial and Ethnic Diversity among Academic and Research Librarians: The Recruitment, Retention, and Advancement of Librarians of Color* (ACRL Board of Directors Diversity Task Force White Paper). http://www.ala.org/acrl/files/publications/whitepapers/ACRL_AchievingRacial.pdf.

Nies, Charles, and Mimi Wolverton. 2000, April. *Mentoring Deans*. Paper presented at the Annual Meeting of the American Educational Research Association (AERA), New Orleans, LA.

Parsons, Jerry L. 1976. "Characteristics of Research Library Directors, 1958 and 1973." *Wilson Library Bulletin* 50 (8): 613–17.

Penny, John, and Laurie Galliard. 2006. "Mentoring African American Women in Higher Education Administration." *Race, Gender & Class* 13 (1/2): 191–200. http://www.jstor.org/stable/41675232.

Rosser, V. J., Johnsrud, L. K., and Heck, R. H. 2003. Academic Deans and Directors: Assessing Their Effectiveness from Individual and Institutional Perspectives. *Journal of Higher Education* 74 (1): 1–25.

Shollen, S. Lynn, Carole J. Bland, Anne L. Taylor, Anne Marie Weber-Main, and Patricia A. Mulcahy. 2008. "Establishing Effective Mentoring Relationships for Faculty, Especially across Gender and Ethnicity." *American Academic* 4 (1): 131–58. http://www.aft.org/pdfs/highered/academic/March08/shollen_bland_etal.pdf.

Smith, Danielle Taana, and Kijana Crawford. 2007. "Climbing the Ivory Tower: Recommendations for Mentoring African-American Women in Higher Education." *Race, Gender & Class,* 14 (1–2): 253–65. http://www.jstor.org/stable/41675208.

Smith, Judith Osgood, Joy S. Whitman, Peggy A. Grant, Annette Stanutz, J. A. Russett, and Karon Rankin. 2001. "Peer Networking as a Dynamic Approach to Supporting New Faculty." *Innovative Higher Education* 25 (3): 197–207. doi: 10.1023/a:1007651632485.

Sorcinelli, Mary Deane and Jung Yun. 2007. "From Mentor to Mentoring Networks: Mentoring in the New Academy." *Change* 39 (6): 58–61.

Turner, Caroline Sotello Viernes. 2002. "Women of Color in Academe: Living with Multiple Marginality." *The Journal of Higher Education* 73 (1): 74–93. http://www.jstor.org/stable/1558448.

Turock, Betty J. 2001. "Women and Leadership." *The Journal of Library Administration* 32 (3-4): 115–37. doi:10.1300/j111v32n03_08.

———. 2003. "Developing Diverse Professional Leaders." *New Library World* 104 (11): 491–98. doi: 10.1108/03074800310508768.

Wheeler, Maurice B. 2000. "Averting a Crisis: Developing African-American Librarians as Leaders." In *Handbook of Black Librarianship*, edited by E. J. Josey and Marva L. DeLoach (Lanham, MD: Scarecrow Press), 169–82.

Wittkopf, Barbara J. 1999. *Mentoring Programs in ARL Libraries* (SPEC Flyer 239). http://www.arl.org/resources/pubs/spec/complete.shtml.

Chapter Five

Academic Library Leadership, Second Wave Feminism, and Twenty-First Century Humanism

Reflections on a Changing Profession

Marta Deyrup

Librarianship in America typically has been regarded as a woman's occupation, and the lack of prestige, low pay, and opportunities for the advancement for women in the profession has been well documented in the library literature. The first area of concern—the lack of job prestige—is still unaddressed and particularly vexing, considering the gains women have made in all the professions generally and the fact that librarianship is transitioning into a technical (e.g., masculine) field. Historically in this country, male-dominated fields have been awarded higher status and better pay. The advances that women librarians have made in terms of economic and professional parity with their male counterparts are a much brighter story. This chapter will focus on the ties between library feminism and second wave feminism that led to this success, and examine the results of a 2012 survey of over 200 academic library women administrators on the impact of feminism on the profession.

Works on recent library history (Moran, Gard-Marshall, Rathbun-Grubb 2010; Hildenbrand 2000) have shown the connections between the struggle for gender equality in the United States and the struggle within librarianship to define itself as both a female-majority and a female-led profession. Moran, Leonard, and Zellers (2009) has described the slow but generally upward rise of women into leadership positions, particularly at the Association of Research Libraries (ARL), where women now make up the majority (60 percent) of library directors. This gain is similar to those made in other women's professions such as nursing and primary and secondary school teaching.

Academic librarianship, the focus of this chapter, is different from nursing and teaching. For most of its history, the profession was male, and its hierarchical organizational structure reflects this. At the top tier—the level of library director or dean—academic librarians are more similar to CIOs or CEOs in terms of their job responsibilities than they are to heads of other academic divisions (Deyrup 2004). Thus, the stakes are much higher than in many other "women's" professions.

Women began to enter the field of academic librarianship in the United States in the mid-nineteenth century. These middle-class, educated women were recruited by male library directors because they were an inexpensive, competent labor force. Fennell, whose dissertation "Career Profile of Women Directors of the Largest Academic Libraries in the United States: An Analysis and Description of Determinants" draws on the work of Justin Winsor, quotes Winsor as saying that "women were wanted in this field because they lighten our labour, they are equal to our work and for the money they cost . . . they are infinitely better than equivalent salaries will produce by the other sex" (Fennell 1978, 1). Their numbers in academic libraries varied according to the economic situation of the time; for example, in the 1920s 90 percent of all librarians were women, whereas after World War II this number fell sharply as women librarians were replaced by male veterans who needed jobs (Fennell 1978, 1). The number of women academic librarians again increased during the 1970s, and in 2013 women again form the majority of the academic library workforce.

Generally, American feminism is seen as having developed in three phases: first wave feminism, which was largely concerned with women's suffrage and the temperance movement of the late nineteenth and early twentieth century; second wave feminism of the 1960s and 1970s, otherwise known as radical feminism, which was involved primarily with gaining economic and civil rights for women; and third wave feminism, which focused on issues such as work-life balance, multiculturalism, and social equity; and what might be called new humanism or post-feminism, which is just taking form.

Of these movements, radical feminism has had the most impact on academic librarianship. The 1960s and 1970s saw major advances for women with the passage of affirmative action legislation, specifically, Title VII and Title IX. Title VII, passed in 1964, prohibits workplace discrimination "based on race, color, religion, sex and national origin" (U.S. Department of Labor Title IX, Education Amendments of 1972). Title IX prohibits discrimination "based on sex in education programs and activities that receive federal financial assistance" (Fast Facts). With the expansion of Title IX, women were allowed to enroll in previously male-only universities and colleges and began to make inroads into professions that were traditionally regarded as male, such as business, engineering, and medicine. They also gained the right to sue their institutions for gender discrimination.

It was also a time of upheaval for many women as they struggled to reconcile having a family and a career. For these women, the personal life could not be separated from the professional life, and the feminist rhetoric of that time accurately reflected their situation. As Mack-Canty writes,

> Feminists of the second wave adopted as their motto "the personal is the political." In so doing they challenged women's exclusion from the public world of politics and economics, while reintroducing the personal experience of being female into the political discourses of the day. They worked to extend the meaning of the "political" to include areas of social life previously treated as "personal" and positioned in the private realm of the household (Mack-Canty 2004, 154).

Radical feminism also coincided with what was in many respects a golden age for U.S. academic libraries; there was money available to spend on books, and libraries were among the most technologically advanced institutions in the country. It was also a time of great frustration for many women who were prevented from entering higher management. Much of the activism of women librarians of that period was in fact rooted in the tactics of radical feminism. Hildenbrand comments that the "upsurge in library feminism . . . [was] attested to by the creation within the ALA" of the Feminist Task Force (1970), Women's Library Workers (1975), and the Committee on the Status of Women in Librarianship (1976) (Hildenbrand 2000, 53). It was only through the actions of organizations like the American Library Association, which gave women the opportunity to gain professional experience through mentoring and networking and by serving in leadership positions on committees, and legislation such as Title IX, that women were able to advance within academic librarianship. Golub writes about the discrepancy between the status of men and women librarians, noting that in 1983 the first comprehensive study of librarians for the ALA's committee on the status of women in librarianship, completed by Heim and Eastbrook in 1983, found that 78.3 percent of ALA's members were female and 21.7 percent were male. While almost half of men and 30.4 percent of women were then categorized as administrators, by 1997 "there was three times the number of women in management positions than men" (Golub 2010).

Men, in fact, have done an extremely good job leading the profession. What is considered today to be the "gold standard" in libraries was a uniquely American (e.g., male) invention. The first private lending library was established in the eighteenth century by Benjamin Franklin; the first national library, the Library of Congress, belonged to Thomas Jefferson; and the current public library system was the result of Andrew Carnegie's generous endowment. Although academic libraries have their roots in German nineteenth-century research universities, and were organized primarily as departmental collections, the influence of a strong civic public library system in this country encouraged university librarians to experiment with new models of service. An example of this is the "open stack" arrangement of collections, which was developed first in public libraries and later adopted by the academic library community.

Male librarians then, as now, were able to advance the profession because they were confident in their own ability to lead—and they continue to do so. In 2011 40 percent of library dean and director positions were still held by men, although men account for 17 percent of academic library positions (Department for Professional Employees, AFL-CIO 2012). Several explanations have been given for this. The first is historical. Women only began to enter the U.S. workforce in great numbers in the 1960s and 1970s, and academic librarianship, although composed of a female-majority workforce, did not become a female-led profession until the twenty-first century. One can argue, therefore, that there have been very few women who could provide leadership models for a younger generation. The second is cultural. Studies have shown that men and women are socialized differently and therefore lead differently. As Helgeson notes, "social role theory states that differences in men's and women's communication styles have to do with the social roles men and women hold in our society, the male role being agentic and the female role being communal." Helgeson (2002) goes on to write that "according to status theory, men's communication of their higher status and women's communication is a function of their lower status. Men's task behavior and women's positive social behavior fit their social roles." Even in today's society, girls are rewarded for being empathetic, nurturing, and collegial, whereas boys are praised for being assertive and self-assured, characteristics that are identified with leadership and still rewarded at the workplace (270–71).

Ambivalence as to whether men and women should be judged by the same criteria has been a consistent theme throughout feminist history. First wave feminism began as a movement that was closely linked to the temperance movement, and a significant argument both for and against universal suffrage was that women were the "better sex" and should be either included (or excluded) from the vote for this reason. The leaders of the radical feminist movement rejected the idea that there were significant differences between men and women and as a result, never satisfactorily addressed family issues, in particular family caregiving—a task that falls primarily on women. In 2012 this issue has not been resolved, although women constitute almost 47 percent of the U.S. workforce (see the statistics provided by Catalyst.org http://www.catalyst.org/knowledge/statistical-overview-women-workplace).

Researchers such as Eagly et al. have argued that differences between men and women are a "culturally constructed phenomenon" and that male and female behavior is determined by the situational position of men and women within society, rather than the result of biological differences. Eagly in particular has done studies that show that in "organizational settings, behavior . . . lose much of its gender-stereotypical character" (Gershenoff and Foti 2003, 171).

What is considered to constitute "good" leadership is largely based upon role models that were established by men. Koenig et al. wrote:

> The implications of the masculinity of leader roles for prejudice against female leaders are straightforward: Men fit cultural constructs of leadership better than women do and thus have better access to leader roles and face fewer challenges in becoming successful in them. Despite some overall change toward more androgynous beliefs about leadership, stereotyping continues to contribute to the labyrinthine challenges that women encounter in attaining roles that yield substantial power and authority. Given the strongly masculine cultural stereotype of leadership quantified by this meta-analysis, these challenges are likely to continue for some time to come (Koenig 2011, 637).

Thirty years ago, it was widely believed that leadership traits were gender-specific. For example, Robert Swisher, Rosemary DuMont, and Calvin Boyer (1985, 230), noted that "professions dominated by women such as librarianship are widely believed to emphasize "'feminine'" qualities such as nurturance, empathy, understanding, helpfulness, and intuitiveness. . . . Managerial positions . . . are characterized by such personal attributes as decisiveness, consistency, objectivity, emotional stability, and analytical ability" More recently, Peter Hernon, Ronald Powell, and Arthur Young published an influential two-part article, "University Library Directors in the Association of Research Libraries: The Next Generation," that examined leadership traits among academic library leaders. These authors concluded that there was very little difference between the leadership styles of men and women. Herbert White refuted the idea that women led differently from men, writing in *Library Journal* that "I think of good management as a sex-neutral process, in which the gender of the participant is irrelevant." He noted that "good library managers" must have characteristics of fairness, consistency, the ability to grasp new ideas when articulated by others, open-mindedness, ambition, the ability to communicate, leadership, idealism, the ability to set priorities and to delegate, and courage" (White 1987, 58).

Unlike their male counterparts, influential feminists such as Betty Turock, former ALA president and professor at Rutgers SCILS, and Paula T. Kaufman, now dean of libraries at the University of Illinois at Urbana-Champaign, took a very different approach. Both women predicted that leadership would indeed change as women became more secure in their role in higher library management. Turock wrote that librarianship was entering a "new stage of leadership" in which "women's values enter leadership paradigms" (Turock 2001, 128). Kaufman believed that "organizational cultures are also being transformed to a gentler, or in terms of stereotypes, to a more 'feminine' style of leadership. Some authors suggest that the nurturing management behavior shown by new library directors, regardless of gender, suggest that women are influencing and changing the library workplace rather than adopting the stereotypical male role model" (Kaufman 1993, 122). In part, Kaufman and Turock were responding to the emergence of third wave feminism in the 1980s and 1990s. *Third wave feminism* was adopted as a term to describe diverse, often localized women's movements that focused on a variety of issues ranging from eco-feminism and postcolonial feminism to youth feminism (Mack-Canty 2004, 167). Most importantly, third wave feminist theory rejected a dualistic conceptual framework (white/black, male/female, etc.), preferring an approach that was more inclusive.

The lack of discussion of third wave feminism in the library leadership and management literature is not surprising. Unlike second wave feminism, which enabled female academic librarians to move into high-level administrative position in the mid- to late-twentieth century, third wave feminism as a movement focuses on inclusiveness and personal choice.

Because the generation who benefited the most from Title VII and Title IX has for the most part now retired, it seemed appropriate to ask how the two subsequent generations of academic library administrators, those born in 1940–1960 and 1961–1980, perceive the feminist movement and what impact it had on their professional careers. To begin to answer these questions, the author conducted a survey of women academic library administrators intended to elicit responses about their perception of gender discrimination or bias at their institutions, whether they had achieved a satisfactory balance between their professional and family life, and how they chose to lead and manage their employees. Although the sample size was small, the data collected provides information about the educational background, personal values, and career choices these women made. Lastly, it provides some evidence, although largely anecdotal, that women library administrators, although aware of the goals and strategies of radical feminism, are actually entering what Turock and Kaufman referred as the next stage of feminism, one focused on humanistic values.

The survey link was posted through listservs of various associations, such as LLAMA, ACRL administrators, ARL administrators, and ALA women's issues lists, and the survey was completed by over two hundred women (Deyrup 2012; see this chapter's appendix). A snapshot of the survey participants shows a group of women who have been extremely successful in their professional careers. Forty-three percent identified themselves as library deans or directors, 16 percent as associate directors or deans, 6 percent as assistant directors or deans, and 34 percent as department heads. One individual was an assistant vice president. The greatest percentage of respondents (43 percent) worked at large (over 10,000 FTE) institutions. Of the 204 individuals who responded, 25 percent identified themselves as working at an ARL library and approximately 65 percent at an ACRL library. The majority (46 percent) had more than eleven years of experience in library administration. Respondents principally were from the Northeast (34 percent) and the South (30 percent). For most of these women, librarianship was their first career (almost 65 percent). The majority of women were in their peak earning years. Seven percent were 65 or older; 40 percent were between the ages 55 and 64, 27 percent were between the ages of 45 and 54, 18 percent were between the ages of 35 and 44, and 8 percent were between the ages of 25 and 34. What follows below is a summary of the survey findings (for full results, see appendix).

Observation 1: Women library administrators value the academic life. The majority of these women administrators were drawn into librarianship because of their desire to work in an academic environment (86 percent). Although the youngest group of women (between the ages of 25 and 34) is a much smaller pool, comprising only a little more than 8 percent of the survey group, they nevertheless constituted the greatest number of women who were drawn into librarianship because of what they saw as the opportunity for administrative responsibilities. They and the 35–44 age group were most drawn to librarianship because of the possibilities for work flexibility (18 percent and 25 percent, respectively). Those drawn to academic librarianship because of the opportunity to work in their subject areas tended to be the oldest, comprising 21 percent of the 55–64 age group and 20 percent of the 65 and older group. It was these groups that were most likely to have a doctorate in their subject area. This stands to reason, as librarianship has changed in the past thirty years from a largely bibliographic to a more technically oriented field. The majority of respondents valued education and were highly educated, with nearly all having a master's degree. This is far higher than the percentage of individuals in the United States who hold master's degrees, which is 9 percent (Perez-Pena 2012).

Observation 2: Academic librarianship is conducive to raising a family. A little over 61 percent of respondents were married, and 16 percent were divorced or widowed. These statistics are different than those reflected by the population as a whole. According to the 2010 U.S. Census, a little over 55 percent of women were married, and approximately 21 percent were widowed or divorced (U.S. Census, Marital Status of the Population by Sex, 1900–2010). The majority of these women academic library administrators (57 percent) have children. There was an increase in number of the children per age category overall, but it is not a simple line. The majority of women were able to juggle both family and a career. This was true as far as the statistical data of the survey showed, and also was apparent from individual responses. The majority of librarians who took time off to care for children were those in the 35–44 age range (50 percent) followed by the 65 and older age range (45 percent), the 45–54 age range (36 percent), and the 55–65 age range (33 percent) In addition, the majority of women who had children shared parenting responsibilities (82 percent).

Observation 3: Women academic library administrators typically report to women directors or deans, who then typically report to male provosts and presidents. Almost three-quarters of the survey respondents said their dean or director was a woman. This corresponds with the literature, which shows a steady increase of the number of women in high-level academic library administrative positions from the 1980s forward. The majority of women reported that they had been mentored during their career (62 percent), with 78 percent reporting that their mentor had been a woman. While a common phenomenon in academia, mentoring has been especially important in academic librarianship because of the opposition women have historically faced in trying to advance their careers through the university structure. Respondents were divided as to whether the appointment of more women academic library deans and directors was the result of the impact of second wave feminism or due to other reasons. The most vocal in their comments were administrators who were 65 and older and those in the 55–64 age range (who also were predominantly deans or directors). Several respondents noted that although administrative opportunities had opened up for women at the academic library level, this was not true at the higher level of university administration. This was certainly true from the statistics generated from this survey. Sixty-nine percent of these academic librarians reported to a male provost and 71 percent to a male president at their institutions.

While many commented on the discrimination female academic librarians had faced in the past, the majority believed that men and women now have an equal chance of advancement at their institutions; 81 percent of respondents believed that women were as likely to obtain top leadership positions at their institution as men; however, there was a difference among the percentage of younger and older women who believed that women were as likely as men to rise to top leadership positions in libraries and that barriers no longer exist, the highest being the 25–34 age range and the lowest the 35–44 and 45–54 age range. Seventy-eight percent stated that they had experienced no discrimination in their career at the library because of their gender. The majority also agreed with the statement that women and men are treated equally at their institutions.

Observation 4: The biggest impediment women face today in rising through the administrative ranks is not gender discrimination. Although 42 percent of the survey respondents who answered this question took gender discrimination seriously as a barrier to advancement, a greater number (60 percent) believed that ageism and family responsibilities (47 percent) were the real problems (see table 5.1). Not surprisingly, the group that felt most discriminated against consisted of those individuals in the 65 or older range (40 percent), while those who felt the least discriminated against were in the 25–34 age range (12 percent). The percent of perception of discrimination increased as the age group increased.

Observation 5: Survey respondents see salary equity as a pressing issue for academic librarians. When asked to rank four issues in order of importance—gender and civil rights; employee benefits such as the family and medical leave act, flextime and childcare; job advancement; and equal pay—the majority of respondents (59 percent) chose salary equity as the most pressing issue for the profession (see table 5.2). Salary equity became more important as age increased; gender equity and civil rights were ranked less important as age increased. Women academic librarians have gotten closer to having parity. In 2012 the average salary for women academic librarians was 96 percent of that for male academic librarians, an increase of almost 2 percent since 2003. However, a 2011–2012 survey showed that men, even if their female colleagues had more experience, still received in 9 out of 10 cases a higher salary" (Fact Sheet 2012, Library Workers).

Observation 6: Survey respondents, independent of age, attribute their professional advancement to a mastery of information technology. Librarians in their 50s, 60s, and early 70s entered the profession at a time when the focus of academic libraries was on collection building; this is reflected in the number of second master's degrees and doctorates held by women from this generation surveyed for this chapter. Today, academic libraries are considered to be a suite of services, many of them driven by information technology. The uneasy relationship between the fields of information technology, which is male-dominated, and librarianship, which is female-dominated, has been explored in the literature with no satisfactory result. This tension is also reflected in the discrepancy between the "higher paying male-dominated IT related jobs and lower-paying female librarian jobs" (n.p.) and, as Golub has noted in speaking of the LIS curriculum, "It is

Table 5.1. Question 41: Do barriers still exist for women who want to rise through the administrative ranks at the library? (n=92)

	n	%
Gender discrimination	39	42%
Ageism	55	60%
Racism	11	12%
Family responsibilities discrimination	43	47%
Other	31	34%

Table 5.2. Question 23: Which of these issues are important to you? Please rank in order of importance. (n = 202)

	1		2		3		4	
	n	%	*n*	%	*n*	%	*n*	%
Equal Pay	119	59%	52	26%	27	13%	4	2%
Job advancement	21	10%	77	38%	56	28%	48	24%
Family issues (family and medical leave act, flextime, childcare, etc.)	26	13%	36	18%	75	37%	65	32%
Gender and civil rights issues	36	18%	37	18%	44	22%	85	42%

argued that the increasing focus on information and technology is an attempt to shift the image of the profession away from the realm of service that has been viewed as feminine to associate the profession with functions considered to be more masculine" (Golub 2010, n.p.).

> Although this shift may be the case, 54 percent of the respondents identified themselves as being proficient and 46 percent as being comfortable with information technology. Over 60 percent believed that their knowledge of information technology had contributed to their career advancement. Many prided themselves as being first or in the lead in adopting technology at their library. Several connected learning new technologies with the ability to embrace change. The youngest age group, 25-34, saw a direct correlation between their technical skill sets and their promotion with their institutions.

Observation 7: The majority of survey respondents describe themselves as feminists. Over three-quarters of the respondents described themselves as feminists, with about a quarter disagreeing. Among the five age groups, the most negative responses came from the 35–44 age group. The least number of women who identified themselves as feminists were from the South (65 percent) and the highest were from the Midwest (83 percent). Of those who did not identify themselves as feminists, almost 14 percent felt that feminist goals had been achieved, 86 percent did not identify with feminist rhetoric, and 17 percent did not identify with feminist objectives.

Observation 8: Women differ in their perception of the impact the women's movement has had on academic librarianship. The majority of women (almost 64 percent) agreed that the women's movement had increased opportunities for women in librarianship; however, the responses of the 25–34 age group were significantly different from all the others; the majority of those who answered this question disagreed. For this question, respondents were also given the opportunity to comment. On the whole, these responses were ambiguous. Several respondents stressed that librarianship was a women's profession and therefore not directly affected by a radical feminist agenda.

Observation 9: Women library administrators are generally aware of significant societal gains achieved by radical feminism, but are largely unaware of the impact federal law (principally Title IX) had on their own chances for advancement in the profession. The passage of Title IX in 1972 probably had a greater impact on shaping gender equity law and furthering the advancement of women academic librarians than any other piece of legislation; however, regardless of their age, the majority of survey respondents either never had heard of Title IX or were confused as to its significance. Women, particularly those of the older generations, had much more of a grasp of the impact radical feminism had had on their profession and of the sacrifices of the women who came before them.

Observation 10: Men and women lead differently. As mentioned earlier, the majority of women who participated in this survey were either deans/directors or associate deans/directors and had a great deal of leadership experience. When asked to rank the qualities they considered most important in a leader, the women administrators placed communication skills first, followed by having a vision for the organization and the ability to tolerate change (see table 5.3). In many respects this ranking is not dissimilar to the results of studies mentioned earlier, such as those undertaken by Hernon, Powell and Young.

Over 60 percent of respondents said they drew on specific "feminine" skills or traits in their leadership. The respondents then were asked to qualify their answers. Although some women felt uncomfortable with the term "feminine," preferring "humanistic," the most overwhelming leadership trait that

Table 5.3. Question 36: What are the qualities you consider most important in a leadership position at any academic library? (n=205)

	n	%
Managerial skills	122	60%
Emotional intelligence	111	54%
Communication skills	177	86%
Vision for the organization	160	78%
Empathy	65	32%
Respect for individuality and diversity	121	59%
Transparent management	120	59%
Ability to tolerate change	136	66%

these women identified as "feminine" was empathy, which was mentioned by 121 respondents. Other common "feminine" traits were consensus-building, listening, and compassion. In their remarks, the respondents stressed that their leadership style focused on collegiality, collaboration, tolerance, and flexibility. Several observed that their maternal experience played a significant role in their managerial career. Others contrasted their own "horizontal" style of management with the "vertical" style of management exhibited by their male colleagues.

Earlier in this chapter, the author addressed some of the effects of second wave or radical feminism on the academic library profession and the difficulties women library administrators had and still have in defining what leadership is and how they should lead. Library literature published between the 1980s and 2000s showed the ambivalence in how librarians of both sexes saw women in academic library leadership positions and whether female or male leadership styles were preferable. These traits were judged as being situational (Eagly et al. 2003), undifferentiated (Hernon, Powell, and Young 2001), and male-centric (Turock 2001). This survey suggests that a younger generation of women, whom the author would refer to as "new humanists," is finding a different way to lead. The survey provides only a snapshot of a particular period of time, 2012, but it gives a complex view of female academic library administrators, most of whom seem to have found a satisfactory balance between work and family. Perhaps one of the more surprising results of the survey was the ability of these women to acknowledge the role second wave feminism has played within the larger society, while being ambivalent as to its impact on librarianship. Equally surprising was the ability of these women administrators to recognize their own leadership traits as being distinctively different from those of men and to use them to promote a humanistic work environment.

In many ways, the milestones that occurred over the last hundred or so years in U.S. women's history and academic library history mirror each other, particularly since librarianship is a "woman's profession." The results of this survey perhaps point to issues the library literature can continue to explore, such as salary equity and professional advancement, while at the same time giving a fresh look at others—such as ageism and the effect of technology on the career trajectory of female academic librarians. More importantly, it may lead to a reexamination of whether there are distinctly male and female leadership traits—one of the original questions that was brought up at the beginning of this chapter.

APPENDIX: FEMINISM AND LIBRARY CULTURE
SURVEY SUMMARY

The following is taken from "Feminism and Library Culture," a survey conducted in the fall of 2012 by Marta M. Deyrup.

1. Are you currently working in an academic library? (If the answer is Yes, please proceed. If No, thank you for your time.)
   Answers: Yes (n=203), No (n=1)
2. Are you a library administrator or do you have significant supervisory responsibilities at your library? (If the answer is Yes, please proceed. If No, thank you for your time.)
   Answers: Yes (n=203), No (n=2)
3. What is your gender? (If you are female or transgender you can proceed, if you are male thank you for your time.)
   Answers: Female (n=202), Male (n=2), Transgender (n=1)
4. Do you have children?
   Answers: Yes (n=116), No (n=88)
5. If so, how many?
   Answers: 1 (n=35), 2 (n=59), 3 (n=19), 4 (n=2), More than 4 (n=2)
6. What are the ages of your children?
   Answers: 0–5 (n=15), 6–10 (n=14), 11–14 (n=7), 15–18 (n=17), 19–24 (n=38), Over 25 (n=58)
7. If you have children, did you take time off from your career to care for them?
   Answers: Yes (n=36), No (n=80)
8. If not, did you share parenting responsibilities?
   Answers: Yes (n=74), No (n=16)
9. Was librarianship your first career?
   Answers: Yes (n=131), No (n=73)
10. Is the academic provost your division reports to female or male?
    Answers: Female (n=64), Male (n=139)
11. Is your academic president female or male?
    Answers: Female (n=56), Male (n=139)
12. Is your academic library director/dean female or male?
    Answers: Female (n=149), Male (n=53)
13. How would you define your library?
    Answers: Academic research Library (ARL) (n=48), College and research library (ACRL) (n=127), Community or junior college library (n=18), Other (please specify) (n=12)
14. What is the job title for your current position?

Answers: Director/Dean (n=77), Associate Director/Dean (n=29), Assistant Director/Dean (n=10), Department head (n=61), Other (please specify) (n=30)

15. What division of the library do you work in?

Answers: Administration (n=110), Archives/Special Collections (n=8), Digital services (n=10), Public services (n=48), Reference services (n=35), Technical services (n=31), Other (please specify) (n=22)

16. How many years of experience do you have as a library administrator?

Answers: Less than 1 year (n=13), 1–3 years (n=27), 4–6 years (n=37), 7–10 years (n=34), 11+ years (n=94)

17. What drew you to the library profession?

Answers: Academic environment (n=157), Opportunity to work in my subject area (n=36), Opportunity for professional advancement (n=38), Work flexibility (n=30), Administrative responsibilities (n=28), Salary (n=10), Benefits (n=17), Other (please specify) (n=33)

18. How familiar are you with information technology?

Answers: Proficient (n=110), Comfortable (n=94), Not proficient (n=1)

19. Did your knowledge of information technology contribute to your career advancement?

Answers: Yes (n=124), No (n=81)

20. If so, how?

Response Count (n=106)

21. Would you define yourself as a feminist?

Answers: Yes (n=154), No (n=51)

22. If not, what are the reasons?

Answers: Feminist goals have been achieved (n=7), Do not identify with feminist rhetoric (n=46), Do not identify with feminist objectives (n=9)

23. Which of these issues are important to you? Please rank in order of importance.

Answers: Equal Pay: 1 (n=119), 2 (n=52), 3 (n=27), 4 (n=4); Job Advancement: 1 (n=21), 2 (n=77), 3 (n=56), 4 (n=48); Family issues (family and medical leave act, flextime, childcare, etc.): 1 (n=26), 2 (n=36), 3 (n=75), 4 (n=65); Gender and civil rights issues: 1 (n=36), 2 (n=37), 3 (n=44), 4 (n=85)

24. Do you agree with the statement, The women's movement has increased leadership opportunities for women in the library profession?

Answers: Yes (n=130), No (n=74)

25. If yes, in what way? Please comment.

Response Count (n=107)

26. If no, why not? Please comment.

Response Count (n=71)

27. Do you draw on any specific "feminine" skills or traits in your leadership role?

    Answers: Yes (n=128), No (n=72)

28. Do you agree with the statement, The women's movement resulted in better benefits for families at my institution?

    Answers: Yes (n=141), No (n=57)

29. Do you consider yourself a beneficiary of Title IX? (Title IX of the Education Amendments of 1972 protects people from discrimination based on sex in education programs and activities that receive federal financial assistance—NCES Fast Facts website.)

    Answers: Yes (n=57), No (n=147)

30. If yes, how so?

    Response Count (n=51)

31. In your view, were you ever discriminated against at the library because of your gender in your career advancement?

    Answers: Yes (n=44), No (n=160)

32. Do you agree with the statement, Men and women are treated equally in my workplace?

    Answers: Yes (n=123), No (n=80)

33. Did you or do you have a mentor?

    Answers: Yes (n=127), No (n=77)

34. What gender is your mentor?

    Answers: Male (n=28), Female (n=99)

35. In your view, do men and women exhibit different styles of leadership?

    Answers: Yes (n=143), No (n=26), Don't know (n=34)

36. What are the qualities you consider most important in a leadership position at any academic library?

    Answers: Managerial skills (n=122), Emotional intelligence (n=111), Communication skills (n=177), Vision for the organization (n=160), Empathy (n=65), Respect for individuality and diversity (n=121), Transparent management (n=120), Ability to tolerate change (n=136)

37. Do you draw on any specific "feminine" skills or traits in your leadership role?

    Answers: Yes (n=121), No (n=78)

38. If so, what are they?

    Response Count (n=121)

39. Do you agree with the statement, The women's movement resulted in better benefits for families at my institution?

    Answers: Yes (n=113), No (n=41), Don't know (n=47)

40. Are women as likely as men to rise to top leadership positions at your library?

   Answers: Yes (n=163), No (n=18), Don't know (n=20)

41. Do barriers still exist for women wishing to rise through the administrative ranks at the library?

   Answers: Gender discrimination (n=39), Ageism (n=55), Racism (n=11), Family responsibilities discrimination (n=43), Other (n=31)

42. Which category below includes your age?

   Answers: 25–34 (n=17), 35–44 (n=36), 45–54 (n=55), 55–64 (n=81), 65 and over (n=15)

43. What is your marital status?

   Answers: Married (n=124), Divorced, separated, or widowed (n=33), Single (n=28), In a committed relationship (n=17)

44. What is the highest level of education you have completed?

   Answers: Bachelors (n=3), Masters in LIS (n=125), Masters in subject area (n=40), Doctorate in LIS (n=7), Doctorate in subject area (n=27), Other (please specify) (n=33)

45. What region is your academic institution located in?

   Answers: Northeast (New England and the Mid-Atlantic States) (n=69), Midwest (East North Central and West North Central States) (n=53), South (South Atlantic, East South Central and West South Central States) (n=62), West (Mountain and Pacific States) (n=20)

46. How many students are at your academic institution?

   Answers: Fewer than 1,000 (n=15), Between 1,001 and 5,000 (n=65), Between 5,001 and 10,000 (n=36), Over 10,000 (n=89)

REFERENCES

Department for Professional Employees, AFL-CIO. 2012. Fact Sheet 2012, Library Workers: http://ala-apa.org/files/2010/02/Library-Workers-Facts-Figures-2012.pdf.

Deyrup, Marta M. 2004. "Is the Revolution Over? Gender, Economic, and Professional Parity in Academic Library Leadership Positions." *College & Research Libraries* 65, no. 3 (May): 242–50. http://crl.acrl.org/content/65/3/242.full.pdf+html.

Fagan, Jody Condit. 2012. "The Effectiveness of Academic Library Deans and Directors." *Library Leadership & Management* 26, no. 1: 1–11. http://journals.tdl.org/llm/index.php/llm/article/viewArticle/5914.

Fast Facts. http://nces.ed.gov/fastfacts/display.asp?id=93.

Fennell, Janice Clinedinst. 1978. "A Career Profile of Women Directors of the Largest Academic Libraries in the United States: An Analysis and Description of Determinants." The Florida State University, 1978. http://search.proquest.com/docview/302954773?accountid=13793.

Gershenoff, Amy B., and Roseanne J. Foti. 2003. "Leader Emergence and Gender Roles in All-Female Groups." *Small Group Research* 34(2) (April): 170–96. Sage.

Golub, Erin Marie. 2010. "Gender Divide in Librarianship: Past, Present, and Future." *Library Student Journal* 5 (January): 2. http://www.librarystudentjournal.org/index.php/lsj/article/view/129/230.

Helgeson, Vicki S. 2002. *The Psychology of Gender*. Upper Saddle River, NJ: Prentice Hall.

Hernon, Peter, Ronald R. Powell, and Arthur P. Young. 2001. "University Library Directors in the Association of Research Libraries: The Next Generation, Part One." *College & Research Libraries* 62, no. 2: 116–45.

———. 2002. "University Library Directors in the Association of Research Libraries: The Next Generation, Part Two." *College & Research Libraries* 63, no. 1: 73–90. http://crl.acrl.org/content/63/1/73.full.pdf+html.

Hildenbrand, Suzanne. 2000. "Library Feminism and Library Women's History: Activism and Scholarship, Equity and Culture." *Libraries & Culture* no. 1: 51–65. http://sentra.ischool.utexas.edu/~lcr/archive/fulltext/LandC_35_1_Hildenbrand.pdf.

Kaufman, Paula T. 1993. "Library Leadership: Does Gender Make a Difference?" *Journal of Library Administration* 18, no. 3/4: 109. doi: 10.1300/J111v18n03_08.

Koenig, Anne M., Alice H. Eagly, Abigail Mitchell, and Tiina Ristikari. 2011. "Are Leader Stereotypes Masculine? A Meta-Analysis of Three Research Paradigms." *Psychological Bulletin* 137, no. 4: 616–42. doi: 10.1037/a0023557.

Kreitz, Patricia A. 2009. "Leadership and Emotional Intelligence: A Study of University Library Directors and Their Senior Management Teams." *College & Research Libraries* 70, no. 6 (November): 531–54. http://crl.acrl.org/content/70/6/531.full.pdf+html.

Mack-Canty, Colleen. 2004. "Third-Wave Feminism and the Need to Reweave the Nature/Culture Duality." *NWSA Journal* 16, no. 3: 154–79. http://www.jstor.org/stable/4317085.

Marital Status of the Population by Sex, 1900–2010—Infoplease.com http://www.infoplease.com/ipa/A0193922.html#ixzz2GeVd3e1khttp://www.infoplease.com/ipa/A0193922.html,

Moran, Barbara B., Elisabeth Leonard, and Jessica Zellers. 2009. "Women Administrators in Academic Libraries: Three Decades of Change." *Library Trends* 58, no. 2: 215–28. doi: 10.1353/lib.0.0088.

Moran, Barbara B. Joanne Gard-Marshall, and Susan Rathbun-Grubb. 2010. "The Academic Library Workforce: Past, Present, and Future." *Library Trends* 59, no. 1–2: 208–19. doi: 10.1353/lib.2010.0030.

Perez-Pena, Richard. 2012. "U.S. Bachelor Degree Rate Passes Milestone." *New York Times*, February 23 (accessed May 5, 2013). http://www.nytimes.com/2012/02/24/education/census-finds-bachelors-degrees-at-record-level.html.

Swisher, Robert, Rosemary Ruhig DuMont, and Calvin J. Boyer. 1985. "The Motivation to Manage: A Study of Academic Librarians and Library Science Students." *Library Trends* 34, no. 2: 219–34. https://www.ideals.illinois.edu/bitstream/handle/2142/7421/librarytrendsv34i2f_opt.pdf?sequence=1.

Turock, Betty J. 2001. "Women and Leadership." *Journal of Library Administration* 32, no. 3/4: 111. doi: 10.1300/J111v32n03_08.

U.S. Department of Labor. Title IX, Education Amendments of 1972. http://www.dol.gov/oasam/regs/statutes/titleix.htm.

White, Herbert S. 1987. "Library Managers-Female and Male." *Library Journal* 112, no. 2: 58.

Part Three

Applying Current Ideas in the Business World to Academic Library Settings

Chapter Six

Leadership and Value Co-Creation in Academic Libraries

Michael Germano

Today's college students have a variety of options for meeting their information needs related to assignments and course completion (Mill 2008, 342–55). Within and without academic library boundaries, research tools and resources have varying levels of efficacy for student researchers, and they may be wholly unaware of the tools and resources' finer points. As a result, academic libraries have become increasingly focused on the need to determine, understand, and predict user needs and perceptions to retain value and competitiveness (Malhan and Rao 2006). Such user-centered value creation efforts are critical to improving student experiences while also facilitating meaningful learning in library environments, because such strategies reflect a combined understanding of student needs and librarian expertise. The resulting value can therefore be thought of as *co-created* by user and librarian. Without leadership, however, the prospect of co-creating value with patrons is highly unlikely. In fact, leadership must focus on establishing and supporting the organizational culture and mind-sets that allow for value co-creation as well as the implementation of programs and services that reflect such shared notions of value (Kefela 2012).

The following chapter will examine the role of library leadership in value co-creation and the critical importance of leadership in the creation and execution of programs and services that matter most to students and librarian-educators alike. Building upon the recent trend of assessing library effectiveness in everything from collection development to instruction, the chapter will also consider the vital role leadership plays in turning assessment into actionable data that produces meaningful changes for student library users.

LEADERSHIP, VALUE CO-CREATION, AND
COMPETITIVE ADVANTAGE

One of the greatest barriers to understanding leadership is its assumed importance. The assumption of importance that surrounds leadership makes it inherently difficult to describe, theorize, or recommend what leadership should or could look like or how and why it might be developed in an individual organization, functional area, or industry (Meindl and Ehrlich 1987). Leadership appears to be something worth pursuing, without question. The problem with this line of thinking, however, is the intangible nature of leadership. More of a process than an actual event and made up of many individual actions, leadership is not always easy to discern (Kempster 2009). One can readily observe the outcome of either poor or beneficial leadership, but it is not always easy to holistically observe the everyday acts of leading or even the short-term benefits of leadership (Schyns and Schilling 2013). This is true in all types of organizations and work environments, including academic libraries.

The assumption of leadership's worth raises many questions for academic libraries. Is leading simply an act of change management? A process for ensuring organizational effectiveness? A means by which strategies are developed and executed? Or is it more? The answer is a qualified yes to all of these things. Leadership is visible when the answers to these questions can be demonstrated with tangible, identifiable, and readily measured results. Leadership without this type of measurable end product is ultimately wasted effort (Yukl 2012). Leading, by definition, is the act of persuading others to pursue a desired goal or result (Lee 2001). The desired result is achieved by the leader, who uses soft skills, including personality, attitude, communication, and ethical behavior, to encourage others to buy in. When the desired outcome has organizational benefits that include measurable results, the process of leading is based on the real, rather than assumed, importance of leadership (Dhar and Mishra 2001, 154).

As service organizations predominantly concerned with supporting and ensuring student success, it seems logical to connect academic library leadership with student success outcomes, whether those outcomes are defined as completing course requirements, degree attainment, or a similar measure. Interestingly, very little research has linked the importance of library leadership to student success. While the causality between leadership and student success may not be fully understood in academic libraries, the connection between leadership and service quality has been explored at length (Clark, Hartline, and Jones 2009; Hui et al. 2007; Yee et al. 2013). If academic libraries truly are service organizations whose main purpose is to support students in pursuit of their educational goals, leadership as a means of improving service quality appears both beneficial and laudable.

When applied to a service organization like an academic library, "value co-creation" is most easily understood as engaging in service delivery premised upon the user's notions of value (Grönroos 2012; Payne, Storbacka, and Frow 2008). Value is critical to the successful delivery of services for a number of reasons related to competitiveness and customer loyalty, which are important outcomes for service organizations. Many academic libraries unfortunately assume users already consider their services valuable (Germano 2011b). Such assumptions are obstacles to value co-creation, since they supplant the users' actual perceptions about the service. Value co-creation requires that the users' perceptions define service value.

Value is co-created when products or services' unique benefits meet stated needs (Grönroos 2012). Value can be price-based when the need is related to income, but in academic libraries, where money is usually removed from any discussion of value, meeting a user's needs is usually considered the major benefit of library service. Co-creating value with student academic library users is highly dependent upon understanding and acting on their short and long-term needs with relevant services. For example, many students have a need to avoid plagiarism, since the negative implications for that act are quite clear. Research and assessment could investigate whether this is an assumed or actual need. Research could also measure the amount of effort students are willing to expend to meet that need. The library could then offer a myriad of services to meet this need, such as library workshops or online tutorials. The student has the option to use library services or public resources such as a website or online video. Unless the library co-creates value with students and makes library offerings' unique benefits clear, students won't perceive the inherent value of the library's plagiarism workshop. Value would derive from the library's ability to show *its* services are best suited to meet the student's need. Libraries can make this clear to students in various ways: convenient accessibility (on-campus location), the possibility of extra credit, certification for attending a workshop, or an explanation about how the library is in the best position to guide and advise students on a particular question. These are all examples of value co-creation, since they reveal a desire and effort to meet the need on students' terms. Considering the above, it becomes clear that co-creating value offers a number of benefits to students and libraries alike.

CO-CREATING VALUE WITH STUDENT ACADEMIC LIBRARY USERS

As previously stated, the clearest way to describe value co-creation is the process of meeting a user's need by offering a service that is uniquely beneficial and capable of meeting that need. Value co-creation is established by uncovering users' needs in a collaborative, interactive way as opposed to assuming or predicting those needs. In academic libraries, uncovering needs can often be achieved through assessing everything from student learning and capabilities to attitudes and desires (Matthews 2012). The key is to analyze data and assess which student needs the library can satisfy in ways that stand out from competing products or services.

Whether academic libraries appreciate it or not, they exist and operate within a highly competitive information industry (Flower 2004). Embracing the need to co-create value represents the library's best hedge against competing forces that encourage students to look elsewhere when it comes to researching, studying, or completing assignments. By co-creating value with student library users, academic libraries can preemptively answer the question, "Why use the library?"

Student patrons of academic libraries have many options when choosing study locations, research sources, and who to consult. When value is co-created with students based upon satisfying their needs, the library is in the best position to compete. For example, one of the easiest choices for students to make when it comes to research is the use of online search engines like Google. Google meets two critical needs of students: availability and ease of use. Librarians and educators often seek to encourage the use of more credible and more effective information sources, like subscription databases and library holdings, without regarding the students' needs surrounding ease-of-use and 24/7 availability. Unless students are provided with a valuable, compelling reason based upon their articulated or discovered needs to use those resources, the end result is predictable.

Academic libraries that choose to operate in a user-value-centered way can expect to see a number of positive results. Chief among them are loyalty from patrons, increased competitiveness, and enhanced credibility in satisfying needs better than competing resources (Helm and Jones 2010). The benefits of co-creating value are not one-way. Co-creating value with students is a student-centered activity that is highly beneficial to them since they are being given a compelling reason to engage in better research habits. In short, librarians who grasp user needs and turn them into value perceptions are in a unique position to guide, counsel, and lead students to successful academic outcomes about research, library use, and studying.

VALUE CO-CREATION AND LEADERSHIP THEORIES

For this discussion, leadership will be defined as the ability to move others toward a desired goal or outcome (Lee 2001). Leadership in service organizations like academic libraries often has two foci: an internal, organizational focus and an external, customer-facing focus. When viewed in this more holistic way, leadership represents a strong connection and mediating force between employee action and customer perception (Heskett et al. 2008). The resulting view of leadership encourages librarians to be leaders at all organizational levels, not just managers and administrators, so services can be improved or optimized. Librarian leadership is needed throughout the academic library to foster value co-creation, including during patron interaction. Leadership, both internal and external, should be directed at improving service quality based on conveying and executing the library's ability to uniquely satisfy user needs. As a result, the remainder of this chapter will examine leadership in academic libraries, including examinations of the critical relationship between leadership and organizational effectiveness and user-centered service delivery that is predicated by value co-creation.

Leadership models have been applied to libraries in a general way to explore leadership's role in organizational effectiveness (Iqbal et al. 2012). However, the nature of the relationship between leadership and library service quality is not yet well understood. A quick review of the leadership literature outside of library science indicates service providers are highly dependent upon leadership as a direct influence upon external perceptions of service quality (Clark, Hartline, and Jones 2009; Hui et al. 2007; Yee et al. 2013; Helm and Jones 2010). Applying such findings to libraries as service organizations suggests that leadership influences user perceptions of quality, relevancy, and the competitiveness of services that are offered.

Leadership can be understood in a number of theoretical ways, but the most common views of leadership focus on purely descriptive, action-based concepts like autocratic, bureaucratic, democratic, laissez-faire, and charismatic, or by examining social interaction or power exchange theories such as situational, transactional, transformational, or servant leadership theories (Nohria and Khurana 2010). While each of these leadership models can help identify the leader's role in organizational effectiveness, they are simply descriptive models and are not necessarily predictive of outcomes. As a result, there is an inherent problem in leadership theory and its application to practical problems (Kaiser, Lindberg Mcginnis, and Overfield 2012). With that said, each model of leadership style can be useful in understanding leadership's influence on value co-creation, especially when predicting which leadership styles might be more effective in fostering and supporting value co-creation in academic libraries.

Before examining leadership models and their specific fit for co-creating value with students, it is useful to consider the beneficial role of leadership in such an endeavor and the key leadership traits required to drive value co-creation. The concept of improving service quality to meet users' stated needs might sound simplistic, but it is a complex undertaking with multiple stages that relies upon multiple organizational and individual mind-sets, skills, and competencies. From understanding the competitive environment to uncovering student needs through research and assessment to analyzing the work required to turn findings into strategic action, co-creating value with student library customers is a complex process that requires leadership to succeed. To engage in such a process, a library must have a culture of analysis, assessment, group learning, user-centeredness, flexibility, creativity, innovation, and a high tolerance for change.

The most easily understood leadership theories are autocratic, bureaucratic, and democratic leadership. Autocratic leadership is something of an oxymoron since the process of telling people what to do based on authority from one's position is somewhat antithetical to modern notions of leadership. Bureaucratic leaders are those who lead by policy or stated rules. Democratic leadership, based upon the notion that the group can decide more fairly than an individual, is followed by participative leaders who seek buy-in. Each has severe limitations when it comes to co-creating value with students.

The obvious problem with autocratic leadership is its dependency upon obligation and the force of authority. Requiring people to engage in creative, strategic innovation to meet a competitive, customer-centric goal like value co-creation is highly improbable. Voluntary buy-in is necessary for a number of reasons, not the least of which is the effect on service quality. Those who believe in a mission deliver better service that is more focused on customer need.

Bureaucratic leadership, or leading by policy, is something of a leadership dead end. Policy-driven leaders think leadership is primarily an exercise in control, not motivation, buy-in, or managing change. Bureaucracy-based leadership also produces negative customer interactions and outcomes. When leaders choose policy or process over people, they are inevitably cutting themselves off from one of the most important organizational attributes needed for value co-creation: flexibility.

In many ways, flexibility is the lifeblood of value creation, since it depends upon both individual and organizational agility to meet constantly changing customer needs. Improving service quality is often a simple matter of flexibility in executing strategic initiatives, especially those that include tactical elements related to direct customer interaction. Bureaucratic leaders do not possess the needed level of flexibility because they are so dependent upon codified rules, processes, and procedures. Leading by policy or bureaucracy is also a documented innovation and creativity killer because it quashes risk taking, learning from mistakes, and entrepreneurial spirit (Amabile and Khaire 2008). For these reasons, those who are most comfortable defaulting to positions of rules, policies, and procedures are in a poor position when it comes to co-creating value with students.

Of the leadership styles mentioned above, democratic or participative leadership is the most promising model for co-creating value, but it has limitations. Democratic leadership defers to group decision making and open, more egalitarian ways of deciding how an organization should act. It promotes openness and transparency while empowering staff at all levels. In some ways, democratic leadership appears extremely fair-minded and thoughtful. Unfortunately, studies have indicated the reality of democratic-led organizations is that other cultural structures like titles, organizational charts, and seniority still wield heavy influence (Kahai, Sosik, and Avolio, 2004). The end result is that democratically led organizations can be less democratic than their members think. Added to this reality is the notion that group decision making is slow and prone to cut off innovation and stifle creativity. Such characteristics are directly at odds with the process of co-creating value.

Ironically, both charismatic and laissez-faire leaders are well-suited for co-creating value—with obvious caveats. Charismatic leaders are those who continually gain buy-in via strength of personality; unfortunately, such leadership is dependent upon the individual (Gary 2002). If a charismatic individual chooses to leave, the process is effectively cut off. Similarly, laissez-faire (or do-nothing) leadership is dependent upon the organization having highly motivated and focused individuals who succeed despite the lack of leadership. Under either form of leadership, the concept of value creation is theoretically possible but practically unlikely.

As seen above, descriptive leadership models are somewhat limited in helping librarians understand the best forms of leadership for co-creating value with students and improving service delivery in academic libraries. An alternative approach is to consider leadership models based upon social power exchange. These include situational, transactional, transformational, and servant leadership. Each presents potential ways for librarians to understand the leadership mind-sets and actions required to co-create value with student library users.

Situational leaders are those who tailor their leadership to meet any given scenario. The driving premise is that no specific type of leadership can satisfy all situations, so leadership must be considered a toolbox, with the leader picking the appropriate tool for the job. Situational leadership theory is seductive, since it avoids the notion of a "best" form of leadership and supplants it with a more practical framework for understanding leadership as a dynamic, dependent process. This makes it difficult to use situational theories to examine the form of leadership needed for value co-creation. Also, the situational approach assumes experienced leaders leading the inexperienced (Yukl 2002, 270–72), which may not be the leadership context for value co-creation. Lack of defined leader behaviors or motivations leave it somewhat inadequate for studying how a leader can support value co-creation.

The most easily understood style of leadership based upon social power exchange is transactional leadership. This view of leadership is based upon a quid pro quo understanding of how organizations function and operate. In some ways it represents a highly pragmatic view of leadership theory, since leaders' abilities or strengths are predicated upon the deals or enticements they can provide followers. The theory may seem cynical because it suggests followers can only be led based upon getting something in return for their efforts. Such an understanding of leadership is highly incomplete and compartmentalized to management functions. Transactional leadership focuses on formal leadership roles such as "manager," since managers are most organizationally equipped to engage in quid pro quo leadership behaviors. However, not all leaders are managers, and many managers are not leaders. Eliminating transactional leadership theory as the best form of leading value co-creation leaves librarians with two leadership models to examine: transformational and servant leadership.

TRANSFORMATIONAL LEADERSHIP, SERVANT LEADERSHIP, AND VALUE CO-CREATION

While both transformational and servant leadership represent useful models for understanding leadership in a library context, a hybridization of the two may provide the best leadership model in the specific context of co-creating value with student library users.

Transformational leaders can exist at any level throughout an organization. These leaders use visionary leadership to create self-replicating, beneficial change within organizations (Grant 2012). Libraries may be well-served by transformational leaders because they face significant competitive and technological forces that often change the way their customers access and use information. Such forces continually shape and alter users' expectations of what libraries should provide to them. Without leadership to drive, guide, and sustain needed change, libraries run the risk of irrelevancy.

The concept of servant leadership underscores the critical role of service to both the organization and its customers (Jaramillo et al. 2009). It has attracted the attention of scholars recently because of evidence that it improves employee retention, customer satisfaction, and profitability (Jones 2012). Because libraries primarily exist as service organizations, servant leadership should be revisited and more closely examined by librarians, since it may represent both a strong cultural and tactical fit for libraries (Anzalone 2007). Both transformational and servant leadership, therefore, represent powerful leadership models for libraries. When merged, they form a compelling theoretical and practical view of leadership that seems ideally suited to libraries in general and libraries who seek to co-create value in particular.

It might be helpful at this point to return to the co-creation of value to examine leadership's role in it more fully. As previously mentioned, value co-creation is a complex, strategic process that requires a deep understanding of customer needs to provide targeted benefits for those needs. To create value for a specific user or customer group, service providers like academic libraries must be intimately aware of what drives user choices and decisions with regards to the library's offerings and those of competitors. The process is predicated upon extensive research and assessment of student needs. Academic libraries must also acknowledge they do not exist in a vacuum, independent from competition in what they offer students. Scanning the external environment to understand what student users like about the competition is also critical. Once data has been gathered and external environments have been scanned, there will be a strong need for analysis coupled with action in terms of creating new services, communicating their benefits, and executing their delivery (Germano and Stretch-Stephenson 2012). Leadership is acutely needed to support these activities. Leading the process described above and shaping the cultural mind-sets that drive value and service delivery is highly dependent on concepts such as innovation, change management, creativity, and customer focus. A transformational-servant leadership model would support all of these.

As previously indicated, the way transformational leaders seek change within an organization is based upon a vision of what an idealized version of the organization might achieve. Value co-creation is a somewhat idealistic vision for academic libraries. It acknowledges the primacy of the library as a service organization that drives student success, since the primary long-term goal of students is a degree or program completion. This makes transformational leadership a good fit. Transformational leadership is also extremely well-suited to fostering innovation and creativity within an organization because it seeks to embrace meaningful change, innovation, and creativity (Gumusluoglu and Ilsev 2009; Germano 2011a). Servant leadership is critical to value co-creation, since it embraces the service and support element of libraries, which is also central to meeting needs to co-create value. Considering the user perspective as the primary driver of service delivery is a central tenet of servant leadership.

CONCLUSION

Co-creating value with student users represents a pathway to relevancy, loyalty, and vibrancy in executing a student-focused mission at an academic library. Value co-creation cannot occur without leadership and may require certain kinds of leadership. Leadership is critical to value co-creation because of its complexity and the reality that all levels of an organization need to be involved in the process. From assessing, researching, and uncovering students' needs to the analysis required to meet those needs through the unique benefits represented by the library's offerings, value co-creation requires both internal and external leadership. Internal leaders drive many of the actions, tactics, and mind-sets that promote the notion of value co-creation and ensure it is realized. External, customer-facing leadership is used to share value with students in ways that compel them to take certain actions related to that value. Transformational-servant leadership represents an idealized form of library leadership that embraces the library's primary need to successfully meet users' needs by providing unique, competitive benefits that are unavailable elsewhere.

REFERENCES

Amabile, Teresa M., and Mukti Khaire. 2008. "Creativity and the Role of the Leader." *Harvard Business Review* 86 (10): 100–9.

Anzalone, Filippa Marullo. 2007. "Servant Leadership: A New Model for Law Library Leaders." *Law Library Journal* 99 (4): 793–812.

Clark, Ronald A., Michael D. Hartline, and Keith C. Jones. 2009. "The Effects of Leadership Style on Hotel Employees' Commitment to Service Quality." *Cornell Hospitality Quarterly* 50 (2): 209–31.

Dhar, Upinder, and Prashant Mishra. 2001. "Leadership Effectiveness." *Journal of Management Research* 1 (4): 154.

Flower, Eric. 2004. "Competition, Technology, and Planning: Preparing for Tomorrow's Library Environment." *Information Technology & Libraries* 23 (2): 67–69.

Gary, Loren. 2002. "In Praise of Pragmatic Leadership." *Harvard Management Update* 7 (12): 3.

Germano, Michael. 2011a. "Library Leadership that Creates and Sustains Innovation." *Library Leadership & Management* (Online) 25 (1): 1–14.

———. 2011b. "The Library Value Deficit." *Bottom Line: Managing Library Finances* 24 (2): 100–6.

Germano, Michael, and Shirley Stretch-Stephenson. 2012. "Strategic Value Planning for Libraries." *The Bottom Line* 25 (2): 71–88.

Grant, Adam M. 2012. "Leading with Meaning: Beneficiary Contact, Prosocial Impact, and the Performance Effects of Transformational Leadership." *Academy of Management Journal* 55 (2): 458–76.

Grönroos, Christian. 2012. "Conceptualising Value Co-Creation: A Journey to the 1970s and Back to the Future." *Journal of Marketing Management* 28 (13–14): 1520–34.

Gumusluoglu, Lale, and Arzu Ilsev. 2009. "Transformational Leadership, Creativity, and Organizational Innovation." *Journal of Business Research* 62: 461–73.

Helm, Clive, and Richard Jones. 2010. "Extending the Value Chain—A Conceptual Framework for Managing the Governance of Co-Created Brand Equity." *Journal of Brand Management* 17 (8): 579–89.

Heskett, James L., Thomas O. Jones, Gary W. Loveman Jr., Sasser W. Earl, and Leonard A. Schlesinger. 2008. "Putting the Service-Profit Chain to Work." *Harvard Business Review* 86 (7): 118–29.

Hui, C. H., Warren C. K. Chiu, Philip L. H. Yu, Kevin Cheng, and Herman H. M. Tse. 2007. "The Effects of Service Climate and the Effective Leadership Behaviour of Supervisors on Frontline Employee Service Quality: A Multi-level Analysis." *Journal of Occupational & Organizational Psychology* 80 (1): 151–72.

Iqbal, Javed, Sumaira Inayat, Madiha Ijaz, and Anam Zahid. 2012. "Leadership Styles: Identifying Approaches and Dimensions of Leaders." *Interdisciplinary Journal of Contemporary Research in Business* 4 (3): 641–59.

Jaramillo, Fernando, Douglas B. Grisaffe, Lawrence B. Chonko, and James A. Roberts. 2009. "Examining the Impact of Servant Leadership on Sales Force Performance." *Journal of Personal Selling & Sales Management* 29 (3): 257–75.

Jones, David. 2012. "Does Servant Leadership Lead to Greater Customer Focus and Employee Satisfaction?" *Business Studies Journal* 4 (2): 21–35.

Kahai, Surinder S., John J. Sosik, and Bruce J. Avolio. 2004. "Effects of Participative and Directive Leadership in Electronic Groups." *Group & Organization Management* 29 (1): 67–105.

Kaiser, Robert B., Jennifer Lindberg Mcginnis, and Darren V. Overfield. 2012. "The How and the What of Leadership." *Consulting Psychology Journal: Practice & Research* 64 (2): 119–35.

Kefela, Ghirmai T. 2012. "Organizational Culture in Leadership and Management." *PM World Today* 14 (1): 1–12.

Kempster, Stephen. 2009. "Observing the Invisible." *Journal of Management Development* 28 (5): 439–56.

Lee, Lee W. 2001. "Leadership." *Encyclopedia of Business and Finance*. Ed. Burton S. Kaliski. New York: Macmillan Reference USA. Vol. 2: 542–45.

Malhan, I. V., and Shivarama Rao. 2006. "Information Marketing: Areas and Practices." *International Information, Communication & Education* 25 (1): 29–45.

Matthews, Joseph R. 2012. "Assessing Library Contributions to University Outcomes: The Need for Individual Student Level Data." *Library Management* 33 (6): 389–402.

Meindl, James R., and Sanford B. Ehrlich. 1987. "The Romance of Leadership and the Evaluation of Organizational Performance." *Academy of Management Journal* 30 (1): 91–109.

Mill, David H. 2008. "Undergraduate Information Resource Choices." *College & Research Libraries* 69 (4): 342–55.

Nohria, Nitin, and Rakesh Khurana. 2010. *Handbook of Leadership Theory and Practice: An HBS Centennial Colloquium on Advancing Leadership*. Boston: Harvard Business Press.

Payne, Adrian F., Kaj Storbacka, and Pennie Frow. 2008. "Managing the Co-Creation of Value." *Journal of the Academy of Marketing Science* 36 (1): 83–96.

Schyns, Birgit, and Jan Schilling. 2013. "How Bad Are the Effects of Bad Leaders?: A Meta-Analysis of Destructive Leadership and Its Outcomes." *Leadership Quarterly* 24 (1): 138–58.

Yee, Rachel W. Y., Peter K. C. Lee, Andy C. L. Yeung, and T. C. E. Cheng. 2013. "The Relationships among Leadership, Goal Orientation, and Service Quality in High-Contact Service Industries: An Empirical Study." *International Journal of Production Economics* 141 (2): 452–64.

Yukl, Gary. 2002. *Leadership in Organizations* (5th ed.). Upper Saddle River, NJ: Prentice Hall.

———. 2012. "Effective Leadership Behavior: What We Know and What Questions Need More Attention." *Academy of Management Perspectives* 26 (4): 66–85.

Chapter Seven

Good to Great for Academic Libraries

Dominique Roberts

A great organization . . . makes such a unique contribution to the communities
it touches and does its work with such unadulterated excellence that if it were
to disappear, it would leave a hole that could not be easily filled by any other
organization on the planet.
—Collins 2005, 8

Academic library leaders currently face many challenges related to identifying and implementing their mission and strategic objectives: deciding which
goals to pursue, effectively communicating strategic objectives to internal
and external stakeholders, obtaining organization-wide buy-in, equipping
staff with the skills and resources to effectively implement organizational
objectives, and measuring the success of specific measures and processes, to
name a few. One evidence-based model that offers insights to organizational
leaders facing the above conundrums is the "hedgehog concept" framework
presented in Jim Collins's *Good to Great*. Collins's research contrasted two
sets of companies, those that went from merely good results to great results
and those good companies that failed to achieve exceptional results. Collins
and his research team found that the most successful companies had implemented what he and his team came to call the hedgehog concept: the good-
to-great companies understood the overlap between three variables—what
their organization could do best, their funding mechanisms, and what they
were most passionate about—and used that understanding to form a strategy
that guided their decisions. The process of creating and implementing the
hedgehog concept can be used by library leaders to clarify and prioritize their
initiatives and strategic objectives, obtain needed economic resources, and
motivate staff members. Specifically, libraries can use the hedgehog concept
to closely examine the specific human resources, funding, and institutional
challenges and opportunities they face when advancing their missions.

For libraries and other social sector organizations, the importance of the hedgehog concept is more pronounced than for businesses because of the funding mechanisms for social sector institutions. The complexity of a non-profit organization's funding sources requires that a nonprofit's hedgehog concept incorporate many of *Good to Great*'s other findings. For example, in *Good to Great and the Social Sectors*, Collins (2005) explains that analysis related to hiring decisions and brand building should be part of a nonprofit's hedgehog concept.

This chapter focuses on the hedgehog concept, and describes how it can be used by academic library leaders to develop and evaluate specific plans aimed at increasing the quality of their library's collections, facilities, human and economic resources, and services. Before getting into the specifics of the hedgehog concept, however, the chapter will briefly review Collins's research methodology and its inherent limitations, the overall goals of Collins's research, and discuss the nature of his findings.

RESEARCH METHODOLOGY

Overview

The impetus behind Collins's research was the following question: Can a good company become a great company and, if so, how? To find an answer, Collins chose several good-to-great companies and a group of merely good comparison companies and examined what the good-to-great companies shared in common that distinguished them from the comparison companies (Collins 2001).

Drawn from an initial pool of all the companies that appeared on the Fortune 500 from 1965 to 1995 (1,435 in all), eleven companies met the good-to-great selection criteria: the company must have fifteen-year cumulative stock returns at or below the general stock market, a transition point, and then cumulative returns at least three times the stock market average over the next fifteen years; and the company must not be part of an industry that showed the same pattern. Two sets of comparison companies were chosen 1) direct comparisons: companies that were in the same industry as the good-to-great companies, and had similar resources and opportunities, but showed no leap from good to great, and 2) unsustained comparisons: companies that made a short-term shift from good to great but failed to maintain their performance. After selecting the good-to-great and comparison companies, Collins and his twenty-member research team conducted a wide range of qualitative and quantitative analyses, including executive interviews, and coded all of the articles published on each company into categories such as strategy, technology, and leadership. After collecting the data, Collins's research team began a series of weekly debates in which the good-to-great businesses were contrasted with the comparison companies (Collins 2001).

The team's findings were organized into a framework of three stages: disciplined people, disciplined thought, and disciplined action. The hedgehog concept fits into the second stage and is based upon the findings that good-to-great companies both "founded their strategies along three key dimensions [what they were passionate about, what they could be the best in the world at, and what drove their economic engine]," and "translated that understanding into a simple crystalline concept that guided all of their efforts" (Collins 2001, 95). The name "hedgehog concept" was derived from Isaiah Berlin's essay "The Hedgehog and the Fox," a work based upon the Greek parable "that the fox knows many things, but the hedgehog knows one big thing" (Collins 2001, 90).

Limitations

In *The Halo Effect*, Phil Rosenzweig (2007) outlined several criticisms of Collins's research methods and findings. First, he explained that retrospective research into successful companies may simply reveal attributions based on company performance, instead of real insight into the reasons for a company's success. He also argued that we don't know if being a hedgehog improves a company's chance of success because, even assuming that all of the successful companies were hedgehogs, less successful companies not included in the study could have been hedgehogs as well. He challenged claims of having found "the immutable laws of organizational performance" because business studies cannot achieve the "precision and replicability of physics" (Rosenzweig 2007, 126). Other criticisms of the research and results in *Good to Great* include concerns regarding the validity and ethical implications of Collins's claims, and the way they are stated. Levitt (2008) asserted that the basic premise of business books such as *Good to Great* is undermined when their implicit message (that the principles discovered have made companies successful and positioned them for continued success) turns out not to be true (i.e., when companies identified as successful fail). An author writing for the University of Pennsylvania's "Knowledge at Wharton" claimed that Collins "leaves out humanity in favor of numbers" when he included Philip Morris on the list of good-to-great companies (University of Pennsylvania 2001). Criticism of Collins's decision to report this result, though, does not bear upon the predictive ability of his research methodology. Others have argued that Collins's claims are not as original as he asserts and that they are hard to disprove because they are so broadly stated (Sutton 2008; Murray 2011).

Collins responded to Rosenzweig's criticism by claiming that the retrospective bias of his study is limited because Collins and his collaborators developed their frameworks "primarily from evidence from the actual time of the events, before the outcome is known" and they "read through the evidence in chronological order, moving forward through time" (Collins 2009, 17). Collins responded to the claim that less successful companies may have also been hedgehogs by explaining that using a data set involving several different industries limited the likelihood of that occurrence, and clarifying that he was not claiming that following the principles in his book will guarantee organizational success, but only that following the principles in his study would improve the probability of success (Collins and Hansen 2011). To Levitt's criticism, Collins responded that "the research [in *Good to Great*] did not attempt to predict which companies would remain great after their fifteen-year run. Indeed, as this work [*How the Mighty Fall*] shows, even the mightiest of companies can self-destruct" (Collins 2009, 4). He also stated that including Philip Morris as a good-to-great company was "difficult to swallow," but "completely supported by the data" (Collins 2001, 215). Collins did not directly respond to the contentions that his findings are unoriginal or so broadly stated that they are hard to disprove, but in his review of *Good to Great*, Michael Skapinker (2001) of the *Financial Times* explained why Collins's seemingly simple prescriptions have been embraced: "The difference [between Collins and other business writers] is how hard Mr. Collins works to arrive at his simple conclusions. They are based on years of detailed, empirical research and are all the more powerful for producing such unexpected results." An examination follows regarding specifics of Collins's hedgehog concept, and considers how leaders in academic libraries may adapt the concept for use in their institutions.

WHAT IS THE HEDGEHOG CONCEPT?

The hedgehog concept originated when the research team realized that although great and comparison companies both had strategic plans, great companies had strikingly simple plans. Take for example, the following good-to-great companies: Kroger had a "superstore" concept, Kimberly-Clark simply moved to paper-based consumer products, and Walgreens decided to focus on building convenient drugstores. Comparison companies, though, seemed to be hindered by their more complex growth strategies. After this basic discovery, the team decided to systematically examine the development and nature of the simple concepts that guided great companies. The ideas that guided the companies were not successful merely because they were simple; they were successful because the companies understood what they were passionate about, what they could be best at in the world, what drove their economic engine and converted that knowledge into a simple concept that guided all of their decisions (Collins 2001).

Isaiah Berlin's essay "The Hedgehog and the Fox" describes the fox as a cunning creature, able to devise a myriad of complex circles around the hedgehog's den, waiting for the perfect moment to pounce. Whenever the hedgehog—a slower and dowdier creature—walks right into one of the fox's traps, though, the hedgehog always wins. Why? Because the hedgehog simply rolls up into a little ball, becoming a sphere of spikes pointing out in all directions, and the fox abandons his attack. Berlin used this story to divide people into two basic groups: foxes and hedgehogs. Foxes chase after many goals simultaneously and see the world in all its complexity. In contrast, hedgehogs see the complexities of the world through the lens of a single organizing idea or basic concept. Some examples of hedgehogs and their unifying concepts throughout history are: Freud and the unconscious, Darwin and natural selection, Marx and class struggle, Einstein and relativity, and Adam Smith and division of labor. Hedgehogs ignore what is not relevant to their hedgehog concept (Collins 2001).

The research team found that the great companies were built by leaders who created a single unifying concept for their organizations. Comparison companies, on the other hand, were "scattered, diffused, and inconsistent" (Collins 2001, 94). The great companies' unifying concepts represented a deep understanding around the intersection of three circles: "best at," "economic engine," and "passion." The first circle, "best at," refers to an awareness of what a company can and cannot be the best in the world at. A core competence may not make the cut: "just because you possess a core competence doesn't necessarily mean you can be the best in the world at it" (Collins 2001, 98).

The next circle is the "economic engine." To become great, companies need to determine what drives their economic engine: "the single denominator—profit per x—that had the greatest impact on their economies" (Collins 2001, 95). Interestingly, here, Collins states that the economic engine metric would be "cash flow per x in the social sector" (Collins 2001, 95). In his 2005 work *Good to Great and the Social Sectors*, however, Collins abandons this idea in favor of a new model, the resource engine (Collins 2005).

The last circle, "passion," finds its basis in the fact that "good-to-great companies focused on those activities that ignited passion" (Collins 2001, 96). Collins notes that companies should not attempt to ignite passion but should discover what makes them passionate. The mechanics of the business do not have to be the basis of this circle; "the passion circle can be focused equally on what the company stands for" (Collins 2001, 110).

THE HEDGEHOG CONCEPT IN ACADEMIC LIBRARIES

In *Social Sectors*, the hedgehog concept was modified to account for the goals and economic realities of the social and not-for-profit sector (Collins 2005). The major difference between the original hedgehog concept and the social sectors version is the conversion of the economic engine to a resource engine. A more nuanced funding-related circle, the "resource engine," was needed for social sector organizations because they "exist to meet social and human needs that cannot be priced at a profit" (Collins 2005, 33). The following sections explore factors relevant to academic libraries searching for their own hedgehog concepts.

Passion

In *Social Sectors* this circle is described as "Understanding what your organization stands for (its core values), and why it exists (its mission or core purpose)" (Collins 2005, 19). This conceptualization is quite similar to the definition of "passion" for the business sector; however, unlike his description of the hedgehog concept for the business sector, Collins clearly intends for "passion" to be the first element considered by social sector organizations: "You begin with passion, then you refine passion with a rigorous assessment of what you can best contribute to the communities you touch. Then you create a way to tie your resource engine directly to the other two circles" (Collins 2005, 20).

A starting point for determining the passion of academic libraries could be an examination of each library's mission statement and strategic plan. Academic libraries, though, are organizations within organizations, so the mission and strategic objectives of the library's parent institution are also relevant. For an academic library that is part of a state's public university system, the system-wide mission statement should also be considered. One example of this is the University of California, Los Angeles (UCLA) library. There are at least three mission statements to consider, those from the UCLA Library, UCLA, and the University of California Regents. Additionally, the UC system is part of the larger California Master Plan for Higher Education—legislation that created a three-tiered educational system including community colleges, primarily master's-granting institutions, and research universities. An understanding of the history and development of the California Master Plan would help UCLA's library to better understand the institutional, socioeconomic, political, and legal contexts it operates within, and to strengthen the library's sense of mission. For academic libraries serving private universities, insight into their founding documents is also essential. For example, the University of Southern California (USC), as a California corporation, is bound by state corporate laws and regulations. USC's founding document is its Articles of Incorporation. It operates primarily on the basis of the Bylaws adopted and periodically amended by its Board of Trustees. Legally, the Articles of Incorporation must be consistent with California corporate law, and the Bylaws cannot violate the Articles of Incorporation. The Board of Trustees is the primary body responsible for university operations. A deeper understanding of the history and development of the university community they support can help enable academic library leaders more effectively articulate their role in advancing the university's mission.

Further insight into the mission of the academic library may also be gained through a systematic comparison of the mission of the university with the mission of its library. Where does the library's mission align with and diverge from the university's mission? Is deviation from the university's mission acceptable or desirable in certain circumstances? One example of at least partial deviation could be when a library takes on expanded roles regarding the preservation and curation of cultural resources. A university's mission may focus more upon the current research needs of its faculty and students, while a library's focus on the preservation of cultural objects (including books) may preference the potential future research needs of all scholars (including the university's own faculty and students) and of the public, in general. Thus, a library that had previously focused on the preservation required primarily for the immediate needs of faculty, students, and staff may slightly depart from the university's core objectives when it takes a more long-term view of its patrons' needs. Even though a focus on broader preservation and access initiatives may deviate from the university's mission, it essentially broadens the mission to include more stakeholders, rather than restricting it or taking it in a new direction. In this case, a broader library mission may be desirable because it does not require completely new knowledge and skill bases for library staff, but merely builds upon existing staff expertise; it broadens the library and university support base; and it energizes library staff because it helps them find more meaning in their work.

In *Redefining the Academic Library: Managing the Migration to Digital Information Services*, the University Leadership Council (2011) argued that the general decline in circulation and reference requests occurring in academic libraries is evidence that their traditional core of services—providing access to books and guiding patrons through research—has moved to the periphery. The Council concluded that "today's users require a new set of services and accommodations from the academic library that necessitate a strategic paradigm shift: from building and maintaining a collection to engaging with students and faculty, as well as providing space for study, collaboration, and creativity" (University Leadership Council 2011, viii). Returning to the UCLA and USC library examples, the strategic plans of both institutions reflect many of the Leadership Council's priorities. The UCLA Library Strategic Plan 2012–17 seems to evidence this new focus on library space and virtual and physical services. The library mission states: "The UCLA Library inspires and supports students, faculty, researchers, and staff in all facets of their pursuits to dream, learn, create, and share knowledge" (UCLA Library 2012). Specific goals in UCLA's strategic plan include, among other initiatives, efforts to 1) support and advocate changes in scholarly publishing, 2) provide services, facilities, and technology to meet research needs, and 3) reconceptualize the library as place (UCLA Library 2012). Similarly, the USC Library's mission and strategic plan is organized around core values such as service excellence, innovation, and "library as a place" (USC Libraries 2011). Thus, major considerations for academic libraries trying to determine the content of their "passion" circle include their library mission statement and strategic plan, their system-wide and/or university mission statement, founding university documents, and goals related to mission statements that will enable library staff to find a sense of meaning to contribute to the greater good of society—through their work.

One way to integrate a library's mission with institution-wide goals is to undertake a formal alignment process. When the library director at Champlain College was asked to create a document explaining how the library advanced college goals, the director used library staff meetings to assist in the department's alignment efforts (Cottrell 2011). The meetings were used to produce a dual-column alignment map that contained one statement or idea from the college's strategic vision in the first column and a statement explaining how the library supports that portion of the college's vision in the other. For example, one statement in the college's strategic vision details the college's commitment to "Educate today's students to become skilled practitioners, effective professionals and global citizens." The library's parallel goal is to "Help educate students to become skilled, effective, responsible information users. That is, people who recognize when they need information, and know how to find, retrieve, evaluate, and use it effectively, efficiently, and ethically" (Cottrell 2011, 518).

"Best At"

In *Social Sectors* this circle is described as "Understanding what your organization can uniquely contribute to the people it touches, better than any other organization on the planet" (Collins 2005, 19). This description is quite similar to the definition of "best at" for the business sector; however, Collins explains that "best at" should be the second element considered by social sector organizations: "You begin with passion, then you refine passion with a rigorous assessment of what you can best contribute to the communities you touch. Then you create a way to tie your resource engine directly to the other two circles" (Collins 2005, 20). Additionally, the "best at" concept in *Social*

Sectors focuses on high performance in a specific activity: the impact the organization will have upon the people it serves (Collins 2005).

What service can academic libraries provide to their patrons better than any other organization on the planet? Consideration of this question requires leaders to first define their library's primary and secondary patron bases, categories that typically include the following groups: faculty, students, staff, alumni, friends, and the general public. The answer to the "best at" question may depend upon which patron base is being analyzed. For example, in *Studying Students: The Undergraduate Research Project at the University of Rochester*, researchers found that students desired different types of study and collaboration spaces than librarians had envisioned (Foster and Gibbons 2007). The University of Rochester library renovation team had decided to put comfy individual chairs next to large library windows, whereas the students wanted large tables to go in front of those windows since they would spend most of their time in the library researching and writing papers on their laptops. Additionally, librarians assumed that large eight-seater tables would seat eight students, but students thought that the tables would seat no more than four or five students—who would each have large working spaces (Foster and Gibbons 2007). By analyzing and implementing the results of studies such as the *Undergraduate Research Project*, libraries have the potential to provide the most user-centered and convenient study and collaboration spaces on college and university campuses.

In contrast to the University of Rochester study, the 2009 *Ithaka Faculty Survey* authors concluded that libraries need to "not only keep up with changing attitudes and practices but also to help *lead* scholars, in order to best support and facilitate scholarship as well as to ensure their own continuing relevance" (Schonfeld and Housewright 2010, 2). The survey found that faculty members were increasingly beginning their research by searching in "a specific electronic research source" or "a general purpose search engine," instead of their library's catalog or building (Schonfeld and Housewright 2010, 5). The study also indicated that more and more faculty view the library's "buyer" role ("the library pays for resources I need, from academic journals, to books, to electronic databases") as increasingly important (Schonfeld and Housewright 2010). When faculty responses were segmented by faculty discipline, researchers found that humanities faculty were more likely to use the library's traditional and new services (including using the library as a gateway to research and turning to the library for curricular and instructional support), than were social sciences and science faculty (Schonfeld and Housewright 2010). From the above findings, researchers concluded that libraries may need to choose between strengthening their traditional services (which are currently highly valued by humanities faculty) and attempting to become more relevant to social science and science faculty (Schonfeld and Housewright 2010). Thus, even within an already unique patron group such as faculty, libraries may need to consider if the degree to which the needs of subgroups within the group align or conflict.

After considering the unique needs of specific patron bases, the next question becomes: What can academic libraries provide better than any other organization on the planet? In this regard, the "Best At" circle is particularly interesting, since it requires that libraries compare themselves to other entities that serve their patron bases. If libraries are merely competent (and have the potential to continue to be competent, not the best) at providing a particular service, then that service cannot form the basis of a library's hedgehog concept. To successfully determine what they are "best at," academic libraries must perform a rigorous, honest self-assessment to discover what they can, and cannot, do best. Collins also points out that what an organization is best at may be something that the organization is not even currently engaged in (Collins 2001). A critical component of the "Best At" circle is that it is "not a goal to be the best, but an *understanding* of what you can and cannot be the best at" (Collins 2001, 98).

> In *Redefining the Academic Library*, the University Leadership Council states that, with the rise of companies like Google and Amazon, as well as nonprofits like Wikipedia and HathiTrust, users now meet most of their information needs through sources outside of the library. The collections . . . made available through these organizations dwarf library collections in size and scope, and content is increasingly accessed virtually through web- and cloud-based distribution portals (University Leadership Council 2011).

In terms of the "best at" circle, the above finding by the University Leadership Council suggests that academic libraries should not focus on building their digital collections, since other organizations are better at meeting that patron need. Instead, according to the Leadership Council, libraries should focus on providing support services to and engaging with patrons, and should provide a space for study, collaboration, and creativity (University Leadership Council 2011). The Leadership Council, though, did not thoroughly examine the role that academic libraries play in collections such as Google-Books and HathiTrust or explore their function as licensors of valuable subscription databases.

In order to determine how they can best serve their current and future users, library leaders need to study their patrons. The methods employed by the librarians at the University of Rochester for their undergraduate research project provide useful examples of patron-centered data-gathering. One aspect of their methodology included a survey of undergraduates who came to the reference desk. The survey was "designed to gather basic information about the student and the assignment that brought him/her to the reference desk, as well as the student's motivation to come to the desk and expected outcomes" (Foster and Gibbons 2007, 7). Students were asked about topics such as sources they checked before coming to the reference desk and what they learned from their reference session. Another technique used by the university librarians was to set flipcharts in various library spaces that asked patrons about why they came to that area of the library and solicited opinions about how that area could be improved. Other methods for studying patrons include creating personae for primary user groups and inviting patrons to participate in group and individual brainstorming sessions for future library services (appendix; Foster and Gibbons 2007).

Resource Engine

The resource engine is comprised of three components: time, money, and brand.

Time

Time "refers to how well you attract people willing to contribute their efforts, or time, for free, or at rates below what their talents would yield in business" (Collins 2005, 18). When compared to the hiring incentives and promotion process in the business sector, the social sector has the following major differences: leaders can more easily use the idealistic passions of people who seek meaning through providing a valuable social good, social sector organizations frequently lack the resources to acquire and retain talent, and tenure systems and volunteer dynamics can make it more difficult for leaders to "get the wrong people off the bus" (Collins 2005, 32).

The "time" or recruitment and retention circle in *Social Sectors* is described in terms of several related principles. To illustrate the principles, Collins cites the example of a public school teacher who became head of the science department at his school, declined to grant tenure to a teacher who was "good, not great," and—because of the open position that resulted from the decline of tenure—was able to hire a great teacher. Thus, the first principle is "you can build a pocket of greatness without executive power, in the middle of an organization" (Collins 2005, 14). This is an important point for academic libraries, since they are positioned within universities. It also suggests that any library managers have the ability to help lead the library in a new direction.

The next principle is that managers should "do whatever they can to get the right people on the bus, the wrong people off the bus, and the right people into the right seats" (Collins 2005, 14). Similar to other social sector organizations, academic libraries' missions appeal to the ideals and interests of potential employees. This appeal allows libraries with clearly defined objectives to "get the right people on the bus" by attracting employees willing to contribute their efforts for less monetary compensation than they would earn in the business sector. Accordingly, before deciding that a current employee is not a good fit for a library, managers may consider whether the employee would help advance the library's mission more effectively if they were "in the right seat" (i.e., in another position or given different areas of responsibility).

The last lesson is that "in the social sectors, where getting the wrong people off the bus can be more difficult than in business, early assessment mechanisms (such as tenure reviews) turn out to be more important than hiring mechanisms" (Collins 2005, 15). This insight is also particularly relevant to academic libraries, many of which have a tenure process or probationary period for new employees. Determining if an employee is "great," however, requires access to metrics that accurately assess the performance of employees. In the academic library context, this is problematic. In "Leadership Evaluation and Assessment," James F. Williams advocates for evaluation primarily based on the opinions of colleagues and supervisors (Williams 2001). While feedback from colleagues is useful, a library leader may want to know, objectively, how well an employee is contributing to the mission of the library. Before such metrics can be obtained, however, leaders must first be able to measure how well the library is carrying out its mission.

One strategy that library leaders can use to track how well their library is carrying out its mission is Balanced Scorecard (BSC) (Kaplan and Norton 1992). BSC seeks to measure and evaluate organizational activities by focusing on performance in four key areas: financial, customer, internal, and learning. The BSC analysis undertaken by the University of Texas at Austin libraries in 2010 is one example of how academic libraries are approaching BSC performance evaluation. Before commencing their BSC analysis, the university hired a consultant to help the libraries conduct a SWOT (Strengths, Weaknesses, Opportunities, and Threats) assessment. This analysis yielded 14 objectives, which were later organized into four perspectives corresponding to the standard BSC objectives (customer, financial, process, learning and growth) (Taylor and Heath 2012, 430). Examples of objectives include goals to "Raise User Satisfaction" (customer objective) and "Reduce Operational Costs" (financial objective) (Taylor and Heath 2012, 430).

The libraries then planned twenty-one initiatives to guide the implementation of their fourteen objectives. For example, the Discovery Institute Initiative task force was charged with the responsibility of identifying methods to make library resources more accessible. Task forces were composed of staff who responded to a library-wide call for participation and also included one member of the libraries' executive management team. Each task force developed recommendations and submitted a final report to the executive management team, which then drafted an implementation plan for the recommendations it chose to accept. After implementation of a plan has commenced, evaluation of the attainment of BSC objectives occurred at the end of each semester. Twenty-eight measures were used to facilitate this evaluation. The results of the evaluation were used by working group members who then drafted and submitted more recommendations to the executive management team. In this way, the University of Texas at Austin libraries used the BSC framework as an integral part of their metrics-based continuous evaluation process.

Money

The money component of the resource engine refers to the main sources of the organization's sustained cash flow (Collins 2005). Businesses have an advantage over social sector organizations in regards to this component, because their profit mechanism makes it easier for them to say "no" or to stop engaging in activities that do not fit their hedgehog concept. In contrast, the social sector desire to "do good'" and the particular focus on donors can lead social sector leaders to make undisciplined decisions (Collins 2005, 33). The idea of the "economic denominator" (if you could pick only one ratio— profit per x—to systematically increase over time, what "x" would have the most significant impact on your economic engine?) cannot be applied to the social sectors. There are three reasons for this: the social sectors do not have rational capital markets that channel resources to those who deliver the best results, there is no one economic formula that applies across all social sector organizations, and the whole purpose of the social sectors is to meet social objectives that cannot be priced at a profit (Collins 2005).

Because of the institutional context they operate within, academic libraries may have limited power regarding which donations and grants they can choose to accept or decline. A university may also require its library to accept funds that do not fit with the library's hedgehog concept. These institutional constraints may require that academic library leaders build stronger and more strategic relationships with administrators and other university decision makers, so that they can carve out the autonomy needed to implement their hedgehog concept.

Collins describes the economic engine in the social sectors in terms of a two-by-two matrix, with one axis representing charitable donations and private grants, and the other axis representing business revenue (fees charged for services and products) (Collins 2005). The matrix contains four quadrants: 1) heavily government-funded, 2) charitable support by private individuals, 3) blend of support from both private individuals and business revenue, and 4) business revenue. Organizations that fall into the first quadrant rely more on political skill and maintaining public support than institutions in the other quadrants. Institutions that are supported mainly by private individuals require fund-raisers to develop personal relationships and have excellent general fund-raising skill. Organizations that are supported by charitable donations and business revenue need both business acumen and fund-raising

skills. Quadrant 4 organizations, those which rely mostly on business revenues, have a resource engine that more closely resembles that of a for-profit
business (Collins 2005).

To create a resource engine, academic libraries must determine which of
the four quadrants they fall into. In *Social Sectors*, Collins places Harvard
College in the third quadrant and UC Berkeley in the fourth quadrant. This
means that colleges with funding structures similar to Harvard need to employ both business acumen and fund-raising skills to renew their resource
engine, whereas institutions whose economic drivers more closely resemble
UC Berkeley's funding mechanisms (more funding through services and
tuition) may have a resource engine that resembles the economic engine of
the for-profit sectors. One issue not addressed by Collins is the impact of the
fact that a significant percentage of university tuition is now paid for by
government-backed loans. If government-backed educational loans and de-
fault rates become an issue of great public concern, then political skill and
maintaining public support may become more important for academic libraries and universities, since educational institutions would now fall into the
heavily government-funded quadrant.

A difference between the strategic objectives of a library and those of its
parent institution may arise if an academic library is in a different economic
quadrant than its university. This situation could make it more difficult for
the library to align its mission with the mission of the university, since—
when the library ties all of the circles of its hedgehog concept together—the
sources of library funding may cause the library to focus on serving its
financial supporters, whether or not those supporters are the primary groups
the university aims to serve. If this is the case, it may be helpful for libraries
to take a broader view of their institution's role as a financial supporter, since
university objectives include supporting the library's primary patron groups.

Brand

Brand "refers to how well your organization can cultivate a deep well of
emotional goodwill and mindshare of potential supporters" (Collins 2005,
18). Collins also refers to this concept as pushing a flywheel because there is
no "miracle moment" when creating a great organization:

> It feels like turning a giant heavy flywheel. Pushing with great effort—
> days . . . with almost [no] progress—you finally get the . . . wheel to inch
> forward. Then, at some point . . . [e]ach turn builds upon previous work,
> compounding your investment of effort. The flywheel flies forward with an
> almost unstoppable momentum (Collins 2005, 23).

A critical component of brand building is discipline, the requirement that an
organization consistently looks to its hedgehog concept when determining

which funds it accepts and how it uses accepted funds (Collins 2005). Collins describes the brand concept in terms of a chart that illustrates the flywheel cycle: the chart has five components which stress that organizations build results by focusing on their hedgehog concept, and that those results, in turn, attract resources and commitment used to build a strong organization that delivers better results, which attracts greater resources. That strong organization then delivers even better results (Collins 2005). Collins explains that, "the key driver in the flywheel is brand reputation, built upon tangible results and emotional share of heart—so that potential supporters believe not only in your mission but in your capacity to deliver on that mission" (Collins 2005, 25). Thus, to attract supporters, social sector organizations must demonstrate results. This is a difficult proposition because, as Collins admits, the social sectors have "fewer easy-to-measure metrics to assess success and stimulate progress" (Collins 2005, 33). This last point is particularly true for academic libraries.

In *Social Sectors*, Collins describes a "good-to-great" symphony that tracked, among other metrics, the number of standing ovations it received. What is the equivalent of a "standing ovation" for academic libraries? How can libraries operationalize their missions?

In *The Value of Academic Libraries: A Comprehensive Research Review and Report*, Megan Oakleaf (2010) provided suggestions for how libraries can demonstrate their value within the context of overarching institutions. She encouraged libraries to define and measure outcomes related to student enrollment, student retention and graduation rates, student success, student achievement, student learning, student engagement, faculty research productivity, faculty teaching, service, and overarching institutional quality. Two ways libraries can track library influences on increased student achievement are by investigating correlations between student library interactions and GPA, and conducting test item audits of major professional/educational tests to determine correlations between library services or resources and specific test questions (Oakleaf 2010). Measuring the success of library instructional programs may be easier than measuring the success of reference work in general. For example, student learning outcomes can be used to determine the effectiveness of library instruction, whereas the success of a reference encounter is more subjective. Users can receive incorrect or incomplete information and still report a reference transaction as successful. The converse is also true (Cook and Heath 2001). In order to fully implement the "brand" aspect of the resource engine circle, academic libraries need to use quantitative and qualitative measures to demonstrate to internal and external stakeholders that they are producing results consistent with their mission.

To demonstrate their institution's value to current and potential supporters, library leaders need access to metrics that track how well they are achieving library-wide and departmental objectives. In "Are They Learning?

Are We?," Meagan Oakleaf identified two steps involved in documenting the impact of library services and collections on student learning: "map[ping] all the intersections between campus needs, goals, and outcomes and library contributions in the form of resources and services" and "assess[ing] and document[ing] library impact" through the use of learning outcomes theory and assessment tools (Oakleaf 2011, 68, 70).

Discussion

To obtain organization-wide support for the hedgehog concept process, library leaders can emphasize the overall goals and specific outcomes they are working toward and clarify the process by which they are moving toward those goals. This approach is consistent with the evidence presented by Bass (1997) that successful leaders "demonstrate the ability to clarify the path to the goals." One way of creating and implementing a hedgehog concept would be to follow "the Council" approach described by Collins (2001), whereby an organization's leading executive creates a standing, informal committee to discuss key issues facing the organization. During periodic meetings, the committee uses the three circles of the hedgehog concept to guide discussions of issues, make decisions, and evaluate results. This chapter's appendix contains questions to help guide individual reflections and group discussion regarding how to apply the hedgehog concept framework to academic libraries.

Throughout the planning and implementation phases of the hedgehog concept, library managers are required to guide their organization through the process of defining objectives and corresponding measures used to anticipate and respond to users' information-seeking needs and behaviors. In the "passion" phase, this process requires engaging in library-wide discussions to better align a library's mission to their parent institution's goals. For libraries considering their unique contribution to their community, leaders need to gather information about their patrons' information-seeking needs and habits. Finally, to effectively manage their organization's human resources and garner support from stakeholders, library leaders need to make decisions based upon metrics that track their library's impact on campus objectives. Tools such as BSC analysis and student learning outcomes assessments can provide leaders with specific questions to consider when implementing their organization's hedgehog concept.

CONCLUSION

Academic library leaders face many challenges related to prioritizing and implementing their organizations' core objectives, including identifying goals, acquiring sufficient resources, effectively communicating their mission to stakeholders, and obtaining data that accurately tracks goal attainment. The hedgehog concept framework provides questions that libraries can use to structure internal discussions regarding the steps needed to implement their strategic objectives. When applying the framework to academic libraries, the importance of the distinctive institutional context in which academic libraries operate becomes clear. For example, when considering the "passion" circle, libraries need to contemplate how their mission aligns with and deviates from their university's mission. As libraries try to determine what they can be "best at" they must consider what products, services, or spaces they can provide to students, faculty, and staff better than any other campus or outside entity, and whether traditional library collections and services fit the "best at" description. In implementing the "resource engine" concept, librarians need to address institutional constraints regarding which funds they can accept and how they allocate donations. Lastly, to build support for their brand among stakeholders, libraries would need to define new metrics that accurately track how well they are accomplishing their missions. To effectively implement the hedgehog concept, then, leaders must facilitate library-wide discussions regarding library performance, user groups, and the library's impact upon their educational institution's objectives.

APPENDIX

The following questions comprise a framework designed to guide libraries' internal discussions regarding the implementation of a hedgehog concept. They draw upon this chapter's treatment of the hedgehog concept's overlapping circles, and the example answers include insights gained from a survey of academic librarians conducted by the author from 2012 to 2013.

Passion

"Understanding what your organization stands for (its core values) and why it exists (its mission or core purpose)" (Collins 2005, 19).

- What interests you most about your library's mission statement? For example, is your mission especially format-agnostic, outcome-based, and/or user-centered?
- If you were going to change the mission statement, what would you add or subtract?
- What interests your users most about your mission statement? What would they add or subtract? For example, one survey response described a simulation project in which students developed mobile applications for the library that they would use. Another response described the process of

creating personae for different types of primary users: typical freshmen, transfer students, adjunct faculty, clinical faculty, and tenure-track faculty.
- What metrics is your library using (or could it be using) to measure the various aspects of its mission statement? For example, some survey responses included using student learning outcomes to measure the effectiveness of library instruction; LibQual; internal progress reports; systematic observation of patrons using library services and spaces; compare individual staff members' goals to accomplishments by means of individual work plans or evaluations; and using queuing theory and reference service capacity data to analyze wait times.
- How well do the metrics identified above track attainment of the imperatives they are intended to measure?
- Which aspects of your library's mission statement are the most difficult to measure? For example, How does your library measure the success of reference transactions?

"Best At"

"Understanding what your organization can uniquely contribute to the people it touches, better than any other organization on the planet" (Collins 2005, 19).

- Is your library currently, or does it have the potential to be, the best at its strategic objectives/services for the communities it serves (especially its primary users)? For example, your library may be best at providing: access to rare books and manuscripts collections; unique instructional support services and collections for faculty; or guides to important resources within and outside of the library's collection.
- If your library has the potential to be the best, what prevents the realization of that potential?

Economic Engine

"Understanding what best drives your resource engine, broken into three parts: time, money, and brand" (Collins 2005, 19).

Time

"Refers to how well you attract people willing to contribute their efforts for free, or at rates below what their talents would yield in business" (Collins 2005, 18).

- What qualities are the most important to you when deciding who to hire? For example, intelligence, ability to innovate, a desire to learn and engage in continuing education, or a desire to contribute to their field.
- In a new hire's first year, what are the early assessment mechanisms? For example, a probationary period or peer review.

Money

"Refers to sustained cash flow" (Collins 2005, 18).

- According to the economic engine chart described in *Good to Great and the Social Sectors*, what economic quadrant is your library in?
- What quadrant is your college or university in? For example, tuition from government-backed student loans could be classified as Quadrant I (government), Quadrant IV (business revenue stream) funding, or both.

Brand

"Refers to how well your organization can cultivate a deep well of emotional goodwill and mindshare of potential supporters" (Collins 2005, 18).

In *Good to Great and the Social Sectors*, Collins describes a good-to-great symphony that tracked, among other output measures, the number of standing ovations it received. What is the equivalent of a "standing ovation" for your library? For example, faculty—because of a record of successful librarian-led instructional efforts—including information literacy courses as an essential component in a curriculum reform proposal without librarians' prior knowledge; university departments thinking of the library at the beginning of a project, rather than the end; or survey results showing that the generally high expectations of library users are met by library collections and services.

REFERENCES

Bass, Bernard. 1997. "Does the Transactional-Transformational Leadership Paradigm Transcend Organizational and National Boundaries?" *American Psychologist* 52 (2): 132. doi:10.1037/0003-066x.52.2.130.

Collins, Jim. 2001. *Good to Great: Why Some Companies Make the Leap . . . and Others Don't*. New York: HarperCollins.

———. 2005. *Good to Great and the Social Sectors: Why Business Thinking Is Not the Answer*. Boulder, CO: HarperCollins.

———. 2009. *How the Mighty Fall: And Why Some Companies Never Give In*. New York: HarperCollins.

Collins, Jim, and Hansen, Morten. 2011. *Great by Choice: Uncertainty, Chaos, and Luck—Why Some Companies Thrive Despite Them All*. New York: HarperCollins.

Cook, Colleen, and Heath, Fred M. 2001. "Users' Perceptions of Library Service Quality: A LibQUAL+ qualitative study." *Library Trends* 49 (4): 548–83. http://hdl.handle.net/2142/8361.

Cottrell, Janet. 2011. "What Are We Doing Here, Anyway?: Tying Academic Library Goals to Institutional Mission." *College and Research Library News*, October.

Foster, Nancy F., and Gibbons, Susan. 2007. *Studying Students: The Undergraduate Research Project at the University of Rochester*. Chicago: Association of College and Research Libraries.

Kaplan, Robert S., and Norton, David P. 1992. "The Balanced Scorecard: Measures That Drive Performance." *Harvard Business Review*, Jan.—Feb., 71–80.

Levitt, Steven. 2008. "From Good to Great . . . To Below Average." *Freakonomics*. July 28. http://www.freakonomics.com/2008/07/28/from-good-to-great-to-below-average/.

Murray, Alan. 2011. "Turbulent Times, Steady Success." *Wall Street Journal*, October 11.

Oakleaf, Megan. 2010. *Value of Academic Libraries: A Comprehensive Research Review and Report*. Chicago: Association of College and Research Libraries.

———. 2011. "Are They Learning? Are We?: Learning Outcomes and the Academic Library." *The Library Quarterly* 81(1): 61–82.

Rosenzweig, Phil. 2007. *The Halo Effect: . . . and the Eight Other Business Delusions That Deceive Managers*. New York: Free Press.

Schonfeld, Robert C., and Housewright, Ross. 2010. *Faculty Survey 2009: Key Strategic Insights for Libraries, Publishers, and Societies*. Ithaka S+R series.

Skapinker, Michael. 2001. "Leadership Shakes Off the Liability of Charisma—Good to Great by Jim Collins." *Financial Times*, October 10.

Sutton, Bob. 2008. "Good to Great: More Evidence That '"Most Claims of Magic are Testimony to Hubris.'" *Work Matters*, December 22. http://bobsutton.typepad.com/my_weblog/2008/12/good-to-great-more-evidence-that-most-claims-of-magic-are-testimony-to-hubris.html.

Taylor, Meredith, and Heath, Fred. 2012. "Assessment and Continuous Planning: The Key to Transformation at the University of Texas Libraries." *Journal of Library Administration* 52: 424–35.

UCLA Library. 2012. UCLA Library Strategic Plan 2012–17. University of California, Los Angeles. http://www.library.ucla.edu/pdf/UCLA-LibraryStrategicPlan2012-19.pdf.

University Leadership Council. 2011. *Redefining the Academic Library: Managing the Migration to Digital Information Services*. Washington, D.C.: The Advisory Board Company.

University of Pennsylvania. 2001. "Good to Great Falls Short of Its Title." *Knowledge at Wharton*. http://knowledge.wharton.upenn.edu/special_sections/121901_ss5.html.

USC Libraries. 2011. The Essential Library: The USC Libraries' Strategic Plan 2011–2013. Los Angeles: University of Southern California.

Williams, James. 2001. "Leadership Evaluation and Assessment." *Journal of Library Administration* 32: 153–76. doi:10.1300/J111v32n03_10.

Chapter Eight

Organizational Culture and Leadership

The Irresistible Force Versus the Immovable Object

Jason Martin

At some time all academic library leaders have wondered, "Why does my library work the way it does?" Academic libraries have similar missions and share important values like service, organization and access to information, and intellectual freedom; however, many libraries differ greatly in how they value the production and dissemination of scholarship by librarians; in the divides between librarians, library staff, public services, technical services, IT, and other departments; and in how well the librarians and staff interact with the university as a whole. Some academic libraries seem to always embrace the newest technology and adapt to change easily, while other libraries seem unable to leave the past and its ways behind. These differences are a product of organizational culture: the shared values, beliefs, and norms of the organization. The culture of a library influences every part of the library including its effectiveness, mission, and goals. Many leaders, both new and veteran, want to change their culture, but the relationship between organizational leadership and organizational culture is complicated, with leadership rarely winning out over culture. This chapter aims to define organizational culture, investigate the relationship between organizational culture and leadership, and explore opportunities for research in the areas of library culture and leadership.

ORGANIZATIONAL CULTURE

Definition

An organization employs people who work under a codified set of policies and procedures in order to achieve its stated mission, goals, and objectives (Freytag 1990, 181; Smirich 1983, 344). A well-functioning organization rationally arranges the tasks and clearly defines the work and responsibility of its employees (Schein 1970). While these criteria define the technical aspects of an organization, an organization can be, and usually is, much more than its policy manual and mission statement. Organizations are "socially constructed realities" whose rules, procedures, and structure provide a frame of reference for seeing and interpreting the world (Morgan 1997, 112, 132). As such, an organization is a miniature society with its own norms, standards, and expectations that influence employee behavior. In short, organizations have a culture all their own, an organizational culture. Academic libraries are no different in this regard.

Culture is a permanent buzzword in leadership literature; however, many executives and managers give a superficial definition to culture when they refer to a "culture of accountability" or a "culture of openness." This is not the same as the deep, rich concept of organizational culture, which is difficult to define. Culture dictates the behaviors and constructs the reality of organizational members who may find it formidable, if not impossible, to express verbally what they know and feel; they just understand how things are done. Organizational culture allows members of an organization to distinguish themselves from others and create a community and sense of belonging through shared values, heroes and heroines, rituals and ceremonies, and a cultural network (Deal and Kennedy 1983, 501–2; Jordan 2003). This chapter will use the following definition of organizational culture created by Edgar Schein, a leading expert on organizational culture:

> A pattern of shared basic assumptions that was learned by a group as it solved its problems of external adaptation and internal integration, that has worked well enough to be considered valid and, therefore, to be taught to new members as the correct way to perceive, think, and feel in relation to those problems (Schein 2004, 17).

Schein (2004) defines five levels of cultural assumptions that, when taken together, create the basic rules of human interaction and behavior in a culture. Analyzing these assumptions generates insight into how the organization's members view themselves, work together, and construct reality. The first level is "assumptions about external adaptation issues" and is concerned with how the organization relates to the environment in which it exists. Important to this level are mission, strategy, goals, and the overall interaction with the larger environment, especially the means by which organizations adapt to their changing external environment. The second level, "assumptions about internal integration," describes how those within the organization define their boundaries, distribute power, develop group cohesion, and allocate rewards. At this level, one is able to discern how the culture shapes the internal workings of the organization. Schein called the third level of cultural assumptions "assumptions about the nature of truth and reality," which for organizations means how decisions are made. The fourth level of culture, "assumptions about the nature of time and space," reveal how a culture views time, both current and historical, and how it allocates and uses space. The final level is "assumptions about human nature, activity, and relationships." On this level culture dictates what it means to be a member of the culture, in what activities members should engage, and how members interact with each other.

Value

Organizational culture fulfills four important needs within an organization. Culture gives members a way to identify and define themselves and to be a part of something larger than themselves, thereby making work more meaningful. Organizational culture creates a stalwart "social system" that ensures all members of an organization adhere to the accepted social norms. Finally, culture guides an organization's members in interpreting reality and understanding the world (Smircich 1983, 345–46). Culture creates sustainability and acts as the single most powerful force for cohesion, a "social glue" creating solidarity amongst its members (Cartwright and Baron 2002, 181). Organizational culture also influences the effectiveness of an organization by affecting the "attitudes" and overall satisfaction of an organization's employees (Gregory et al. 2009, 678–79).

Creation

Organizational culture is a product of the environment in which the organization is located (for academic libraries this is the college or university in which they are located), the history of the organization, and the daily interactions of the organization's members. Culture is influenced by the steadfastness of the organization, the shared events of the organization's history, how culture is imparted to newcomers, and the founder's assumptions. An organization with no long history, no shared important events, or frequent turnover will have a weak culture (Schein 1990, 111). Values, the building blocks of organizational culture, are derived from "organizational traditions." When an organization encounters a problem, its leaders or founders form an approach to solve the problem. Once that approach has been validated through repeated success, it becomes a shared value. After enough validation and success, the shared value becomes taken for granted and develops into an underlying assumption. This "assumption creation" process is a long one, and emphasizes the importance of tradition and history in the creation of culture. These underlying assumptions guide not only behavior, but how members perceive, interpret, and react to the environment around them. When confronted with an idea that does not conform to these underlying assumptions, the culture rejects the idea outright, and any challenge to an organization's assumptions produces defensive behavior from its members. An organization's underlying assumptions are difficult to diagnose, confront, or change because they are rarely articulated, yet they form the foundation of culture (Schein 2004, 30–36). When faced with the problem of how to educate its patrons on using the library, one library decided the best solution was to offer "one-shot," face-to-face library instruction. When the librarians and library staff determined this method worked well, they continued to offer library instruction. Over time, this assumption about the effectiveness of library instruction became so strong that when faced with research and empirical evidence showing different methods of instruction produced better results, the librarians simply rejected it outright. They preferred to continue with what they had always done rather than employ new methods of instruction.

Organizational culture is learned. It can be learned through formal training programs as well as through informal means such as employee stories, ceremonies, and myths, and the learning begins during the hiring process (Goffee and Jones 1998, 45; Schein 1990, 115). How well the culture is imparted to new librarians and library staff is critical for the strength and effectiveness of the culture. If those who are new to the organization learn the culture fully and embrace it willingly, then the culture becomes stronger. But if newcomers do not learn and embrace the culture of an organization, or do so only partially, then the culture will weaken over time.

No one right culture exists; culture is derived from the history of the organization and must fit the organization, its mission, and surrounding community. A culture is right for an organization when it helps the organization accomplish its mission and relate to the external environment, and a culture is wrong when it hinders an organization from doing these things. No matter what the culture, the stronger it is the more integrated its beliefs and values systems are in the organization (Smart and St. John 1996, 220). The concepts of sociability, friendliness in the organization, and solidarity, common tasks and shared goals, are prominent in every culture. High sociability is beneficial in that it creates a pleasurable work environment, helps creativity, and creates an environment where people are likely to go "above and beyond." The drawbacks of high sociability include toleration of poor performance due to friendship, too great an emphasis on consensus, and the creation of cliques and informal networks (Goffee and Jones 1998, 25–27). High solidarity helps to create unity in the organization, but too much solidarity makes for an oppressive work environment for anyone who may stand in the way of achieving common goals (Goffee and Jones 1998, 28–31).

Some researchers have tried to place cultures into specific types. Cameron and Quinn (2011), using their competing values framework, developed four specific culture types: clan (collaborate), adhocracy (create), market (compete), and hierarchy (control). Goffee and Jones (1998) likewise created four culture types called networked, mercenary, communal, and fragmented. Wilkins and Ouchi (1983) argued for three distinct cultures: market, bureaucracy, and clan. Much of the research on organizational culture in academic libraries makes use of these typologies of cultures (Brooks 2007; Kaarst-Brown et al. 2004; Shepstone and Currie 2008), and most have found those working in libraries tend to prefer clan and/or adhocracy cultures and high sociability. This typology of cultures appeals to a need to neatly place an idea in a compartment but is a superficial understanding of culture; organizational culture is much deeper and more complex than a "type." Few organizations have only one culture, and some organizations do not have any culture (Schein 1986, 31).

Expression

Deal and Kennedy (1982) detailed ways in which an organization's culture may be understood: learn the organization's sagas, study the physical setting, read what the company says about itself, observe how the organization greets and interacts with strangers, study how those within the organization spend their time, and understand how careers progress within the organization and how long members stay. Organizational culture may also be seen and understood through cultural expressions and the use of cultural artifacts like symbols, sagas, and rituals; however, it is crucial to not mistake the artifact for the culture. The artifact allows access to the underlying values and assumptions and should never be substituted for those assumptions; doing so would reveal only a superficial understanding of organizational culture (Schein 1986, 30–31). The key is to discern the meaning behind the forms in which culture is expressed (Katopol 2006, 10).

Symbols are objects, not necessarily physical, which hold a meaning for the members of the organization and are perhaps the most crucial aspect of a culture. Jordan (2003) defines a symbol as any object or event that represents or stands for another object or event. A symbol can be a physical object, but it can also be a logo, slogan, story, action, visual image, or metaphor. Jordan (2003) argues culture is composed of symbols and learning their meaning is the key to understanding culture. Symbols reveal the hidden and underlying assumptions of an organization's culture and can unite its members and incite them to action (Deal 1995, 120). A book holds a functional purpose, but to an academic librarian a book is symbolic of knowledge. Librarians place a great deal of importance on books because of their deeply ingrained values to protect and preserve knowledge. This may explain why an academic librarian would resist a shift to the use of e-books. In changing the format of the book, the symbol has been destroyed.

Rites and rituals are an integral part of an organization's culture and have the most impact on workplace behavior (Deal and Kennedy 1982, 60). A ritual generally contributes to the operating procedure of an organization, but it also has a symbolic role that embodies the values of the organization. Rites and rituals are important because they reinforce the values of an organization through the active participation of the organization's members. Rituals are pre-planned social and public events of varying formality and have both manifest and latent purposes. The manifest purpose of the ritual generally contributes to the workings of the organization and helps the organization achieve its mission and accomplish its daily tasks. The latent purpose is where the celebration of the sacred occurs. Rituals create order and community and can be used to both instill new values into the culture and change the organization's culture. A library faculty meeting is a public, pre-planned event guided by set rules and procedures. Its manifest purpose is for librarians to discuss faculty governance, but its latent purpose could involve rites of integration (a bringing together), enhancement (elevation in standing of a member), and renewal (learning).

Stories, myths, and sagas are one of the earliest and most enduring aspects of human culture. Sagas are central in studying and understanding organizational culture. Discovering an organization's culture is longitudinal in nature as the researcher looks to find past events that still influence an organization's present actions (Samuels 1982, 150). Sagas are stories that blend the history and heritage of an organization in order to explain its current practices. Sagas often arise from an organization in chaos. As the hero leads the organization to success (or failure, depending on the nature of the saga and the organization), the story explains how an assumption came to be widely held among an organization. A saga can be viewed as the answer to why an organization does what it does or values what it values (Clark 1971). While sagas have great benefit for an organization, they can also be negative if an organization's past is filled with so many great heroes that it is difficult to get members to stop clinging to the past (Samuels 1982, 145). The stories told within the walls of the library, stories of the "good old days" or of terrible bosses, are sagas. One library in particular likes to tell of the time it underwent a renovation, and its staff spent a very cold winter missing one external wall. This story tells of struggle and hard work to overcome adversity.

In summary, organizational culture is a deep, all-encompassing force in an organization. Culture is created over the long history of an organization and takes for its foundation the values and assumptions of that organization. It directs the behavior and worldview of all those in the organization, gives a sense of meaning and belonging to an organization's members, and is expressed through cultural artifacts like symbols, sagas, and rituals. How effective an organization is at meeting its mission is ultimately a result of its culture. Understanding an organization's culture is the key to understanding what the organization values and what motivates those in the organization. This cultural understanding can lead to better relationships between employees and management and the organization and external environment.

LEADERSHIP

Culture and Leadership

One of the first things many new leaders proclaim is their desire to change an organization's culture. This is naïve at best. In one study, a regional manager attempted to change the shared values but only succeeded in changing how the existing values were expressed (Siehl 1985). Granted, if a new leader walks into an organizational culture that is dysfunctional and toxic, where those in the culture want a new culture and direction, change will be much easier, but this is not always the case. Changing the value system requires the participation and willingness of all the members of the culture (Frost et al. 1985, 139). The relationship between an organization's leadership and its culture is complex and can be a source of great frustration for leadership. Culture is the main influence on the goals an organization selects and the strategies it uses to meet those goals (Schein 1986, 31). Culture not only affects how well the organization runs but defines what the organization does. Leaders often feel restrained by their organization's "structures and processes" (Maloney et al. 2010, 330). They cannot achieve all they would like because organizational culture dictates what types of managerial theories and practices are implemented and used in the organization (Pors 2008).

Pfeffer deftly argues organizational culture is a "social system" that "constrains behavior" of not only the frontline employees but the organization's leaders as well. Culture sets limitations on what the leader can do and influence in the organization. Organizational culture also decides who will be selected as a leader. People are attracted to other people and organizations that share the same values, so candidates for leadership positions will select the organizations to which they will apply based on similarities in values. A librarian from a small college that values one-on-one student engagement may not feel she would be a good fit as an administrator at a large university library that values research, so she decides not to apply. In addition, organizations develop their own leadership paradigm, and only those candidates who match the socially constructed criteria will be hired for the position

(Pfeffer 1977, 106). Even if an organization wants to go outside its culture and ignore its own preference for a leader, the new leader will be thwarted by the values already present in the culture. A large research library decides it wants to be more student-focused, so they hire a librarian from a small school as a new administrator. But once she starts to advocate for weeding the collection to create more student space, she is likely to face a great deal of resistance since weeding is anathema to a research library. This means organizational culture dictates who will be considered and selected as a leader, constrains the leader's behavior once she is chosen, and limits what areas of organizational effectiveness the leader can influence. More often than not, the culture changes the new leader, rather than the new leader changing the organization's culture (Pfeffer 1977).

In the worst cases, a leader can be undermined, thwarted, or even fired because of an organization's culture. Carly Fiorina became the chief executive officer (CEO) of Hewlett-Packard in 1999. Immediately she began a restructuring of the company and a controversial acquisition of Compaq, an action that never really bolstered HP's bottom line. But more damning to Ms. Fiorina's tenure was her inability to become part of the "HP Way." Hewlett-Packard, like most tech companies, is informal and collegial with an open, two-way flow of communication. Ms. Fiorina was seen by many in HP as being aloof and unapproachable, thereby bucking the company's culture (Said 2005; de Vries 2009). She resigned as CEO in 2005 and presents a cautionary tale for all new leaders and the respect they must have for organizational culture.

Managing Culture

Leaders do have some effect on culture, however. Founders play a substantial role in the creation of the organization's culture by setting the initial values that ultimately become cultural assumptions (Schein 1990, 112). Founders also prescribe how the organization will relate to the external environment, develop internal integration, and meet its stated mission, goals, and objectives (Schein 1984, 13 and 17). This is true even in academic libraries and higher education, where many of the founders lived and worked generations ago. Even though they are far removed from the present, their presence is still felt on campus. Strong cultures with consistent leadership can survive high turnover because the assumptions are stable at the top (Schein 1984, 7). In a young company, if the employees are unhappy with the shared values and dissatisfied with the company, then a culture change could be successful since members would be responsive to change in their current state (Frost et al. 1985, 128). But as an organization matures, a leader has less and less influence on the values, norms, and beliefs shared by the culture's members, thereby making culture change more difficult (Schein 1990, 115). Therefore leaders should spend time and energy managing their organization's culture.

Perhaps the best way for a leader to manage culture is through the management and creation of meaning in the culture. When a leader wants to create meaning, she must emphasize core values by rewarding and championing members who demonstrate and hiring employee candidates who already share these values. This celebration of role models provides "courage" to those within the organization and is vital to the culture (Dill 1982, 314–15; Frost et al. 1985, 129). If a library dean would like librarians to focus more on creation and dissemination of scholarship, then she could weight scholarship more heavily in annual reviews and the promotion process and hire librarians with a proven track record of publications.

In managing the culture and creating meaning, leaders must work to preserve the unique identity of the organization while also giving meaning to the work performed. Leaders can manage meaning in a culture by reinforcing, emphasizing, or deemphasizing existing rituals and symbols. The risk involved with managing meaning is that the reception and perception of the symbol may be far different than the intention of the leader. Symbols can often be abstract, which causes difficulty in relating meaning to the members (Dill 1982). As Dandridge (1985, 151) so eloquently writes, "belief manages, not the manager."

Transformational Leadership

The previous section described what James MacGregor Burns refers to as "transactional leadership" in his seminal 1978 work *Leadership*. Transactional leadership consists of a series of exchanges, what Burns calls "exchanging gratifications," between leader and follower. Management strikes a bargain with the organization's employees to perform in a certain way for a certain reward. This system helps the organization achieve its goals and its members achieve their goals. Change in transactional leadership is merely substituting one thing for another, and the bartering done between leader and follower over behavior and reward is usually superficial (Burns 1978, 169).

The opposite of transactional leadership is transformational leadership. Transformational leaders seek to unite their followers in achievement of "higher goals," to connect means and ends through the values of the organization, and to look beyond the interests of the individual to the "collective interests" of the group (Burns 1978, 425; Bass 1990, 21; Garcia-Morales et al. 2012, 1040). For academic libraries, librarians and staff may realize they are not simply a piece within the library but are contributing to the education of the students and working to make them information literate and lifelong learners. Leadership is not neutral; it consists of values (Burns 2003). Transforming leaders emphasize the values of their organization (Garcia-Morales et al. 2012, 1040). The stronger these values, the stronger the relationship is between leader and follower; the stronger the leader/follower relationship, the more the leader and follower can accomplish together (Burns 2003, 211). At its core, transformational leadership is about building relationships among people and creating real, significant change.

A transformational leader demonstrates the "Four I's": idealized influence, inspirational motivation, intellectual stimulation, and individualized consideration (Bass and Avolio 1994, 3–4). As an influencer, the transformational leader acts as a role model. The leader communicates well, develops a high level of agreement on organizational goals and buy-in on mission and vision, and encourages members to be part of something larger than themselves (Bersona and Avolio 2004; Bass and Avolio, 1994). As a motivator, the transformational leader challenges those in the organization to achieve at "higher levels" and inspires and challenges them (Bass and Avolio 1994; Bass 1990). As a stimulator, the transformational leader generates creativity and intellectual stimulation. One study found those in an organization who have a "collectivist" mind-set create more ideas under a transformational leader (Jung and Avolio 1999). By mentoring, building strong relationships with those in the organization (both their employees and their supervisors), and meeting the emotional needs of followers, the transformational leader provides individualized consideration.

Transformational leadership is not without its critics. The concept of transformational leadership covers a broad area of leaderships and encompasses a wide range of skills for the leader to possess (Northouse 2007). Transformational leadership seems to be mainly focused on personality traits of leaders, making it a difficult leadership concept to teach (Bryman 1992). More serious criticisms of transformational leadership call it "elitist" and "antidemocratic" (Avolio 1999; Bass and Avolio 1993) with the potential to create a cult of personality around the leader who works to change the values and vision of followers without any checks on whether these changes are for the good (Yukl 1999; Northouse 2007).

Most research and writing on transformational leadership, however, is positive. One study showed the combination of transformational leadership and a commitment to organizational learning increases the overall effectiveness of an organization (Garcia-Morales et al. 2012, 1045). Another study by Gumusluoglu and Ilsev (2009) found transformational leadership positively influences creativity and intrinsic motivation, psychologically empowers employees, and enhances organizational innovation. Those within the organization tend to work harder for transformational leaders, and the leaders themselves make a greater "contribution" to the organization (Bass 1990, 2). What could transformational leadership mean for organizational culture change? Could a transformational leader do more than merely manage culture?

Changing Organizational Culture

A leader cannot simply command the organization to think, act, and see the world differently. Even external threats and new members, including leaders, are not enough for members to relinquish their culture (Schein 2009, 266; Schein 1990, 116). Being part of a culture with its shared assumptions, values, norms, and behavior reduces anxiety by creating a frame through which to see and understand the world (Schein 1990, 11). Changing culture and the shared assumptions inherent in culture creates anxiety, stress, and worry since now members must learn a new way to interpret the world (Schein 1986, 32). People do not willingly and readily move toward more stress and anxiety; people like stability, and culture gives it to them. Change is threatening to a culture and to its members. People become attached to the expressions of their culture and can become "confused, insecure, and often angry" when they are changed (Deal and Kennedy 1983, 157).

A real leader, however, knows cultural change is inevitable. They understand in order to maintain success in the wake of external change internal change is necessary (Maloney et al. 2010, 323). Real cultural change, changing the way people behave and express their culture, is long and difficult. What makes it even more difficult in culture itself is the "barrier to change" (Deal and Kennedy 1983, 158–59). Deal and Kennedy (1983) describe five scenarios that necessitate cultural change: external environment is undergoing deep change; a quickly changing professional environment; poor performance by the organization; a good organization on the brink of being a great organization; and rapid growth by the organization (159–60).

When faced with one or more of these scenarios, how does an organization go about making the change needed to survive? First the leaders need to look at the basic ways in which culture is created and transmitted, such as mission statements, modeling of behavior, and "what leaders pay attention to" (Schein 1984, 22). Rewards demonstrate in a very tangible way what the leader and the organization value. The leader also needs to take action to move the change forward. Schein outlines steps a leader can take to manage cultural change, including creating a new direction and new artifacts to express the organization's newfound values and assumptions. Leaders need also to build consensus, encourage two-way communication, train and build a skill base among employees, allow time for the change to become permanent, be flexible, and invest heavily in the change (Deal and Kennedy 1983, 162, 164–66). Most importantly, whatever reason prompted the cultural change must be "credible" (Deal and Kennedy 1983, 162).

Transformational leadership could be the key to organizational culture change. The qualities of the transformational leader align well with what organizational culture is and does. The transformational leader may be seen as the cultural leader, and therefore particularly adept at changing culture.

Transformational leaders are interested in the organization as a whole and how to build unity among its employees and create a higher purpose and meaning in their work. This is done in part by creating a shared mission and vision, which is also one of the first steps in changing culture. The transformational leader uses values to build relationships and help the organization grow. Values are, of course, the building blocks of culture. By modeling desired behavior and then rewarding that behavior in employees, a transformational leader really begins to make serious change in an organization. The combination of strong values, role modeling, and relationships allows the transformational leader to build credibility in the organization, which is another important aspect of cultural change. Using the "Four I's," the transformational leader motivates and stimulates employees. Transformational leadership enhances creativity and innovation and empowers members of an organization. All of these are crucial to help an organization survive and thrive during cultural change. At its heart, transformational leadership is about meaningful and sustainable change.

ORGANIZATIONAL CULTURE, LEADERSHIP, AND ACADEMIC LIBRARIES

Previous Research

Little research has been performed on the organizational culture of academic libraries. The findings of two case studies, one by Ostrow in the "Minerva Library" (1998) and one by Lee in the "New Millennium Library" (2000), appear to have a great deal in common. The similarities led Lee to conclude that insiders may be able to distinguish between different library cultures, but outsiders may not (Lee 2000, 123). Both libraries were slow to change and were reluctant to offer new services such as library instruction and increased technology throughout the library. This attitude contributed to the overall passivity present in the libraries. The librarians working at the Minerva Library and New Millennium Library felt inferior to the teaching faculty and that their work was overall underappreciated. They tended to view themselves through negative stereotypes and position themselves in opposition to the rest of the university. A subcultural divide existed in both libraries between the librarians working in technical services and those working in public services. Further divides were present among new and old librarians, professional librarians and paraprofessional staff, and librarians at main campus and those in regional locations.

Another study by Martin at the "Metropolitan Academic Library" (2011) found different results. The culture of the library was "in the process of becoming" and was therefore neither rich nor deep, but the shared values of service, including the desire to offer more services, and campus engagement were present in the librarians and library staff. The members of the library viewed themselves positively and did not feel inferior to the teaching faculty. Recent administrative hires made change the focal point of the library's story. The dean was working on an aggressive change schedule in order to make the library more modern in its services, organization, and technology. No divides between departments, staff, and librarians were found.

Cultural Change in Libraries

Of the five scenarios for cultural change previously discussed (Deal and Kennedy 1983), three of them, poor performance, rapid growth, and the move forward to greatness, apply to the specific situations of an organization. But the other two, deep change in the external environment and a quickly changing professional environment, apply to all academic libraries. Higher education, the external environment of the academic libraries, has undergone great change in the past few decades and will continue to change into the foreseeable future. Decreased funding, increased enrollment, and a focus on return on investment have all made *accountability* the buzzword on campuses across the country. Small, private liberal arts colleges and large state research universities alike have developed metrics to evaluate programs, departments, and colleges on a number of criteria including retention of students, student credit hours generated, return on investment, fiscal responsibility, and overall contribution to the university. Libraries are included in these studies and must find ways to demonstrate their value to the university. Gone are the days when an academic library could prove its worth by simply declaring itself the heart of the university. Now academic libraries must demonstrate what roles they play in the education, retention, and engagement of students, and what value they add to classes, campus activities, and the overall running of the institution. While service is still an extremely important value for libraries, new values of campus engagement, leadership, innovation, and scholarship must take hold and grow in the library's culture. Librarians must learn new skills in order to contribute to the development of online classes; to serve the increasing number of distance, international, and nontraditional students; and to creatively find ways to take part in campus life.

The profession of librarianship is also changing. The explosion of digital publishing has permanently altered how students, faculty, and staff access information, how libraries develop collections, and how librarians teach research and library skills. This new generation of college students has very different wants, needs, and expectations of the library than the previous generation of students, and libraries are struggling to find ways to serve, reach, and teach these new students. All of this is compounded by stagnant or shrinking budgets and the "do more with less" ethos so prevalent on college and university campuses today. In order to successfully navigate these changes and stay afloat in today's world of higher education, academic libraries need to undergo significant cultural change.

Of the three studies above, one library (New Millennium) did not undergo any cultural change; one library (Metropolitan Academic) was undergoing a great amount of organizational change, which, if successful, could lead to cultural change; and one library (Minerva) underwent a successful change in culture. The Minerva Library succeeded in their change by buying out the contracts or offering incentives for early retirement to those librarians and library staff who did not embrace the new cultural values, replacing them with librarians and staff who did. And while some may argue this is the best way to implement a successful change in culture, a special set of circumstances must be in place for academic libraries to engage in this practice. A better method for cultural change is through the process of transformational leadership. Granted, this is not easy and takes special leaders who, sadly, may be lacking in librarianship, but it is nonetheless a worthy and reachable goal.

Suggestions for Research

Before any of the changes discussed in this chapter can happen, academic libraries need to know themselves and higher education better. Below are suggestions for research that would help the library profession to better understand organizational culture and leadership in academic libraries:

- Studies of a wide array of academic libraries' organizational cultures. Libraries must understand how they work, what they value, and what motivates them to act and behave as they do. Organizational culture studies are the only way to accomplish this understanding. Along the way researchers may also be able to develop an understanding of the professional culture of librarianship. Examples of these studies exist for academic libraries (Lee 2000; Martin 2011; Ostrow 1998), higher education (Clark 1970; de Zilwa 2007), and other industries (Heracleaus 2001; Hofstede, Bond, and Luk 1993).
- Case studies of organizational culture change. While every organization and culture is different, case studies of cultural change can help shed light on what potentially works and what does not. Learning from the success and failures of other libraries is important.
- Critical evaluation of the state of librarianship. Too often criticisms of librarianship are met with defensiveness from librarians. In order to successfully change and navigate the uncertain waters of the future, librarianship needs to become more self-aware of the profession's strengths and weaknesses and take steps to build on the former and correct the latter.

- Analysis of leadership types currently holding leadership positions in academic libraries. If transformational leadership is the key to successful cultural change, then it is imperative to study and understand the types of leaders in librarianship and whether any of them are transformational leaders.
- Study of leadership development, especially the development of transformational leadership. Again, if transformational leadership is the key to successful cultural change, then the profession must find ways to develop this type of leadership.
- Analysis of the viability of bringing in transformational leadership from outside the library field. Bringing in a nonlibrarian to lead an academic library is a bold step that flies in the face of both the library's and librarianship's culture; however, this type of brash action might be needed in order to successfully navigate cultural change.

CONCLUSION

Why does a library work the way it does? Organizational culture. Culture is the force responsible for an academic library's effectiveness and norms and is built on the values and history of the library. Seemingly every library leader wants to change at least some part of the library's culture, but very few succeed. This is because organizational culture exerts a greater influence on the leader than the leader exerts on the culture. Transformational leadership may be the key to successful cultural change. Transformational leaders emphasize values and are more attuned with culture; they seek real, meaningful change. In order for academic libraries to thrive in the future, they must meet the new demands of higher education. This means they must make cultural changes. More research is needed in the areas of academic library culture, cultural change, and leadership.

REFERENCES

Avolio, Bruce. 1999. *Full Leadership Development: Building the Vital Forces in Organizations*. Thousand Oaks, CA: Sage.

Bass, Bernard. 1990. "From Transactional to Transformational Leadership: Learning to Share the Vision." *Organizational Dynamics* 18: 19–32. doi:10.1108/01437730410538671.

Bass, Bernard, and Bruce Avolio. 1993. "Transformational Leadership: A Response to Critiques." In *Leadership Theory and Research: Perspectives and Directions*. Edited by Martin Chemers and Roya Ayman, 49–80. San Diego: Academic Press.

———. 1994. "Introduction." In *Improving Organizational Effectiveness through Transactional Leadership*. Edited by Bernard Bass and Bruce Avolio, 1–9. Thousand Oaks, CA: Sage.

Bersona, Yair, and Bruce Avolio. 2004. "Transformational Leadership and the Dissemination of Organizational Goals: A Case Study of a Telecommunication Firm." *The Leadership Quarterly* 15: 625–46. doi: 10.1016/j.leaqua.2004.07.003.

Brooks, Monica. 2007. "Organizational Leadership in Academic Libraries: Identifying Culture Types and Leadership Roles." EdD diss., Marshall University. http://mds.marshall.edu/cgi/viewcontent.cgi?article=1013&context=etd.

Bryman, Alan. 1992. *Charisma and Leadership in Organizations*. London: Sage.

Burns, James MacGregor. 1978. *Leadership*. New York: Harper & Row.

———. 2003. *Transforming Leadership*. New York: Atlantic Monthly Press.

Cameron, Kim, and Robert Quinn. 2011. *Diagnosing and Changing Organizational Culture*. San Francisco: Jossey-Bass.

Cartwright, Susan, and Helen Baron. 2002. "Culture and Organizational Effectiveness." In *Organizational Effectiveness: The Role of Psychology*. Edited by Ivan Robertson, Militza Callinan, and Dave Bartram, 181–200. Chichester, NY: Wiley. doi: 10.1002/9780470696736.ch8.

Clark, Burton. 1970. *The Distinctive College: Antioch, Reed, and Swarthmore*. Chicago: Aldine Publishing Company.

———. 1971. "Belief and Loyalty in College Organization." *The Journal of Higher Education* 42: 499–515.

Dandridge, Thomas. 1985. "The Life Stages of a Symbol: When Symbols Work and When They Can't." In *Organizational Culture*. Edited by Peter Frost, Larry Moore, Meryl Reis Louis, Craig Lundberg, and Joanne Martin, 141–53. Beverly Hills, CA: Sage.

Deal, Terrence. 1995. "Symbols and Symbolic Activity." In *Images of Schools: Structures and Roles in Organizational Behavior*. Edited by Samuel Bacharach and Bryan Mundell, 108–36. Thousand Oaks, CA: Corwin Press.

Deal, Terrence, and Allan Kennedy. 1982. *Corporate Cultures: The Rites and Rituals of Corporate Life*. Reading, MA: Addison-Wesley.

———. 1983. "Culture: A New Look through Old Lenses." *Journal of Applied Behavioral Science* 19: 498–505. doi: 10.1177/002188638301900411.

de Zilwa, Deanna. 2007. "Organisational Culture and Values and the Adaptation of Academic Units in Australian Universities." *Higher Education: The International Journal of Higher Education and Educational Planning* 54: 557–74. doi: 10.1007/s10734-006-9008-6.

Dill, David. 1982. "The Management of Academic Culture: Notes on Management of Meaning and Social Integration." *Higher Education* 11: 303–20. doi: 10.1007/BF00155621.

Freytag, Walter. 1990. "Organizational Culture." In *Psychology in Organizations: Integrating Science and Practice*. Edited by Kevin Murphy and Frank Saal, 179–96. Hillsdale, NJ: Lawrence Erlbaum Associates.

Frost, Peter, Larry Moore, Meryl Reis Louis, Craig Lundberg, and Joanne Martin, eds. 1985. *Organizational Culture*. Beverly Hills, CA: Sage.

Garcia-Morales, Victor Jesus, Maria Magdalena Jimenez-Barrionuevo, and Leopoldo Gutierrez-Gutierrez. 2012. "Transformational Leadership Influence on Organizational Performance through Organizational Learning and Innovation." *Journal of Business Research* 65: 1040–50. doi:10.1016/j.jbusres.2011.03.005.

Goffee, Robert, and Gareth Jones. 1998. *The Character of a Corporation: How Your Company's Culture Can Make or Break Your Business*. New York: Harper Business.

Gregory, Brian, Stanley Harris, Achilles Armenakis, and Christopher Shook. 2009. "Organizational Culture and Effectiveness. A Study of Values, Attitudes, and Organizational Outcomes." *Journal of Business Research* 62: 673–79. doi:10.1016/j.jbusres.2008.05.021.

Gumusluoglu, Lale, and Arzu Ilsev. 2009. "Transformational Leadership, Creativity, and Organizational Innovation." *Journal of Business Research* 62: 461–73. doi:10.1016/j.jbusres.2007.07.032.

Heracleaus, Loizos. 2001. "An Ethnographic Study of Culture in the Context of Organizational Change." *The Journal of Applied Behavioral Science* 37: 426–46. doi:10.1177/0021886301374003.

Hofstede, Geert, Michael Bond, and Cheung-leung Luk. 1993. "Individual Perceptions of Organizational Cultures: A Methodological Treatise on Levels of Analysis." *Organization Studies* 14: 483–503. doi: 10.1177/017084069301400402.

Jordan, Ann. 2003. *Business Anthropology*. Prospect Heights, IL: Waveland.

Jung, Dong, and Bruce Avolio. 1999. "Effects of Leadership Style and Followers' Cultural Orientation on Performance in Group and Individual Task Conditions." *Academy of Management Journal* 42: 208–18. doi: 10.2307/257093.

Kaarst-Brown, Michelle, Scott Nicholson, Gisela Von Dran, and Jeffery Stanton. 2004. "Organizational Culture of Libraries as a Strategic Resource." *Library Trends* 53: 33–53. https://www.ideals.illinois.edu/bitstream/handle/2142/1722/Kaarst-Brown3353.pdf?sequence=2.

Katopol, Patricia. 2006. "We Don't Do That Here: Using Cognitive Work Analysis to Learn about Organizational Culture." *Bulletin of the American Society for Information Science and Technology* 33: 9–11. doi: 10.1002/bult.2006.1720330104.

Krefting, Linda, and Peter Frost. 1985. "Untangling Webs, Surfing Waves, and Wildcatting: A Multiple-Metaphor Perspective on Managing Organizational Culture." In *Organizational Culture*. Edited by Peter Frost, Larry Moore, Meryl Reis Louis, Craig Lundberg, and Joanne Martin, 155–67. Beverly Hills, CA: Sage.

Lee, Soyeon. 2000. *Organizational Culture of an Academic Library*. PhD diss., University of Texas. Austin: ProQuest/UMI (publication no. AAT 9983275).

Maloney, Krisellen, Kristin Antelman, Kenning Arlitsch, and John Butler. 2010. "Future Leaders' Views on Organizational Culture." *College and Research Libraries* 71: 322–45. http://eprints.rclis.org/14822/1/FutureLeaders.pdf.

Martin, Michael. 2011. *In the Process of Becoming: The Organizational Culture of the Metropolitan Academic Library*. PhD diss., University of Central Florida. Orlando: Available at etd.fcla.edu/CF/CFE0003585/Martin_Michael_J_201105_EdD.pdf.

Morgan, Gareth. 1997. *Images of Organization*. Thousand Oaks, CA: Sage.

Northouse, Peter. 2007. *Leadership: Theory and Practice*. Thousand Oaks, CA: Sage.

Ostrow, Rona. 1998. *Library Culture in the Electronic Age: A Case Study of Organizational Change*. PhD dissertation, Rutgers The State University of New Jersey. New Brunswick: ProQuestUMI (publication no. AAT 9900685).

Pfeffer, Jeffrey. 1977. "The Ambiguity of Leadership." *Academy of Management Review* 2: 104–12. doi:10.5465/AMR.1977.4409175.

Pors, Niels. 2008. "Management Tools, Organizational Culture, and Leadership: An Explorative Study." *Performance Measurement and Metrics* 9: 138–52. doi: 10.1108/14678040810906844.

Said, Carolyn. 2005. "Where Do They Go from Here?." *San Francisco Chronicle*, February 10.

Samuels, Alan. 1982. "Planning and Organizational Culture." *Journal of Library Administration* 2: 145–48. doi:10.1300/J111V02N02_11.

Schein, Edgar. 1970. *Organizational Psychology*. Englewood Cliffs, NJ: Prentice-Hall.

———. 1984. "Coming to a New Awareness of Organizational Culture." *Sloan Management Review* 25: 3–16.

———. 1986. "What You Need to Know about Organizational Culture." *Training and Development Journal* 40: 30–33. http://cmapspublic.ihmc.us/rid=1GSGS9M3P-8BFNGM-Q8Z/what%20you%20need%20to%20know%20about%20org%20culture%20schein.pdf.

———. 1990. "Organizational Culture." *American Psychologist* 45: 109–19.

———. 2004. *Organizational Culture and Leadership*. San Francisco: Jossey-Bass.

———. 2009. "The Leader as Subculture Manager." In *Organization of the Future 2: Visions, Strategies, and Insights on Managing in a New Era*. Edited by Frances Hesselbein and Marshall Goldsmith, 258–67. San Francisco: Jossey-Bass.

Shepstone, Carol, and Lyn Currie. 2008. "Transforming the Academic Library: Creating an Organizational Culture that Fosters Staff Success." *Journal of Academic Librarianship* 34: 358–68.

Siehl, Caren. 1985. "After the Founder: An Opportunity to Manage Culture." In *Organizational Culture*. Edited by Peter Frost, Larry Moore, Meryl Reis Louis, Craig Lundberg, and Joanne Martin, 125–40. Beverly Hills, CA: Sage.

Smart, John, and Edward St. John. 1996. "Organizational Culture and Effectiveness in Higher Education: A Test of the 'Culture Type' and 'Strong Culture' Hypotheses." *Educational Evaluation and Policy Analysis* 18: 219–41. http://www.jstor.org/stable/1164261.

Smircich, Linda. 1983. "Concepts of Culture and Organizational Analysis." *Administrative Science Quarterly* 28: 339–58. http://www.jstor.org/stable/2392246.

de Vries, Lloyd. 2009. "The Rise and Fall of Carly Fiorina." *CBSNews.com*, February 11. Accessed February 27, 2013. http://www.cbsnews.com/2100-500163_162-672809.html.

Wilkins, Alan, and William Ouchi. 1983. "Efficient Cultures: Exploring the Relationship between Culture and Organizational Performance." *Administrative Science Quarterly* 28: 468–81. http://www.jstor.org/stable/2392253.

Yukl, Gary. 1999. "An Evaluation of Conceptual Weaknesses in Transformational and Charismatic Leadership Theories." *Leadership Quarterly* 10: 285–305.http://dx.doi.org/10.1016/S1048-9843(99)00013-2.

Part Four

Case Studies of Successful Leadership

Chapter Nine

The Entrepreneurial Leadership Turn in Higher Education

Agency and Institutional Logic in an Academic Library

Kristen E. Willmott and Andrew F. Wall

Entrepreneurship in higher education has become a topic of contrasting scholarly positions between promise and peril. Advocates claim entrepreneurial leadership is a pragmatic response to fiscal constraint in higher education, as a means whereby student learning and institutional missions can be maintained or enhanced to serve society's economic development needs (Clark 2001; Etzkowitz and Leydesdorff 1997; Zemsky, Wegner, and Massy 2005). Conversely, critics argue entrepreneurial leadership practices promote market-centered values that erode the core academic ideals associated with learning, free knowledge distribution, and the public good (Apple 2008; Giroux 2005a). The arguments of advocates and detractors both have merit that ultimately represents the reflexive nature of the structures that frame change within higher education institutions. In advancing the tension, the authors eschew a resolution, seeking to embrace the tension between the positions to illuminate how both have legitimacy and peril. This chapter outlines two contrasting views of entrepreneurship leadership in higher education, framing their analysis in sociological and institutional theory. A case study of an entrepreneurial academic leader provides a basis for illuminating how entrepreneurship can lead to organizational leadership success and supports the critique that entrepreneurship advances a dominant market legitimizing logic in higher education. For the purposes of this case, *legitimizing logic* refers to the process whereby an ideology, in this case entrepreneurial action and market-related shifts, becomes legitimate (and accepted) by its attachment to the norms and values of an organization.

TWO CONTRASTING POSITIONS

The authors frame two contrasting positions: one position forwarded by advocates of entrepreneurship in higher education and social entrepreneurship; the other offered by critics of entrepreneurship and related market-like behavior. Advocates of entrepreneurship in higher education have developed their position at both the individual and institutional level (Mars and Metcalfe 2009). At the individual level, emerging scholarship points toward the potential to use entrepreneurial attitudes, beliefs, and behaviors to instigate organizational change in higher education. Advocates believe entrepreneurship is vital in addressing fiscal tensions, quality concerns (and therefore accountability), and changing social expectations placed upon higher education in an information economy.

Scholarship focusing on entrepreneurship by individuals points toward the promise of what Max Weber (2003) has called "the entrepreneurial man" by focusing on how individual leaders or managers can act to foster organizational advancement toward the capital development. The entrepreneur as an individual has been grounded in Schumpeter's 1947 article, which defines entrepreneurship as "the doing of new things or the doing of things that are already being done in a new way (innovation)" (151). Schumpeter's and Weber's focus on entrepreneurial action toward economic growth represents a view that entrepreneurship advances society through the development of wealth, a view shared by contemporary proponents of entrepreneurship, particularly in business applications (Schramm 2006).

In the context of education or social programs, the promise of entrepreneurship is seen as both an economic activity that advances society and one that directly fosters action toward social betterment (Borasi and Finnigan 2010). Florin, Karri, and Rossiter framed a social definition for entrepreneurship as "the desirability and feasibility to proactively pursue opportunities and creatively respond to challenges, tasks, needs, and obstacles in innovative ways" (2007, 18–19). A higher-education-specific definition casts entrepreneurship as "the process of creating and implementing innovation-based solutions and responses to economic or societal problems and gaps" (Mars and Metcalfe 2009, 2). Jacobs, Lundqvist, and Hellsmark (2003) conceive of entrepreneurship in higher education as processes of commodification and commercialization, particularly of science, rather than the more socially oriented definition offered by Mars and Metcalfe (2009). Picking up on the promise of individual entrepreneurial action connected to leadership in higher education, Fisher and Koch (2004) examined entrepreneurial presidents whom they find to be "individuals who generate synergy in their institutions and seem almost mysteriously to draw the best from their colleagues" (143). Entrepreneurship is not simply seen in individual action but is also viewed as a mind-set, a way of thinking to guide decisions where opportunity and potential are seen as key dispositional assets (McGrath and MacMillan 2000). For advocates of the promise of entrepreneurial action, the visions of heroic opportunists are akin to scholarship on trait or behavioral leadership (Kezar, Carducci, and Contreras-McGavin 2006).

At the organizational level, a contextually complex view of entrepreneurial action nested within contemporary social, political, and economic circumstances in higher education emerges. Clark (2001) stated the entrepreneurial university emerged as an institutional response to changing economic and political support for the modern university. Clark (1998) also argued it is equally important to secure the position of basic research and the values and morals attached to this core function of the university, which he calls "the academic heartland." Thus, Clark (1998) maintains the two kinds of values and morals—academic and market-oriented—can be accommodated so they coexist within academia. To be responsive to financial tensions and changing global labor dynamics, higher education institutions are seeking ways to further connect their faculty, students, and outside communities in a strategic infrastructure where ideas flow, new initiatives blossom, flexibility abounds, and global reputations expand; entrepreneurialism has been seen as a way to move forward (Wood 2007). Zemsky, Wegner, and Massy (2005) proposed using revenues from entrepreneurial profit centers within a university to develop revenue to support mission-critical cost centers, thereby using entrepreneurial action to enhance institutional mission.

Entrepreneurship in higher education has also been critiqued. The discourse of entrepreneurship has been rooted in economic rationality and related management and organizational approaches (Gumport 2000). Criticism from researchers and scholars challenges the inevitability and superiority of the underlying ideology of economic rationality and identifies how market rationales place higher education as an industry and not a social institution interested in serving democracy's interests. Harvey (2005) identifies entrepreneurialism with neoliberal thought, an ideology that rejects governmental intervention in the domestic economy and promulgates materialism, consumerism, and the commodification of many public goods.

Neoliberalism has become a powerful force that has come to dominate the discourse and behaviors of many aspects of the United States (Apple 2008; Giroux 2005b). Researchers like Slaughter and Rhoades (2004) have investigated the rise of academic capitalism as a manifestation of neoliberalism in colleges and universities. Academia's apprehensions about increased engagement of universities in academic capitalism as a response to decreased government funding, the commodification of knowledge, and the increased interplay between universities and the private sector have risen (Ylijoki 2003). Some scholars believed increasing market orientation has given rise to a new research culture that has displaced traditional academic values and norms. For example, Ylijoki (2003) referenced Zinman by saying:

Intellectual property displaces communalism of results, universalism in research is turned into problem solving in local contexts, disinterestedness is
transformed into a mix of commercial, political, and social interests, disciplinary context is giving way to multidisciplinary context, and individualistic
working patterns are replaced by working in entrepreneurial teams. (308)

Jacobs, Lundqvist, and Hellsmark (2003) concurred: "The new emphasis on
commercialization and commodification of knowledge creates some degree
of role uncertainty for universities" (1555). A lack of awareness at the faculty
level, ill-defined leadership, and borderless infrastructure further complicate
an institution's entrepreneurial turn (Jacobs, Lundqvist, and Hellsmark 2003;
Nelles and Vorley 2010). Barnett (2011) describes the emergence of the
entrepreneurial university as part of the evolution of higher education in
modern society.

In a specific critique of the framing of entrepreneurialism in education,
Holmgren et al. (2004) said current advocates position entrepreneurialism
primarily as an individual action rather than a social construction. Holmgren
et al. set up a classic tension between seeing educational entrepreneurship
primarily emanating from organizational structure or from individual agency
(Bourdieu 1980; Giddens 1979). Ultimately, advocates of academic entrepreneurialism highlight a pragmatic or utilitarian view, even obscuring the role
of the social field and its associated underlying ideology. However, critics
question the inevitability of the pragmatic view, pointing instead toward the
nature of economic rationality that guides the approach to entrepreneurialism
as the correct response to contextual challenges.

ENGAGING CONCEPTUAL TENSIONS

This study's examination of academic entrepreneurship is focused on how an
individual self-described entrepreneurial leader uses entrepreneurial ideas
and what that means in a particular instrumental case example (Stake 1995).
The authors selected the case of a leader of an academic library because the
library context specifically engages academic entrepreneurship's potential
and is rife with tensions associated with knowledge production, publication,
and dissemination that bring the academic library—and in turn the university—closer to the knowledge economy (Hayes 2004). This study's analysis
employed institutional theory to acknowledge how library history and norms
inform individual action, but it also considered how individual agency can
transform the library's institutional logic and ultimately its structure (DiMaggio 1988). Institutional theory's push to illuminate contextual changes connects to transformational leadership. Thus, this study focuses on the transformation process as it both aligns with and affects leadership and entrepreneurialism.

The authors centered their analysis on exploring two broad research questions: First, what is entrepreneurial action within the context of leadership in higher education? Second, toward what structure does entrepreneurship move the academic library?

The authors framed their analysis within the conceptual framework of institutional entrepreneurship as introduced by DiMaggio (1988) and in the academic restructuring and academic capitalism work of Gumport (2000) and Slaughter and Rhoades (2004). In addition, research that subscribes to institutional theory "comprises a variety of perspectives, [and] common to all of them is the existence of persistent and resilient patterns of social interaction" and social leadership (Glynn and DeJordy 2010, 144). Thus, leadership theory, with an emphasis on what Costa and McCrae (1988) refer to as social leadership structures, was also employed in data analysis. This study's conceptual and theoretical framework guided the examination of case-study data as the authors aimed to see agency in action (meaning how social leadership and social entrepreneurial action create value) and examined how agency reflexively interacts with organizational structure. In line with Mair and Martí (2006), the authors looked for areas in the case study that advanced entrepreneurial action as an activity taken to create social value. In particular, this study adopted a critical realist approach to examining entrepreneurship within an institution that is concerned with both agency as an empirical domain and the structure as more abstracted actual and real domains (Blundel 2007). Ontologically, the use of critical realism promotes the examination of both the observable, empirical world and structures in the social and natural world that exist independently of knowledge, are often obscured, and are not directly observable (Blundel 2007).

To highlight the social and natural world that is obscured and not directly observable, the authors employed the lens of academic restructuring and academic capitalism to offer a critical viewpoint through which to illuminate the structure that frames entrepreneurial action in higher education. In conceptualizing academic structure and restructuring, this study draws upon Gumport's (2000) three-part thesis that sees restructuring as:

1. moving the legitimizing idea of higher education from that of a social institution to an industry,
2. the rise of academic management, academic consumerism, and re-stratification of the academy, and
3. the reconciliation of competing institutional logics as an ongoing challenge.

Building upon the conceptualization of restructuring, this study employs the theory of academic capitalism, specifically in examining how the library is entering into new knowledge networks, serving as its own marketer to students, and moving to see knowledge as a commodity rather than a public good (Slaughter and Rhoades 2004).

METHODS

The authors examined the results of a single case study of a self-described entrepreneurial leader in higher education as evidence of the tension between the pragmatic aspects of entrepreneurship (or engaging the "domain of both the empirical and actual") (Leca and Naccache 2006, 635). The domain of the empirical is seen here as what can be actually observed, while the actual and real is the domain of the broader set of structure or field that cannot be directly observed (Bhaskar 1979; Sayer and Morgan 1984). The case examined here is one of eight Research Subjects Review Board-approved cases of educational entrepreneurs developed as a research project funded by the Kauffman Foundation (see Borasi and Finnigan 2010). In each case study, the authors first followed the procedures of Yin (2002), as cases were developed around an individual to describe in detail how the individual functioned within a particular environment. This approach's advantage was that it allowed for a rich understanding of individuals' actions, their specific agency, and the structure surrounding their actions. Data collection involved interviews with the head of libraries lasting at least four hours and interviews with professionals identified as his collaborators lasting at least two hours. All interviews followed a semi-structured interview protocol, were recorded and transcribed, and sought to illuminate initiatives or activities that the head of libraries perceived to be entrepreneurial. While all interviews were semi-structured, it was essential to follow the story as it emerged in the interviews (Stake 1995). Supporting documents were also reviewed to better understand the case's context; documents examined included library histories, photos, library web pages, and extensive materials provided by the head of libraries and his collaborators.

The research team, including the project investigator and two graduate assistants, completed an iterative analysis process. Initial analysis was completed using line-by-line coding that followed a common coding framework (Babbie 1995; Bogdan and Biklen 1992) identified from the initial case (not this specific case) of the eight case studies the authors researched in conjunction with a review of entrepreneurship literature. The team used pattern-level analysis and developed common themes (LeCompte and Schensul 1999). This initial analysis was insufficient for understanding the reflexive nature of how individual action transforms the domain of the actual or real (Blundel 2007; Laclau and Bhaskar 1998). To explore the data at a higher level of abstraction, the critical realist strategy of retroduction (or inference) was employed to put forward the institutional logics that inform the connection between empirical findings and the library transformation. Inferential analysis offers a critical view of entrepreneurship within the context of higher-education institutional logics. The case of the head of libraries will first describe the actions of the entrepreneur's practice and then discuss the tensions associated with how one accesses institutional logics and resources to transform an organization toward values he and the organization hold important.

Description of the Case of the Head of Libraries

The selection of the head of libraries as the individual upon which to build a case analysis reflects his perception as a self-reported entrepreneurial leader in an era when the idea of the library is being transformed. The head of libraries served in that position from 1997 to 2008, a time of constant change when advances in digital information were reshaping how individuals conceive of library collections—be they books, journals, or other artifacts. The head of libraries led a central library that boasts more than 2.5 million volumes and an extensive collection of electronic resources and is literally and figuratively an unofficial symbol and community landmark at a research-extensive university. The library has a storied history from its inception in 1850, and during the leadership of the head of libraries, it remained in the top 50 research libraries in the United States and Canada.

The library and higher education are two things the head of libraries knows extremely well. The head of libraries spoke somewhat longingly of his first professional appointments in university libraries, of the mentors he had along the way, and the lessons he learned about the role the library plays in students' lives and in maintaining an archive of knowledge. He described the library as being filled with the hopes and dreams of students who toil in its stacks and scholars whose ideas fill its shelves. Based upon this study's interviews, the authors developed three vignettes, which relay three stories of institutional entrepreneurship led by the head of libraries.

Vignette One: Restructuring the Budget and Library Collection

The head of libraries arrived at the university at a time of significant fiscal tensions. One of his first challenges—the need to make a budget recommendation in a time when cuts were imminent—was emblematic of his entrepreneurial spirit. He began his leadership at the library with the goal of increasing the library collection's quality despite the institution's extreme budget constraints at the time. He began this process by recognizing that, to increase the library collection's quality over time, he needed to garner the support of institutional leaders. To garner support in a difficult budget year, he decided to propose a library budget cut, saying:

So I wrote to the Provost and said, I want the 2 percent cut, and my thinking was, one, it makes me a better partner with the college for later; two, it gives me an opportunity to create extensive urgency in the library for doing something different; and three, if we did it right, we would never again have to hear the argument from the college administrators or anybody else that the collection we were purchasing did not match what was going on at the university.

The urgency of budget cuts created the context for the head of libraries to go to his librarians and explain that each of them would need to make a 35 percent budget cut. He asked his staff to come up with a list of core materials that were essential to support the faculty and curriculum. Subsequent cuts would then be made after first and foremost fulfilling the faculty's must-have items, thus making reductions to the collection from what the faculty did not need. The change in thinking was important as it focused not on continuing past material collections but rather refocused the library collection on what the faculty and curriculum must have to complete their current and future activities. In his own words:

You're going to take a 35 percent cut to your budget, and what you must do is come up with a core collection for the discipline you support, meaning serials and lists of publishers where we buy everything, [so] that if we did not buy them you couldn't say we supported this discipline at all and you couldn't even really offer degrees in this discipline because you're not following the standard things. So . . . you, the librarian, must go to the faculty and come up with a list of what are the standard titles, [and] you then must come back to the head of collections and convince that head of collections that you have done that.

The library was then committed to buying collections that faculty reported they must have, but everything else that had been previously purchased was open to removal. Once the collection had been trimmed to include only items the faculty needed, faculty members were asked for a list of wants. The head of libraries reported expenditures were $200,000 less than the previous year, even after the requests were purchased; funds were reallocated even with a 2 percent overall budget cut.

Vignette Two: Restructuring Academic Space

The budget was not the only challenge the head of libraries faced in his new position, as it was evident that the existing facility was not inviting to students. Rather than focusing on the bleak facilities, the head of libraries began to put forward a vision of the library that would invite students to participate in literature and active learning and ultimately restructure the idea of the use of library space itself. He articulated his efforts to transform the library as:

It seemed to me that if you wanted to focus as a librarian on bringing students to the literature, to support what was going on in the classroom and going on in the major, then you needed to go back to the issue of facilities because the facilities had to reflect the same quality as what was going on in the literature that was in the library.

The head of libraries' strategy related to library facilities reflected his entrepreneurial leadership approach and large personality. He used storytelling to gain resources and transform library culture (Lounsbury and Glynn 2001). He told the story of the library facilities at every possible venue, including in front of the university trustees. His approach was to talk about the need for facilities upgrades to transform the library into a place for students to engage in learning. His vision of the library was not simply as a collection of books and a knowledge repository but as a uniting experience for students. The head of libraries took this vision seriously, and to realize the vision, he sought new relationships with businesses and donors to fund the transformation. The following passage articulates how he made his case to a university trustee to support a remodeling project:

He [the university trustee] came to see me, and he said, "I understand what you want to do. What could you do for $250,000 in the periodical reading room?" . . . So we began to look at it, and we said, you know, the chairs were old and worn down, the floor was cork and worn out, there were fluorescent lights on the ceiling so you couldn't see the art on the ceiling, so it looked like a space that was very tired. It didn't have lights on the tables, it didn't have Internet access, it didn't have anything basically, and it was pretty empty. We said for $250,000 we could do this, but for $500,000 we could do much more and so he gave us $500,000.

The library's transformation into a space that truly invites students in has been a core initiative of the head of libraries' leadership. Remaking the library facility was key to achieving the vision of the library as a student-centered space that contributed to student learning and growth. This study's final interview with the head of libraries concluded with a tour of the entirely new library space focused on what students indicated they needed in a study space. The room was filled with movable lounge furniture, television screens, movable white boards, and laptop computer connections, with adjacent space for the new Starbucks. The library, in his vision, has become the hub of campus academic life, and the librarian, by extension, is not a keeper or locator of material but an educator who is a learning partner of faculty and students. Depicting this vision was part of the head of libraries' leadership, and selling that vision was central to the fund-raising necessary for achieving facilities transformation. He articulated his approach to fund-raising in the following statement:

> You don't just ask for money. You build a relationship and you create an
> excitement, you get people interested in what they can do and then you make
> the ask, and then you celebrate them and then you keep them informed. So
> there's a process.

Ultimately, the head of libraries did not just transform a few rooms but
changed the form and function of the library space. In one swift and symbolic
move, the head of libraries opened the library to student use of food and
drink since it was what students wanted. He sought not simply to transform
the appearance of the library space and to bring students in to engage with
the collection, but he also marketed the library as a student-friendly space
that served as the hub of campus life, complete with food and drink to better
meet student desires. This restructuring has brought students to the library
collections and marketed the library to students as consumers.

Vignette Three: The Marketing and Technology Initiative

The head of libraries envisioned integrating the university library with student life on campus; he knew that for students to use library resources effectively, they needed to visit the library. The head of libraries emphasized a
proactive approach for his librarians and routinely shared his belief that
"librarians are educators" with his colleagues and staff. As he stated:

> Librarians have a very set way of thinking about things, and they're very
> passive, they wait for students to come. . . . They view the library as a delivery
> service to the campus so that when you come in, I will assist you because I
> deliver a service. . . . I disagreed with that perspective.

To initiate and establish a rapport with the student community, the head of
libraries encouraged ideas such as hosting a breakfast for incoming students'
parents and an annual Halloween event, called the "Scare Fair." He saw it as
the library's role to market itself to students, to make the library an outreach
and student service-oriented culture.

Sensing the need for upgrading and integrating technology into library
processes, the head of libraries identified staff who could develop and lead a
digital library initiative. Despite his skepticism about the cost and legal issues of library digitization, he perceived the need to engage in new ways of
accessing and thinking about library collections. He provided the required
freedom and the permission to be entrepreneurial, to innovate and develop
solutions that would benefit the library and by extension the university community. In the following passage, the head of libraries discusses the library's
research offerings before technological updates were implemented in the
mid-2000s:

> Students who were doing this kind of Google searching, they might be writing papers, but they weren't writing papers that really modeled the life of an academic, and therefore they really weren't becoming engaged in discipline. So the question became would there be a way that we could make the library approach, the catalog to the library, more like Google? And so we began testing how students used the catalog.

Here we see the head of libraries was very astute in assessing and understanding the changing role of technology in the world of the library. He was aware of the constraints that kept the library from making larger investments in technology and thus sought creative solutions, some of which trace to private industry, that would make the technology initiative sustainable.

> We realized that we had to invest in making the technology more user-friendly, more student-friendly. . . . We can't make that product any different than what is sold to us, but we can change the front end, so we began inventing different ways of getting into the catalog. . . . We cut back on their [staff members'] other duties, outsourcing training, and that gave the same number of people freedom then to do the kinds of work that the library was coming to count on because we were [be]coming more and more the technological center.

The head of libraries allowed his team the freedom to be creative and approach problems and constraints as improvement opportunities; he calls this "painting a vision." A vision that embraces entrepreneurial ideas and action provides individuals with the opportunity for agency to transform the organization. The head of libraries' vision for the digital library, developed in part out of his staff's agency to be institutional entrepreneurs, prompted a major change in how individuals access and are considered to access the library. For instance, visits to the library count whether they are physical visits or digital visits through the online portal. The library space is not simply the physical space but includes the virtual space accessed through the Internet.

ANALYTIC RESOLUTION

Given these three vignettes within the head-of-libraries case study, this study's findings are relayed, first in the empirical domain and then at greater levels of abstraction that examine the structures associated with organizational transformation. By identifying the practice of entrepreneurial action and more abstracted institutional logic systems employed by the head of libraries, the tension between structure and agency associated with institutional transformation is examined, thereby moving the examination of entrepreneurship from processes primarily conceptualized within an individual to a reflexive interaction between the individual and his social context.

In accordance with Blundel (2007) and Leca and Naccache (2006), the authors first identified observed practices of entrepreneurship that emerged from a review of the literature related to the entrepreneurial process. The final broad practice categories included: visioning (Bygrave 2004), developing opportunities (Bygrave and Zacharakis 2004; Timmons and Spinelli 2007), identifying resources (Baron and Shane 2005; Stevenson and Jarillo 1990; Timmons and Spinelli 2007), taking risks (Busenitz 1999; Palich and Bagby 1995), decision making and problem solving (Bygrave 2004), and managing growth (Kelley and Marram 2004). These categories were then used as the beginning coding scheme of interview transcripts.

The authors see entrepreneurship as a practice rather than a set of traits, but they still see the identified elements of practice as limited, incomplete definitions of the more abstract, reflexive relationship between the structure and an individual's agency in developing institutional transformation. The abstract relationship is further highlighted given social leadership processes and the presence of "leader emergence" and implementation (Judge et al. 2002, 768). Below are brief articulations of the entrepreneurial practices identified as central to library innovations under the head of libraries' leadership:

Visioning. The head of libraries articulated a clear vision to guide action, something he shared at every opportunity; as he said, "My approach with major change is to articulate a vision, give a broad statement, a broad feeling to generate energy around doing something."

Opportunities. Identifying and pursuing opportunities is at the core of several definitions of entrepreneurship; the head of libraries took developing opportunities very seriously. He said to us: "Years ago I wrote an article for a financial journal in librarianship arguing that libraries needed to invest in R&D. If we look at companies who remain viable, they tend to invest between 4 and 5 percent of their annual assets in R&D, and we should too."

Resources. As a part of his entrepreneurial practice, the head of libraries made resource identification a core element of his efforts. In doing so, he moved to become a fund-raiser, be it through advancing grant making or fostering relationships to solicit donations. He seemed to relish the role of generating resources: "Along the way we ran into Virginia Smith, who did the Smith Room upstairs, and we got to know Amy and Bill Clark, who are the primary board directors of the Clark Foundation. The Clark Foundation generously gave us the money to renovate the Great Hall and to renovate the back of the first floor, but you don't just ask for money; you build a relationship and you create an excitement."

Risk-taking. Entrepreneurs are often considered risk-takers; in the head of libraries' case, he saw risk in calculated terms, as exemplified in his description of risk associated with developing the library's digital reserves: "Janelle [a student worker] brought forward a proposal to do digital reserves.

She had been reading about it. She thought it was easy to do, and I was reluctant [be]cause I thought you know, this is going to be a lot more expensive. We're going to need new equipment, we're going to need servers, there might be some legal issues. I said, 'Well, why don't you do a test and come back and tell me what it's going to cost?' and she never did. She just did it and then came back and said, 'It's working, and it didn't cost anything,' and I said 'Terrific, you're the employee of the year.'"

Decision making and problem solving. Two interrelated ideas emerged from the practice associated with decision making and problem solving. First, the head of libraries embraced being the person who "decided," often doing so quickly when he identified strategic advantage (as in his overnight decision to allow students to have food and drink in the library). Second, he often used problems as opportunities for innovation or restructuring, as seen in his budget realignment and as articulated in the following: "To sustain that collection meant that we need[ed] on average 9 percent new money every year just to buy the same things that the faculty have told us we must have. Every year since then I've gotten the money that we've needed to sustain that collection plus some additions. So that overcame a reluctance on the faculty to deal with resizing the collection, because now they were in charge. It showed the college and the provost I was the team player because never in our provost's entire academic life had he ever had anyone take a 2 percent cut, ever."

Growth. Just as Bornstein (2004) reported the social entrepreneurs he studied were not satisfied when their ideas succeeded at a small scale, the head of libraries was grand in his desire to be a leader in reshaping the library, including the redesign of library space, and in his desire to be a true leader in the move toward the library's digital formatting.

Theoretic Re-description and Retroduction

This study offers a beginning insight into the complexity of entrepreneurial practice and related organizational transformation under the head of libraries' leadership. A more abstract re-description of the library during the head of libraries' tenure identified three major structures that were simultaneously acting upon institutional change. The first structure was the legitimizing logic of entrepreneurial action and the related shifting legitimizing logics of higher education generally. For the purposes of this case, *legitimizing logic* refers to the process whereby an ideology, in this case entrepreneurial action and market-related shifts, becomes legitimate (and accepted) by its attachment to the norms and values of an organization. The second structure is the broader set of social change associated with information in the new economy and in particular how information technology has influenced the idea of the library within higher education. The third structure is the local institutional emergent context, specifically as aligned with social leadership and leader emergence (Judge et al. 2002), including underlying beliefs and values.

The dominant legitimizing logic associated with entrepreneurship has been associated with economic development (Alvord, Brown, and Letts 2004; Holmgren et al. 2004). Entrepreneurship has primarily been conceptualized to facilitate economic value; this would include the logic of entrepreneurial action increasing human capital with the aim of having that capital transform individuals into entrepreneurs who generate economic value (Guedalla et al. 2001). More recently, examinations of social entrepreneurship have striven to expand the legitimizing logic of entrepreneurial action to include social value, where social value might still be seen as economic (as in sustaining not-for-profit organizations) or as value in the form of alleviating social problems (Alvord, Brown, and Letts 2004; Austin, Stevenson, and Wei-Skillern 2003; Mair and Martí 2006). As Holmgren et al. (2004) said, ultimately it is difficult to separate entrepreneurial action from a political ideology associated with market and capital-generating legitimizing logic.

The structure of entrepreneurial action and the value, whether social or economic, is framed by legitimizing thinking associated with the correctness of market (or capital) development-focused behavior. A logic of legitimization associated with market thinking is not new to higher education, and as Gumport (2000) said, it has become an increasing component of the legitimizing logic of higher education as primarily an industry. The move to legitimize higher education as an industry also reflects the broader national neoliberal public policy context (Harvey 2005). However, as Slaughter and Rhoades (2004) stated in describing public good and academic capitalist knowledge regimes, more than one legitimizing logic of action in higher education are operating simultaneously. Examining what logics are pervasive in which situations helps to illuminate the restructuring of higher education. The consideration of entrepreneurial practices operates within its legitimizing structures and is a reflexive practice in the contemporary higher education landscape.

The head of libraries' entrepreneurial practices rest within a reflective structure of legitimization and within the emergent information technology environment. From 1997 to 2008, information technology rapidly advanced digitization and access. The library, as a literal and figurative holder of archived volumes of information, transformed the way individuals in higher education accessed scholarly information. Similarly, the emergence of knowledge itself as a commodity had a direct role on changing the library's role as a gateway to the free exchange of information. Increasing access to information was seen not as public good but rather a commercial activity. New innovations in searching information have all but replaced card catalogs and early digital information access systems in the library. The head of libraries' push to consider how Google might be integrated into library searches reflects the broader changes in information technology. Within the entrepreneurial scaffolding in modern academia, there is evidence of what Nelles and Vorley (2010) termed "the Third Mission," meaning the mission-driven academic movement to center on not only teaching and research but also commercial engagement (the third mission). Collective consideration of teaching, research, and commercial engagement becomes part of an institution's entrepreneurial architecture; universities weave each of the three missions together in flexible, interconnected ways that accurately reflect an institution's strengths and culture (174).

A third emergent element of the structure that informed and acted upon the head of libraries' entrepreneurial practice takes form in the local institutional context. The head of libraries arrived at an institution that was experiencing significant financial tensions, had unattractive library facilities, held a strong commitment to undergraduate liberal arts education, and was within a decentralized decision making and organizational governance culture. The emergent culture also included a president-initiated plan to limit enrollment as a means to increase institutional selectivity and raise the perceptions of institutional quality. The head of libraries entered an institutional context that directly informed his possibilities for action. In addition to an institutional commitment toward the drive for prestige, limited funds were available to initiate change, and the library needed to satisfy the institution's colleges that were, in the head of libraries' words, "taxed" by the central administration to support the library. The agency of the head of libraries' entrepreneurial practice was set within an emergent structure informed by abstract legitimizing logics of action, broad information technology changes, and specific institutional dynamics. Further, as social leadership theory highlights, the head of libraries' leadership processes included "valuing" (Banerjee 2004, 2) in which activities and pursuits were analyzed regarding their value and meaning to the organization, the institution, and its members. There is an established leadership structure in the daily consciousness of the head of libraries that is central to entrepreneurial practice as a causal mechanism.

DISCUSSION

The final phase of applying a critical realist framework to analysis is to consider this study's initial empirical findings in light of a more abstract discussion of the case; this allows us to draw some conclusions as to the role of entrepreneurial practices in shaping organizational transformation. In the case study of the head of libraries, the authors examined two broad findings for further elaboration. First, this study highlights how the head of libraries used simultaneous legitimizing logics and in so doing legitimized his entrepreneurial practice and engaged his own agency in legitimizing the logic of the library as increasingly market-oriented. Second, each of his self-described initiatives emerged from social context reflective of the broader structure of the environment; thus, in defining his innovations, his agency was akin to steering a boat with a current that was already flowing. He steered the boat toward increased public-private knowledge networks, increasingly seeing faculty and students as consumers and information as a commodity to be brokered by the library.

In each of the head of libraries' innovations, he illustrated two simultaneous legitimizing logics. First, in reflecting his vision, he called upon the institutional commitment to liberal learning; he repeatedly described his commitment to in-depth student engagement in the disciplines where learning is valued for the sake of learning. The authors were compelled by his commitment to and personal love of learning; he often legitimized his innovations as necessary to bring students to the library to serve the purpose of deep liberal learning that includes broad discipline reading and writing. Secondly, he called upon a market-based legitimizing logic where the student, faculty member, or collaborator is a consumer with needs to be met by the library. The needs of the "users," as he described them, are seen as legitimate and something the library should seek to understand, appreciate, and be nimble in responding to. Marketing the library and repositioning the library's role in an outreach capacity were core elements of serving students and faculty alike. The head of libraries was particularly utilitarian in his thinking; his innovations were less about process and more about the outcome of ensuring the library as a vital and attractive element in the view of key consumers. In pursuit of his utilitarian intentions, he reflected the simultaneous and ongoing tension associated with whichever logic of legitimacy was preeminent, reflecting his own tension and the broader structure associated with differing and coexisting legitimizing logics. Ultimately, the application of his entrepreneurial practice played an important role in restructuring the norms of the environment toward an entrepreneurial culture and associated legitimizing logic, as illustrated in the following statement:

> One of the reasons that few people [employees] leave here is because they can't find any place else to go that will give them that same amount of freedom or have an open enough vision that they will accept what they are now.

Entrepreneurial practice rests within an emergent context that informs and constrains individual agency. As an example, altering the budgeting and purchasing process was highly informed by the emergent institutional context, but it also reflected how responding entrepreneurially within that context steers an organization further down a course it is already on. In this case, the budget realignment freed up resources to allow the organization to be steered toward supporting research and development and restructured the view of the collection as being responsive to the consumer needs of faculty research. While sold as supporting faculty research, the budget realignment repositioned the library legitimizing logic toward that of an industry responsive to external (through research and development) and internal (primary consumer) needs—Nelles and Vorley's (2010) third mission. Participation in research and development brought library staff in contact with new knowledge networks via grant-making activities and via partnering with private companies involved in information technology development. Faculty support was fostered through asking faculty for input on their needed scholarly materials, with materials used by faculty retained in the collection and less useful materials dropped from the continuing collection. Faculty's needs as consumers of particular knowledge were met, so the type of collection that developed was one that was responsive to current faculty work. The library sought to serve faculty work and shifted into being a broader collection of knowledge. As new areas of knowledge were required, the cost was passed along to the respective department needing new materials in the form of an increased institutional levy. New library resources in the new budget model came with a user fee attached, thus pushing the library to see its collection as a commodity to be leveraged for funding.

Entrepreneurial practice in this case reflects action associated with an emergent structure, where the leader's agency is akin to steering the organization further in a direction it is already heading. The head of libraries' entrepreneurial practice and social leadership processes did generate results in the form of new facilities, a change in the organizational culture that placed emphasis on outreach and student learning, and advancement of the information technology capacity of the organization, but these innovations also flowed from structural pressures. The head of libraries' agency is best described in the degree and type of legitimizing logic with which he steered the organization. The authors' data analysis found his agency is reflected in the extent to which he operationalized an underlying entrepreneurial and market-based legitimizing logic that pushed the library toward being part of the industry of higher education, while at the same time making meaningful and important changes to space, technology, and practice that benefited students, faculty, and the institution.

CONCLUSION

This is a single case study and as such, it illustrates a view of entrepreneurial practice that is constrained by time and context. The case's value is to raise a series of issues for further consideration across contexts. This study aims to engage the tension that emerges between the practical positions of advocates, reflected here as individual entrepreneurial agency, and the critiques of detractors, reflected here in the structure of the library context. The head of libraries' leadership is a case-in-point example of the potential of entrepreneurial thinking and social leadership action when applied to the challenges of leadership in higher education.

The head of libraries was effective in addressing the emergent context of his leadership through entrepreneurial initiatives to update library space, advance information technology capacities, and shift the library toward serving students' interests; moreover, he navigated the library through troubled financial times. However, using fiscal resource tensions and the broader emergent context to drive change is indicative of the notion that entrepreneurship marches academia toward capitalist market values. As Gumport (2000) said, academics must consider how modern colleges and universities are engaging in "academic restructuring." Higher education institutions are increasingly using production and consumerist metaphors that point to corporate settings and business contexts; the case of the head of libraries illustrates this shift. This study's case study findings revealed the head of libraries engaged in risk management, sought funding from donors to modernize and technologically revolutionize library space, invested in research and development using a budget model, and aimed to connect his vision to the university's mission. As educational institutions engage in academic restructuring and thus move to respond and adapt to the evolution of the consumer—or in this study's case, students and faculty—they are absorbing adopted versions of academic capitalism. As Gumport (2000) argued:

> Higher education is increasingly using market discourse and managerial approaches to restructure in an attempt to gain legitimacy; yet, in so doing, they may end up *losing* legitimacy by changing their business practices to such a degree that they move away from their historical character, functions, and accumulated heritage as educational institutions" (87).

The fiscal realities of higher education make it clear the academy needs leaders who can hold, rather than simply resolve, the tensions inherent with entrepreneurial action as a strategy toward organizational change, renewal, and advancement (Toma 2011). This case illustrates how entrepreneurial leadership is both a strategy for instigating new change initiatives toward organizational mission and goals and a means by which ideology is reflected in shifting legitimizing logics. Ultimately, entrepreneurial action remains part of the university, just as it was when educational entrepreneurs were starting new institutions of higher education concerned about both operating revenues and instruction. The challenge for researchers and practitioners in contemporary higher education is to more clearly identify the means by which entrepreneurship might uphold ends that are desirable to maintain a view of education that appreciates, but is not solely based in, market rationality.

This research was funded in part by the Ewing Marion Kauffman Foundation.

BIBLIOGRAPHY

Alvord, Sarah, L. David Brown, and Christine Letts. 2004. "Social Entrepreneurship and Societal Transformation: An Exploratory Study." *The Journal of Applied Behavioral Science* 40 (3): 260–83. doi: 10.1177/0021886304266847.

Apple, Michael W. 2008. "Between Neoliberalism and Neoconservatism: Education and Conservatism in a Global Context." In *Globalization and Education: Critical Perspectives 2008*, edited by Nicholas C. Burbules and Carlos Alberto Torres, 57–77. New York: Routledge. http://www.southalabama.edu/coe/faculty/fregeau/615readings/BetweenNeoliberalismNew-conservatism.pdf.

Austin, James, Howard H. Stevenson, and Jane Wei-Skillern. 2003. "Social Enterprise Series No. 28, Social Entrepreneurship and Commercial Entrepreneurship: Same, Different, or Both?" *Harvard Business School Working Paper*, no. 04-029, November.

Babbie, Earl R. 1995. *The Practice of Social Research*. 7th ed. Belmont, CA: Wadsworth Publishing.

Banerjee, Anjana. 2004. *Theories of Social Leadership*. Enclave, Delhi: Global Vision Publishing House.

Barnett, Ronald. 2011. *Being a University*. New York: Routledge.

Baron, Robert A., and Scott A. Shane. 2005. *Entrepreneurship: A Process Perspective*. Canada: Thomson South Western.

Bhaskar, Roy. 1979. *A Realist Theory of Science*. 2nd ed. Leeds: Leeds Books.

Blundel, Richard. 2007. "Critical Realism: A Suitable Vehicle for Entrepreneurship Research?" In *Handbook of Qualitative Research Methods in Entrepreneurship 2007*, edited by Heele Neergaard and John P. Ulhøi, 49–74. United Kingdom: Edward Elgar Publishing.

Bogdan, Robert C., and Biklen, Sari Knopp. 1992. *Qualitative Research for Education*. 2nd ed. Needham Heights, MA: Brunner/Mazel.

Borasi, Raffaella, and Kara Finnigan. 2010. "Entrepreneurial Attitudes and Behaviors That Can Help Prepare Successful Change-Agents in Education." *The New Educator* 6: 1–29. http://www1.ccny.cuny.edu/prospective/education/theneweducator/upload/1st-article-3.pdf.

Bornstein, David. 2004. *How to Change the World: Social Entrepreneurs and the Power of New Ideas*. Oxford: Oxford University Press.

Bourdieu, Pierre. 1980. *The Logic of Practice*. Stanford, CA: Stanford University.

Busenitz, Lowell W. 1999. "Entrepreneurial Risk and Strategic Decision Making: It's a Matter of Perspective. *Journal of Applied Behavioral Science* 35 (3): 325–40. doi: 10.1177/0021886399353005.

Bygrave, William D. 2004. "The Entrepreneurial Process." In *The Portable MBA in Entrepreneurship 2004*, 3rd ed., edited by William D. Bygrave and Andrew Zacharakis, 1–27. Hoboken, NJ: John Wiley & Sons.

Bygrave, William, and Andrew Zacharakis. 2004. *The Portable MBA in Entrepreneurship*, 3rd ed. Hoboken, NJ: John Wiley & Sons.

Clark, Burton. 2001. "The Entrepreneurial University: New Foundations for Collegiality, Autonomy and Achievement." *Higher Education Management* 13 (2): 9–24.

———. 1998. *Creating Entrepreneurial Universities: Organizational Pathways of Transformation*. Guildford: Pergamon.

Costa, Paul T., Jr., and McCrae, Robert R. 1988. "Personality in Adulthood: A Six-Year Longitudinal Study of Self-Reports and Spouse Ratings on the NEO Personality Inventory." *Journal of Personality and Social Psychology* 54: 853–63. http://psycnet.apa.org/index.cfm?fa=fulltext.journal&jcode=psp&vol=54&issue=5&page=853&format=PDF.

DiMaggio, Paul J. 1988. "Interest and Agency in Institutional Theory." In *Institutional Patterns and Organizations: Culture and Environment 1988*, edited by Lynne G. Zucker, 3–22. Cambridge, MA: Ballinger.

Etzkowitz, Henry, and Loet Leydesdorff. 1997. "Introduction to Special Issue on Science Policy Dimensions of the Triple Helix of University–Industry–Government Relations." *Science & Public Policy* 24 (1): 2–5. doi: 10.1093/spp/24.1.2.

Fisher, James, and James Koch. 2004. *The Entrepreneurial College President*. Westport, CT: American Council on Education & Praeger Publishers.

Florin, Juan, Ranjan Karri, and Nancy Rossiter. 2007. "Fostering Entrepreneurial Drive in Business Education: An Attitudinal Approach." *Journal of Management Education* 3: 17–42. doi: 10.1177/1052562905282023.

Giddens, Anthony. 1979. *Central Problems in Social Theory: Action, Structure and Contradiction in Social Analysis*. London: Macmillan.

Giroux, Henry A. 2005a. "Academic Entrepreneurs: The Corporate Takeover of Higher Education." *Tikkun* 20 (2): 18–23. http://www.tikkun.org/article.php/Giroux-AcademicEntrepreneurs.

———. 2005b. "The Terror of Neoliberalism: Rethinking the Significance of Cultural Politics." *College Literature* 30 (1): 1–19. http://www.jstor.org/stable/25115243.

Glynn, Mary Ann, and Rich DeJordy. 2010. "Leadership through an Organization Behavior Lens: A Look at the Last Half-Century of Research." In *Handbook of Leadership Theory and Practice 2010*, edited by Nitin Nohra and Rakesh Khurana, 144. Boston: Harvard Business School Publishing.

Guedalla, Martin, Henrik Herlau, Mike Armer, and Shazeen Qasier. 2001. "The KUBUS system: An Holistic Approach to Enterprise and Entrepreneurship." In *Entrepreneurship Education: A Global View 2001*, edited by Robert H. Brockhaus Sr., Gerald E. Hills, Heinz Klandt, and Harold P. Welch, 104–27. Burlington, VT: Ashgate.

Gumport, Patricia J. 2000. "Academic Restructuring: Organizational Change and Institutional Imperatives." *Higher Education* 39: 67–91. http://citeseerx.ist.psu.edu/viewdoc/download?doi=10.1.1.183.3485&rep=rep1&type=pdf.

Harvey, David. 2005. *A Brief History of Neoliberalism*. New York: Oxford University Press.

Hayes, Helen. 2004. "The Role of Libraries in the Knowledge Economy." *The Journal for the Serials Community* 17 (3): 231–38. doi: 10.1629/17231.

Holmgren, Carina, Jorgen From, Anders Olofsson, Kristen Snyder, Hakan Karlsson, and Ulrika Sundström. 2004. *Entrepreneurship Education: Salvation or Damnation?* Information Center for Entrepreneurship Nordic Education Research Association.

Jacob, Merle, Mats Lundqvist, and Hans Hellsmark. 2003. "Entrepreneurial Transformations in the Swedish University System: The Case of Chalmers University of Technology." *Research Policy* 32 (3): 1555–68. http://dx.doi.org/10.1016/S0048-7333(03)00024-6.

Judge, Timothy A., Remus Ilies, Joyce E. Bono, and Megan W. Gerhardt. 2002. "Personality and Leadership: A Qualitative and Quantitative Review." *Journal of Applied Psychology* 87 (4): 765–80. http://tamu.edu/faculty/bergman/judge2002.pdf.

Kelley, Donna, and Ed Marram. 2004. "Managing a Growing Business." In *The Portable MBA in Entrepreneurship 2004*, edited by William D. Bygrave and Andrew Zacharakis, 405–26. Hoboken, NJ: John Wiley & Sons.

Kezar, Adrianna J., Rozana Carducci, and Melissa Contreras-McGavin. 2006. *Rethinking the "L" Word in Higher Education: The Revolution in Research on Leadership*. San Francisco: Jossey-Bass.

Laclau, Ernesto, and Bhaskar, Roy. 1998. "Discourse Theory vs. Critical Realism." *Alethia* 1 (2): 9–14.

Leca, Bernard, and Philippe Naccache. 2006. "A Critical Realist Approach to Institutional Entrepreneurship." *Organization* 13 (5): 627–51. doi: 10.1177/1350508406067007.

LeCompte, Margaret D., and Jean J. Schensul. 1999. *Analyzing and Interpreting Ethnographic Data*, 5. Walnut Creek, CA: Altamira Press.

Lounsbury, Michael, and Mary Ann Glynn. 2001. "Cultural Entrepreneurship: Stories, Legitimacy and the Acquisition of Resources." *Strategic Management Journal* 22: 545–64. doi: 10.1002/smj.188.

Mair, Johanna, and Ignasi Martí. 2006. "Social Entrepreneurship Research: A Source of Explanation, Prediction, and Delight." *Journal of World Business* 41 (1): 36–44. http://dx.doi.org/10.1016/j.jwb.2005.09.002.

Mars, Matthew, and Amy S. Metcalfe. 2009. "The Entrepreneurial Domains of American Higher Education." *ASHE Higher Education Report* 34 (5): 1–110.

McGrath, Rita Gunther, and Ian C. MacMillan. 2000. *The Entrepreneurial Mindset: Strategies for Continuously Creating Opportunity in an Age of Uncertainty.* Boston: Harvard Business School Publishing.

Nelles, Jen, and Tim Vorley. 2010. "Constructing an Entrepreneurial Architecture: An Emergent Framework for Studying the Contemporary University beyond the Entrepreneurial Turn." *Innovative Higher Education* 35: 161–76. http://link.springer.com/article/10.1007%2Fs10755-009-9130-3#page-1.

Palich, Leslie E., and D. Ray Bagby. 1995. "Using Cognitive Theory to Explain Entrepreneurial Risk-Taking: Challenging Conventional Wisdom." *Journal of Business Venturing* 10: 425–38. http://www.utexas.edu/law/journals/tlr/sources/Issue%206/Peterson/fn134.palich.pdf.

Sayer, Andrew, and Kevin Morgan 1984. "A Modern Industry in a Declining Region: Links between Method, Theory and Policy." In *The Politics of Method 1984*, edited by D. Massey and R. Meegan, 133–55. London: Methuen.

Schramm, Carl J. 2006. *The Entrepreneurial Imperative: How America's Economic Miracle Will Reshape the World (and Change your Life).* New York: Harper Collins.

Schumpeter, Joseph. 1947. "The Creative Response in Economic History." *Journal of Economic History* 7: 149–59. http://www.jstor.org/stable/2113338.

Sharma, Pramodita, and James J. Chrisman. 1999. "Towards a Reconciliation of the Definitional Issues in the Field of Corporate Entrepreneurship." *Entrepreneurship Theory and Practice* 23 (3): 11–27.

Slaughter, Sheila, and Gary Rhoades. 2004. *Academic Capitalism and the New Economy: Politics, Markets, State and Higher Education.* Baltimore, MD: Johns Hopkins University Press.

Stake, Robert E. 1995. *The Art of the Case Study.* Thousand Oaks, CA: Sage.

Stevenson, Howard, and J. Carlos Jarillo. 1990. "A Paradigm of Entrepreneurship: Entrepreneurial Management." *Strategic Management Journal* 11: 17–27.

Timmons, Jeffrey A., and Stephen Spinelli. 2007. *New Venture Creation: Entrepreneurship for the 21st Century.* 7th ed. Boston: McGraw-Hill.

Toma, J. Douglas. 2011. *Managing the Entrepreneurial University: Legal Issues and Commercial Realities.* New York: Routledge.

Weber, Max. 2003. *The Protestant Ethic and the Spirit of Capitalism.* New York: Charles Scribner's Sons. Original work published 1958.

Wood, Van R. 2007. *Globalization and Higher Education: Eight Common Perceptions from University Leaders.* New York: Institute of International Network.

Yin, Robert K. 2002. *Case Study Research: Design and Methods.* 3rd ed. Thousand Oaks, CA: Sage.

Ylijoki, Oili-Helena. 2003. "Entangled in Academic Capitalism? A Case Study on Changing Ideals and Practices of University Research." *Higher Education* 45: 307–35. http://link.springer.com/article/10.1023%2FA%3A1022667923715#page-1.

Zemsky, Robert, Gregory R. Wegner, and William F. Massy. 2005. *Remaking the American University: Market-Smart and Mission-Centered.* Piscataway, NJ: Rutgers University Press.

Ziman, John. 1996. "Post Academic Science: Constructing Knowledge with Networks and Norms." *Science Studies* 9 (1): 67–80. http://www.sciencetechnologystudies.org/v9n1/ZimanPDF.

Chapter Ten

Marriage between Participatory Leadership and Action Research to Advocate Benefits Equality for Lesbian, Gay, Bisexual, and Transgendered People

An Extended Human Rights Role for Library and Information Science

Bharat Mehra and Donna Braquet

Contemporary trends and media attention related to the information needs of minority and marginalized communities have created public expectations that academic libraries will provide more representative services for people and issues that are traditionally considered on the margins of society (Hanna, Cooper, and Crumrin 2011; Mehra and Braquet 2011; Wood, Miller, and Knapp 2006). This case study focuses on queer leadership in academic library circles and shares select strategies for "leading from below" to further social justice and social equity in library and information science (LIS) on behalf of disenfranchised lesbian, gay, bisexual, and transgendered (LGBT) populations in the conservative buckle of the Bible Belt. A significant element of such a new model in LIS integrates participatory leadership and action research principles beyond those found in traditional conceptualization and practice. Drawing on the intersections between these two concepts using a case study approach helped academic information professionals lead by following, becoming more effective as social justice advocates on discrimination issues.

The authors, an LIS educator and an academic librarian, explored an extended leadership role with a proactive commitment to LGBT rights. Select episodes from the authors' story as two "out" faculty members at the University of Tennessee–Knoxville illustrate an LIS leadership role using research findings from a domestic partnership benefits study to mobilize institutional policy development and implementation at the individual, group, and community levels in a multilevel, interactional mode of analysis (Anand et al. 2011). The authors' goal has been to develop a more socially progressive and accepting academic community based on democratic ideals of equality, justice, and fairness for all human beings, irrespective of their married status, sexual orientation, or gender identity. While learning to nurture the skills and capacities within an extended leadership role, the authors used specific formal and informal leadership strategies to succeed in a multilayered environmental context. A significant difference from past LIS academic leadership work was gathering and using research-based evidence (e.g., the findings from a domestic partnership benefits study) to propose that campus stakeholders take action to promote a marginalized population's human rights.

In this chapter, the term "library and information science" identifies the authors' roles as educator and practitioner in the information creation, organization, management, and dissemination processes in an academic library setting and beyond. A broad use of the term represents the authors' efforts to not only tap into the services, programs, and experiences available within an administrative department at an institution of higher learning and an academic library, but also to use the information-related opportunities offered to them by being embedded in the larger setting of a land-grant, flagship university. Such work has helped the authors extend their presence as LIS educators and practitioners beyond the academic library into the campus and surrounding local community to build positive partnerships and potential allies to further LGBT issues and concerns.

AN EXPANDED LEADERSHIP THEORY

Scholars writing about leadership in business, corporate, and academic organizational environments have recently recognized that abstract and general statements about leadership theories without reference to a particular setting are often invalid and irrelevant (Jackson and Parry 2008). Such a "groundedless" approach misses the details of the contextual situational realities (Jones 2005), develops disconnect from the social and cultural context of the organization (Hogg, Martin, and Weeden 2003), overlooks the differences in a variety of settings, and minimizes the "richness and complexity of the phenomena it supposedly refers to" (Alvesson 2011, 151). The authors recognize the value of these gaps and consequently identify the nuances of their experiences and specific actions as LIS professionals using an influencing process to provide an extended understanding of leadership in the realm of human rights, social justice, and community context. The chapter highlights an understanding of leadership "to include influencing task objectives and strategies, influencing commitment and compliance in task behavior to achieve these objectives, influencing group maintenance and identification, and influencing the culture of an organization" (Yukl 1989, 253). This research connects with the emerging scholarship on leadership and organization theory (Parry 2011), namely in areas of organizational learning, innovations, and knowledge management; context and process instead of examination of individual traits and behaviors (Uhl-Bien 2006); and methodological preference toward qualitative approaches and strategies. Adopting traits from participatory leadership concepts and action research allowed the authors to adopt a qualitative ethnographic methodology that reveals the complexities and challenges involved in the influencing process to make a difference in the given social and cultural community context.

Participatory leadership is the "extent to which a leader involves others in making decisions for which the leader has formal authority and responsibility" (Yukl 2011, 286). This leadership paradigm is a democratic approach based on promoting engagement to harness diversity, build community, and create shared responsibility for action (Rooke and Torbert 2005). The conceptualization applies to some of the authors' collaborative efforts in building allies and partnerships with members of various university stakeholders and the external community to further the adoption and implementation of benefits equality at the University of Tennessee–Knoxville. The research also integrated certain elements of situational leadership. For example, the relationship behavior (e.g., telling, selling, participating, and/or delegating), individual/group maturity levels (e.g., high, moderate, low), and the immediate and short-term activities, resources, opportunities, members, functions, and tasks emerged in an ad hoc and spontaneous manner in response to specific situations based on mutual dialogue and discussion with new stakeholders, keeping the bigger goal of promoting benefits equality as a driving force that shaped ongoing interactions and communications (Blanchard, Zigarmi, and Zigarmi 1985; Hersey 1985; Hersey and Blanchard 1971). Adopting different strategies and leadership styles based on the different stakeholders and the tasks at hand reflected dimensions of contingency theory in how the situation and context altered the path adopted, influence on the group and individual, flow of work, distribution of activities, and allocation of resources and time (Fiedler 1971; House and Mitchell 1974).

Stephen Kemmis and Robin McTaggart (1998) identified the object of action research as social practice and its transformations along with the changes that occur in the social institutions and relationships that support it.

Action research is defined as collaborations between a "professional action researcher and members of an organization or community seeking to improve a situation" (Greenwood and Levin 1998, 4). The trustworthiness of action research is established by reporting on credibility, transferability, dependability, and confirmability (Stringer 1999). Action research characteristics fitting this chapter's research experiences include varied levels of participation in research and action, learning in collaboration, community inquiry into everyday experiences and potential impact, online-offline efforts, use of mixed methods, and situated nature of applications and concrete outcomes (Mehra 2006; Rahman 2008).

From these brief descriptions of participatory leadership and action research, readers will recognize their expected overlap and intersection in shared characteristics and underlying values. The marriage between the two concepts supported the adoption of elements from both approaches, creating a highly relevant frame for the research experiences in this chapter. Participatory action research, where "communities of inquiry and action evolve and address questions and issues that are significant for those who participate as co-researchers" (Reason and Bradbury 2008, 1), also relates to these research experiences since it includes the element of participation in conjunction with action research, although the focus in participatory action research is not on leadership issues (Bishop et al. 2003; Mehra et al. 2002). Hence, a theoretical understanding of the alliance between participatory leadership and action research better reflected the authors' research experiences in furthering LGBT rights issues at the University of Tennessee–Knoxville. The participatory component was explicit not only in the authors' roles as faculty members who were proposing the benefits of equality initiatives but also in their role as "out" faculty members who are participants and members of the LGBT community. Additionally, the authors' LIS position shaped their role as leaders and professionals in terms of their knowledge, experiences, and skills associated with the information creation, organization, management, and dissemination processes within the university. An educator and practitioner's perspective further complements and integrates their roles in leadership within the LIS milieu while drawing intersections between theory, practice, and community action.

THE ACADEMIC CONTEXT FOR HUMAN RIGHTS

Historically, prejudice, institutionalized discrimination, and a denial of equal rights and fair representation are considered violations of human rights (Clapham 2007; Hunt 2008). Recent political, cultural, social, and media attention have dragged LGBT experiences to the forefront of the human rights debate at all levels (Obama 2012; Clinton 2011), calling for progressive leadership in varied settings to take concrete actions, mobilize resources, and support community activism to promote LGBT rights "as the proper cause of justice" (Larney 2009; Moyn 2012, 21). Accordingly, this section identifies select contextual and administrative developments at the University of Tennessee–Knoxville to present the nuances of how the academic culture has affected the discourse surrounding the denial of a LGBT rights initiative and the queer academic leadership strategies the authors pursued in response.

During 2004, an International and Intercultural Awareness Initiative Task Force was formed in an effort to make diversity planning at the University of Tennessee–Knoxville more specific and accountable, thereby strengthening the institution's reaccreditation application to the Southern Association of Colleges and Schools (SACS). This task force's purpose was to create an "inclusive campus community by fostering demographic and intellectual diversity" and "to ensure that all University of Tennessee graduates possess the knowledge, attitudes, and skills necessary to succeed in today's complex, pluralistic world" (Papke 2005, 4); the task force's planning documents identified the following salient limitations of the university's diversity commitment:

1. lack of institutionalization of diversity at all levels;
2. lack of diversity included in mission statements;
3. lack of sensitivity by faculty, staff, and administration for the needs and feelings of minorities;
4. consultation with underrepresented groups only when incidents arise making them seem like problems and not an integral part of the campus community; and
5. the university's narrow interpretation of diversity in terms of only race, specifically as African American (Papke 2005).

The task force's Quality Enhancement Plan (QEP), released in January 2005, outlined specific actions that would "create a climate of intercultural vitality" and diversify the university's students, faculty and staff, student activities, and curriculum (Papke 2005, 12). Yet this 71-page document mentioned LGBT issues only once when referring to a long list of area studies (such as Asian studies/Asian American studies, Arabic studies/Middle Eastern studies, Latino/Latina studies, Native American studies, etc.) that were lacking in the curricula. The failure of the task force to significantly acknowledge LGBT as part of the campus's diversity was eye-opening. Further, interactions with task force members and others on campus also helped the authors realize the group's definition of diversity was very narrow, as it did not initially recognize sexual orientation and gender identity as valid identity constructs similar to race, gender, ethnicity, and religion. As a result the authors found it essential to hone their leadership skills and strategically begin creating awareness and advocacy regarding LGBT concerns and representation on the University of Tennessee–Knoxville campus.

The library staff in the University Libraries at the University of Tennessee–Knoxville are known as leaders on campus related to diversity initiatives (Dewey 2010). The University Libraries established a diversity committee in 2001 (http://www.lib.utk.edu/diversity/) and a minority residents program in 2003.[1] The University Libraries' offering of family circulation privileges was the institution's first benefit offered to those other than spouses.[2] Overall, LGBT-related initiatives were limited in the University Libraries, even within its diversity committee. Donna Braquet, a member of the committee, often brought LGBT issues into the conversation, disrupting the committee's trend of silence on the topic and its tendency to focus on only race and ethnicity.

One such suggestion was for the libraries' diversity committee to sign a poster in support of an inclusive nondiscrimination policy. The banner, which hung in the University Center, quickly became a controversial issue for the committee. Unlike other efforts, a full vote of each member of the committee was required, and when a majority agreed, the request went to the library dean for approval.[3] While the committee's name eventually joined hundreds of other signatures, this hesitancy to see LGBT issues as an aspect of diversity illustrates how the narrow definition of diversity and its effect on LGBT issues was reflected in some librarians' mind-set, contributing to perpetuate a chilling impact across campus.

The research and action-oriented efforts in this chapter are part of the authors' use of findings from a benefits equality study to initiate policy adoption and implementation. In response to the University of Tennessee–Knoxville's and its library's limited understanding of diversity, the authors became LIS action researchers to develop initiatives on behalf of LGBT people, developing culturally appropriate information resources and services; creating greater visibility and representation; and promoting positive decision making, progressive legislative and policy development, and community action. Other venues and publications document some of these initiatives and activities (Mehra 2011; Mehra and Braquet 2011; Mehra and Braquet 2007a; Mehra and Braquet 2007b; Mehra and Srinivasan 2007; Mehra and Braquet 2006; Braquet and Mehra 2006). Table 10.1 provides a short historical context to the research in this chapter by highlighting a few key activities and developments from 2005 to 2010 that the authors participated in and led.

The chapter is not about the benefits equality study per se. Instead, it examines the authors' roles in academic library queer leadership and the resulting process they are pursuing to implement some of the reported research findings. The benefits equality research evaluated the websites of 2011 *U.S. News & World Report* top public universities in January and

February 2012 and compared the University of Tennessee–Knoxville's performance with these schools in its representation and offering of domestic partnership benefits.[4] Research findings revealed that twenty-four of twenty-six universities offered some form of domestic partnership benefits for same-gender—and occasionally opposite-gender unmarried—employees and students. This fact revealed that domestic partnership benefits were considered important for LGBT and other non-LGBT people alike. The study found thirty-three specific types of benefits offered at these universities, which fell into six main categories—health benefits, financial assistance, leave, insurance, counseling, and campus services. On its various campuses, the University of Tennessee–Knoxville offered domestic partnership benefits in only two of these categories. The University of Tennessee–Knoxville offered domestic partnership benefits in only three of the thirty-three specific criteria. This performance placed the University of Tennessee–Knoxville among the lowest ranks.

The authors realized "domestic partnership benefits" should not be taken as a blanket term since the benefits equality study's rich dataset revealed a range of implementable offerings within each category. Many offerings were within the individual campuses' administrations' internal jurisdictions, and recognition of a range of domestic partnership benefits left room for making progressive efforts in individual campus settings and negotiating approval of some (if not all) benefits when seeking support of local political and administrative authorities.

This key understanding motivated the authors to find avenues and opportunities at the University of Tennessee–Knoxville to implement some of the benefits offered at other top universities. The qualitative content analysis of the authors' experiences in participatory leadership in this case study illustrated an extended role for LIS professionals (including but not limited to academic libraries) as action researchers that goes beyond traditional conceptualizations of information service providers and LIS educators. The effects of participatory leadership and action research are deeply integral to reconceptualizing an extended role for LIS. This leadership model aids LIS professionals in becoming active supporters of human rights by strongly affirming their commitment, via concrete and tangible actions, to diversity of all forms and by developing a socially progressive community based on democratic ideals of equality, justice, and fairness for all human beings.

LEADERSHIP STRATEGIES TO SUPPORT BENEFITS EQUALITY

The case study approach has long been a valid research tool in leadership practices (Yin 2008). It draws from a rich naturalistic, holistic, ethnographic, phenomenological, and biographic research tradition (Stake 1995) to intensively analyze, in a descriptive and/or explanatory fashion, an individual unit or case such as a person, group, event, period, or other system while focusing on its developmental factors in relation to context (Thomas 2011; Yin 2011). This chapter draws on the case study method in its emphasis on select episodes from the authors' leadership experiences, weaving a narrative to track the process and progress made, capture the developmental and temporal dimensions of the phenomena, and reflect the authors' participatory leadership role discussed here. This chapter adopts and embraces selective storytelling as a conscious methodological strategy to transfer knowledge and transmit values about the given social and cultural context (Archibald 2008), to share and interpret experiences (Evenson 2006), and to document the research processes and findings undertaken by the authors' (Feak and Swales 2009).

LIS LEADERSHIP FOR SOCIAL ACTION

Toni Samek (2007) challenges the notion that libraries should remain neutral in the light of human rights conflicts around the globe and calls for a more proactive LIS leadership that gets involved in promoting critical social action and community-wide progressive changes. An underlying thread that emerges in the authors' narrative is how their LIS background supported their leadership roles and provided the impetus for mobilizing politically motivated social action. The authors' roles, responsibilities, and skills as part of an LIS professional leadership mandate were significant, though not necessarily only in terms of a formal capacity as managers of processes related to information creation, organization, and dissemination or curators of world knowledge (Shera and Egan 1953; Rayward 1975). Leadership in participation with community stakeholders involved additionally "helping people help themselves" beyond traditional notions in LIS to merely helping people as if they are completely "needy, impoverished, and asset-less" (Mehra, Albright, and Rioux 2006; Mehra, Rioux, and Albright 2009; Mehra 2011, 306). The authors' work also integrated social justice ideals and developed action-oriented goals, objectives, agendas, and outcomes differing from past LIS work that has distanced itself from advocacy to maintain its objectivity and neutrality (Mehra 2009; Mehra and Sandusky 2009). Moreover, sometimes the marriage of participatory action and action research for LGBT social change meant adopting an informal mode of leadership practice as facilitators, which allowed connections and developments to emerge based on how others played leading roles and took charge when the authors encouraged them to step up.

In 2007, the authors led the research committee of the Chancellor's Commission for LGBT People in an effort to compare support for LGBT students and employees as displayed through the University of Tennessee–Knoxville's and its peer institutions' websites.[5] This resulted in a report, titled "Website Analysis of the University of Tennessee's Peer Institutions to Assess Their Support for Lesbian, Gay, Bisexual and Transgender People."[6] Support was judged by the presence of twenty-three different variables on the websites, such as LGBT advisory committees, LGBT student groups, LGBT inclusion in nondiscrimination policies, offers of domestic partner benefits, LGBT resource centers, and LGBT educational and social events. The report also included a quantitative checklist that provided a quick translation of complex and new ideas to administrators, busy academics, the media, and the general public. This checklist served as a powerful visual that showed the lack of support LBGT people received at the University of Tennessee–Knoxville compared to other institutions. As LIS professionals, the authors used their research skills to gather evidence and highlight the inequities at the University of Tennessee–Knoxville in comparison to other institutions. Involvement at the administrative level in the institutional structure (i.e., the Commission for LGBT People) was important for the authors to integrate participatory leadership and action research in LIS so they could share the research findings with other like-minded individuals and agencies and build allies and support for the cause.

In January 2010, Tennessee's governor Phil Bredesen challenged the University of Tennessee–Knoxville to become a top 25 public research institution. The university's response, *VOL Vision 2015: The Pursuit of the Top 25*[7] was developed in January 2011 and had five strategic priorities: 1) undergraduate education; 2) graduate education; 3) research; 4) faculty; and 5) infrastructure and resources. With the institution's focus on the top 25 initiative, the authors decided to conduct a website analysis of these public universities to determine how their support for LGBT people compared to the University of Tennessee–Knoxville's (Mehra and Braquet, under review). The report, compiled during the summer of 2011, surveyed how twenty-two LGBT supportive variables were portrayed on the websites of the top schools. These criteria were grouped into three main categories: administration and policy, teaching and research, and services. The range of criteria across the categories was significant to show that a variety of domestic partnership benefits were being offered in different campuses in all the significant work domains pursued in an academic institution of higher learning. As LIS professionals in leadership roles, identifying elements, language, and policies from the strategic planning documents that the University of Tennessee–Knoxville's administration was using to shape the institution' present and future directions (e.g., VOL Vision and Top 25) and contextualizing these in relation to research-based evidence was extremely important in helping the authors garner support and propose steps the administration and initial detractors could not ignore. The authors acknowledge that adopting and co-opting the language of the opposing administrators was a politically motivated response to the emotionally charged resistance of an LGBT-unfriendly administration that wanted to avoid a controversial issue, as it was fearful of politicized wrath of the conservative state legislature, which controls the university's purse strings.

In August 2011, both authors were elected to the university's Faculty Senate and were appointed to its Benefits and Professional Development Committee. This increased the authors' potential to support benefits equality, extending their role and capacity for social action as part of the LIS leadership. During the committee's initial meeting, members brainstormed issues that should be considered for the coming year. Domestic partnership benefits for LGBT employees soon came to the forefront as a topic worth pursuing, in part because of the University of Tennessee's VOL Vision Top 25 Plan for the university to attract and retain stellar, diverse faculty and staff.[8] To compete with the top universities for the best and brightest students, faculty, and staff, the university would require competitive benefit offerings. In subsequent committee meetings, the authors informed other members about the website analysis conducted earlier that summer that tracked the domestic partner benefits of the top 25 institutions. The committee found the report promising and assigned the authors to work on an in-depth analysis of domestic partner benefits, while several other members drafted a resolution that would be brought before the Faculty Senate to address the matter. Excerpts from this analysis served as an addendum to the committee's final resolution in support of benefits equality at the University of Tennessee–Knoxville. As LIS leaders, the authors were able to apply their knowledge of web resources, awareness of rubrics and metrics in evaluation and assessment, and research skills in developing benefits equality datasets to mobilize faculty support and initiate social action.

Analysis of human resources on the top 25 schools' websites revealed a variety of benefits offered to domestic partners, which included university discounts, library privileges, recreational facilities membership, housing, dual career hires, sick and bereavement leave, and health insurance. The authors felt it imperative to provide a detailed listing of benefits, some of which were under individual campus control, to address administrators' counterargument that since Tennessee's constitutional amendment restricted marriage to be between a man and a woman, no benefits could be offered on the campus. As LIS professionals involved in integrating participatory leadership and action research in their social justice efforts, the authors' identification, recognition, and subsequent categorization of benefits, showing that some were the purview of the state and others could be implemented at the campus level, allowed them to convince others that the administration needed to take a more flexible approach. Several faculty members' subsequent pressures on the administration were based on arguments that many offerings were within the internal jurisdiction of the individual campuses' administration.

The Benefits and Professional Development Committee's resolution[9] was brought before the Senate's executive committee in March 2012 and then to the Faculty Senate in April 2012. To the authors' surprise, the resolution caused little debate once introduced. One friendly amendment requested that a timeline be given for the chancellors of the two relevant campus units (namely, the University of Tennessee–Knoxville and the Institute of Agriculture) to respond with their plan for benefits equality. The resolution passed unanimously and asked that a response be given during the first faculty meeting the following fall.[10] Local news media provided noteworthy coverage to the consideration and passage of the resolution (Boehnke 2011, 2012a, 2012b).

Members of the Benefits and Professional Development Committee, along with other faculty senators, eagerly awaited the chancellors' response at the first senate meeting in September 2012. Neither chancellor attended; the Faculty Senate president read a letter that had been sent.[11] The brief letter was not well received by faculty senators, and during the discussion, the brevity of the letter was described as "shocking and inconsistent with statements that diversity is valued on this campus" and "unacceptable."[12] Soon, the story about the chancellors' inadequate response became more newsworthy than the resolution itself, with news media as far away as Hawaii, San Francisco, Oregon, Florida, New Jersey, New York, and Europe reporting on the controversy (Boehnke 2012c; Butera 2012; Cardona 2012; DeSantis 2012; *Hawaii News Now* 2012; Lake 2012; Local8now.com 2012; McCormick 2012).

The dismissive tone of the chancellors' letter caused an outcry on campus, and students, faculty, and staff held a forum within two weeks to prepare a strategy for continued pressure; the University of Tennessee–Knoxville chancellor's own advisory group, the Commission for LGBT People, released a letter calling for dialogue with the administration.[13] At the Faculty Senate's second meeting on October 22, 2012, the University of Tennessee–Knoxville chancellor apologized for the letter and mentioned that a second, more detailed letter would be released soon.[14]

The news media contacted the authors, known on campus as "out" faculty members who worked on the resolution, for comment. The Graduate Student Senate, looking to bring up a similar resolution for student benefits, invited the authors to speak at its meeting. The concept of a coordinating committee to plan further action came from the open forum, and the authors assisted the effort. Using their skills as organizers and managers of information, the authors created a blog to capture information surrounding the issue and to help educate employees, administrators, students, and the general public about the concerns.[15] In their efforts on the coordinating committee, the authors also helped maintain a listserv and Facebook page on benefits equality.[16]

The coordinating committee also planned a "Speak Out event," where members of the campus community were invited to share how the lack of benefits affected them and their families, on November 29, 2012. *The Daily Beacon*, the campus newspaper, covered the event ("Forum Held to Discuss Equal Benefits for Faculty Domestic Partners" by Justin Joo) in its December 3, 2012, issue.[17] By the end of 2012, the chancellors still had not issued the promised letter. To keep the issue in the spotlight, members of the coordinating committee, including the authors, painted a message on the "The Rock," the campus' free speech area.[18] In early 2013, the authors supported plans to collect, broadcast, and archive video interviews, as a personal story can be a very compelling and powerful tool to humanize the issues of civil rights, equality, and fairness.

The chancellor's long-awaited letter,[19] dated January 10, 2013, was finally posted to the Faculty Senate website on January 22, in advance of the February Faculty Senate meeting. The letter stated the chancellors' had taken their position "only after consideration of the very complex political, fiscal, and legal issues presented by the issue of domestic partner benefits." The letter mentioned Tennessee Code and the 2006 state constitutional amendment recognizing one man and one woman as the only legally recognized marital contract. The letter concluded the university's pursuit of domestic partner benefits "would have significant political implications" and "significant fiscal implications" and that the chancellors, "as leaders of a publicly funded institution . . . are responsible for acting in the best interests of the entire institution." Minutes from the February Faculty Senate meeting contain the statement of Jimmy G. Cheek, chancellor of the University of Tennessee–Knoxville: "There is no way seen to be able to move forward with any such proposal at this time."[20]

Following this response, the Faculty Senate asked the professional development and benefits committee to respond with a letter[21] forcefully explaining the Senate's disappointment. The letter cites the 'university's much-touted climb to the "top 25" and the disenfranchisement of a group of already employed faculty and staff. One year after the resolution's passage, senators reaffirmed their commitment to the issue of benefit equality at the April 2013 meeting. Meanwhile, in March 2013 the Graduate Student Senate passed a resolution similar to the Faculty Senate's resolution, supporting domestic partner benefits for graduate students. Since graduate student insurance is not part of the state's insurance program, the authors are interested to see how the university deals with this issue.

The Benefit Equality Campaign group, of which both the authors are members, is collecting video testimonials to keep the issue at the forefront of the public's attention. It is also worth mentioning that, at the end of March

2013, the state university rescinded nearly $12,000 of funding from a week-long, student-planned, educational and awareness initiative called "Sex Week," just two weeks prior to the event. Two Tennessee state senators threatened to take away the University of Tennessee's funding if the "Sex Week" activities used state funds, which included funding from the College of Arts and Sciences and other departments on campus. In a written statement, Chancellor Cheek said, "We support the process and the students involved, but we should not use state funds in this manner" and stated that some of the activities "are not an appropriate use of state tax dollars."[22] While the students were successful in filling the financial gap through private donations, this administrative decision set the precedent that any topic seen as controversial, objectionable, or "not appropriate" by a few in the legislature might be cancelled or defunded by the university. In the April 2013 Faculty Senate meeting, senators made the connection from "Sex Week" to domestic partner benefits and LGBT issues in general. As LIS professionals in leadership roles, the authors wonder, with trepidation, at the implications of a loss of academic freedom and stifling of intellectual curiosity at the hands of conservative politicians on issues that do not appeal to the majority's values and religious beliefs. As LIS professionals in leadership roles, the authors will continue to draw attention to the loss of basic rights in the academy and beyond, making efforts to mobilize community-wide actions to resist and challenge the imposition of such dictatorial measures.

LEADERSHIP IN ACTION: EIGHT RECOMMENDED DIRECTIONS

This section briefly identifies key themes that have emerged based on the authors' experiences as LIS action researchers involved in furthering LGBT human rights at their institutions. The following eight themes can be seen as significant components in integrating a participatory leadership and action research role in LIS settings that extends an understanding of the services, programs, and functionalities the professions should deliver in local communities by generating positive outcomes for people existing on the margins of American society.

Strategize Your LIS Role in Meeting the Needs of Marginalized Populations in Your Community

An important step in participatory leadership and action research in the LIS context involves identifying who the community leaves out of the distribution of power, prestige, resources, social acceptance, information access, and other variables, and strategically thinking of how LIS professionals can help mitigate those imbalances and inequities based on the opportunities available within and beyond our institutional settings. As "out" LIS professionals, the authors are directly affected by the lack of benefits their heterosexual colleagues take for granted. This inequity in benefits is not fair because homosexual and heterosexual employees are doing the same work; it means unequal pay for equal work for people in the two categories, which is discrimination. The authors recognized their roles and responsibilities in the academy involved the traditional expectations in American universities and colleges: research, teaching, instruction, and service (Thelin 2007). They decided strategically to identify what options and activities they could purse within this framework to help meet the needs of the marginalized LBGT population in their constituencies.

Organize Participation and Action to Further Advocacy and Human Rights

People in LIS are recognized as experts who bring their knowledge, experiences, and skills in information creation, organization, management, and dissemination processes to any professional encounter (Mehra and Robinson 2009). An extended role in participatory leadership and action research requires LIS researchers to apply their expertise in planning and mobilizing human and technical resources toward efforts and activities that further advocacy and human rights issues for disenfranchised communities. For example, Braquet was the key leader in organizing various meetings of the coordinating council and planning concrete actions (e.g., the "Speak Out" event and painting on "The Rock") where both authors participated with several students, faculty, staff, and community members to further benefits equality and LGBT human rights.

Use Research-Based Evidence to Justify Your Social Justice Proposals and Actions

It has been very important for the authors to use research-based evidence to justify their proposals and actions to further benefits equality for LGBT and opposite-sex unmarried couples working at the University of Tennessee–Knoxville. The research-based evidence has provided a solid basis for channeling the authors' efforts to translate benefits equality into action. The authors' efforts have found much acceptance and support because of their research-based findings for social justice proposals and actions. In several instances, it was difficult for people to deny the importance of LGBT benefits equality when the authors presented evidence showing how far behind the times the University of Tennessee–Knoxville was compared to other nationally recognized colleges and universities.

Collaborate and Partner with Agencies and Individuals Outside Your Traditional Zones

For the authors, a significant element of participatory leadership and action research has meant viewing each individual and group with whom they have interacted as potential collaborators who could help them further benefits equality. This has required conducting a self-reflective strengths-weaknesses-opportunities-threats (SWOT) activity following every interaction with an individual/group and analyzing each encounter to figure out what possible collaborations and partnerships can be developed toward furthering benefits equality. The authors' initial appointment to the university's Faculty Senate and its Benefits and Professional Development Committee is an example of how they initially presented the concern about domestic partnership benefits, and from there, the committee took the leadership role in formulating the resolution based on the willingness and enthusiasm of the members; the resulting partnership went beyond anything the authors had originally conceptualized.

Become Involved in Political Decision Making and Administrative Policy Development

Venturing outside their traditional LIS-related comfort zones and spaces has also included moving into the realms of political decision making and administrative policy development within LIS agencies and beyond in the institutional settings. Being elected to the Faculty Senate and appointed to its Benefits and Professional Development Committee provided the authors a rich insider's perspective regarding the political climate and administrative processes in the academy. It also helped the authors understand how to use their knowledge about the political realities within higher education, the institution, units, and the Tennessee state legislature to their advantage in challenging human rights violations. It also made the authors sensitive to timely decision making and to expect barriers in the process while finding ways to persevere via negotiation, building ally networks, and going around the challenges. For example, one individual the authors encountered tried desperately to get them off the LGBT benefits equality campaign. It was thanks to the strong values, democratic spirit, faith in the mission, support, and communication of the other committee members that the authors were able to continue without getting frustrated or distracted from the path toward fairness and justice for all employees at the University of Tennessee–Knoxville.

Exposure to the administration's priorities, goals, and strategies helped the authors realize the need to articulate their social justice proposals in a language and rhetoric based on the administrative agenda and mind-set. Initially, when the authors had proposed setting up a Commission for People of Diverse Sexual Orientations to Chancellor Loren Crabtree in 2005, their argument was that the university was not able to attract the best of students, faculty, and staff owing to the lack of visible administrative support toward all forms of diversity, including LGBT people; the authors also pointed this limitation caused the University of Tennessee–Knoxville to miss out on corporate and business capital investments. This experience helped the authors recognize the priorities and language the administration viewed as important. The valuable lesson helped them craft the benefits equality report, developing allies and supporters by articulating the human rights advocacy in terms of what was perceived to be important to administrative stakeholders. Placing the benefits equality campaign in the context of the University of Tennessee's VOL Vision Top 25 Plan was one such strategy.

Develop Communication Channels with the News Media to Provide Coverage for Your Activities

The authors were extremely fortunate to develop and nurture positive communication channels with the news media, which provided support and coverage of the various benefits equality activities and events. This added pressure on the administration and spread awareness to the public about the developments in the benefits equality process at the university. The news coverage indicated to the administration that news agencies considered this an important matter that would not go away on its own.

Use Multiple Information Creation, Organization, Management, and Dissemination Channels

As LIS professionals, the authors were directly able to apply their expertise in information creation, organization, management, and dissemination processes in multiple channels (offline and online) and social and communication technologies to share information about different activities and events in the benefits equality campaign. Braquet set up a Facebook account and blog to engage the public on the matter, present a repository of resources and information, and share a historical timeline associated with the benefits equality campaign in the context of earlier LGBT advocacy and developments. The LGBTANet (see table 10.1) also disseminated information and elicited participation of allies and members in the LGBT community during various benefits equality events.

Document the Process and Leave a "Paper" Trail Available in the Public Record

Having worked on LGBT advocacy at the University of Tennessee–Knoxville and in local communities since 2005, the authors have been exposed to rumors, hearsay, gossip, and mixed signals from administration stakeholders at different times. During these interactions, the authors have also encountered a high level of bureaucracy and a lack of clarity and transparency in the decision-making processes associated with LGBT concerns (Mehra and Braquet 2007b). For any kind of feedback about decisions being proposed, both generally and about LGBT issues, the key information sources were based on "who knew who" and had personal communication contacts with people in the top-level administration. In response to this administrative climate, the authors learned to make sure they left a "paper" trail documenting the steps, decisions, and communications from various top-level administrators and others. Such publically archived paper-based or digital sources include minutes of meetings, responses shared on blogs, press releases, electronic mail exchanges, posts on electronic mailing lists, publically available resolutions, and letters from administrators. Now the authors and others have both formal and informal public sources to cite when they share the nuances of the story of the benefits equality campaign. The evidence can be used to support their observations and analysis of the social and cultural environment. Future advocates and others can trace the steps via the public record to deepen their understanding of the campus and community climate and take appropriate steps to further their missions and agendas.

CONCLUSION

This chapter provided a personalized story of the authors' efforts to advocate benefits equality via particpatory leadership and action research in LIS circles and beyond. The story integrated a strong social justice mission in the narrative to address the perceived human rights violations at the University of Tennessee–Knoxville. In this storytelling process, the authors intentionally chose to stay focused on the policy development and implementation experience at the university level though they have been very much also supported (directly or indirectly) by the administrative leadership efforts taken in their own departmental units and colleges. For example, as part of the College of Communication and Information's Diversity and Inclusion Week from October 1 to 4, 2012, Mehra organized and moderated a panel on diversity and sexuality where benefits equality was touched upon by five LGBT panelists in the light of greater individual, social, political, and community-wide support for people of different sexualities in the east Tennessee region. Similarly, Braquet is a member of the Women's Leadership Program at the University of Tennessee–Knoxville and was invited by her library dean to apply for the Leading Change Institute, a week-long leadership program for librarians and other information professionals.

An expanded leadership approach, which allowed the authors to integrate particpatory leadership and action research, was important to adopting relevant and meaningful action-oriented steps while navigating academic policies and administrative protocols. It also let the authors document the nuances of their experiences as a narrative that was reflective and self-critical in analyzing what worked in leadership efforts, learning of community advocacy processes, and organizational learning. Additionally, the authors were able to study the factors and variables asscoiated with the external social and cultural environment of the academy and community as they played a role in determining the course of action, the challenges and barriers encountered, and the opportunities and options that became available. Some of these variables included the interactions with facilitating allies or detracting opponents, availability of resources and committee alignments, and support of interested news agencies, to name a few. The authors' responsibilities and contributions, positions and competencies, and adopted approaches ranged between active, semi-active, semi-passive, and passive as circumstances and situations emerged and other players did or didn't take ownership in specific actions and activities. Their professional training as LIS educators and practitioners allowed the authors to apply their knowledge, experiences, skills, and understanding in traditional domains related to information creation, organization, management, and dissemination and the use of information and communication technologies towards nontraditional leadership in community advocacy to address human rights agendas.

Figure 10.1 generalizes the authors' experiences in the case reported in this chapter so readers can apply the human rights frame for LIS professionals to address social justice issues in their own libraries and communities. The frame consists of the following interlated components: 1) context in which LIS professionals are embedded and grounds for application of their information-related competencies to reveal the dimensions of the context better; 2) methods of participatory leadership and action research; and 3) human rights outcomes and results. LIS professionals can apply their knowledge of information creation, organization, management, and dissemination; experiences in information-related work; expertise of case study and other methodologies; and use of research-based evidence to analyze, respond to, and potentially change the contextual dimensions of the environment (e.g., social and cultural aspects of the organization or community, details of situational realities, unique characteristics, and the richness and complexity of the phenomena being studied). LIS professionals can tap into the intersections between the methods of participatory leadership and action research approaches to effectively achieve human rights outcomes and results that lead

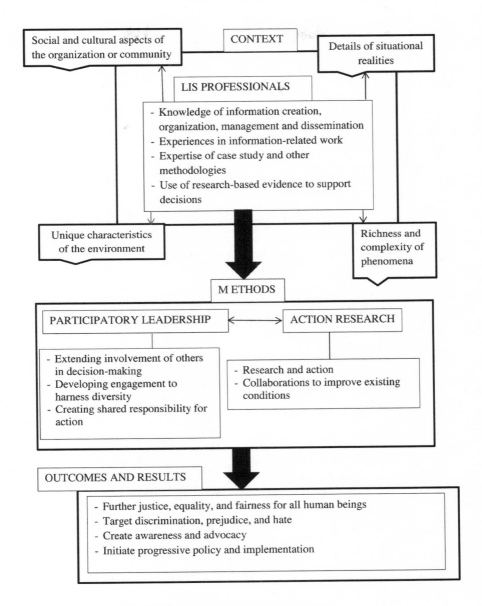

Figure 10.1.   Human Rights Frame for LIS professionals

to progressive changes in society and localized communities. Outcomes and results are articulated in terms of furthering justice, equality, and fairness for all human beings by targeting discrimination, prejudice, and hate, creating

Table 10.1.   LGBT Activities and Developments Involving the Authors' Participation and Leadership (2005–2010)

LGBT Activities and Developments	Timeframe
1. Initial contact and beginning of collaborations between Mehra and Braquet based on shared understanding as "out" LIS members in the academy.	Spring 2005
2. Partner and communicate with members of internal university units: the Chancellor's Ready for the World initiative (initially known as the Quality Enhancement Plan, URL: https://san4.dii.utk.edu/pls/portal30/docs/FOLDER/SACS/SACSQEP/qep0 3.html), Office of Equity and Diversity (OED), Diversity Council, and the Diversity Experience Workshop Advisory Group to develop key allies, gain support, and promote advocacy for LGBT issues.	Spring 2005
3. Partner and communicate with members of external community agencies: Unitarian Universalist Church (local religious institution, Knoxville Out&About (local LGBT newspaper, URL: http://outandaboutnewspaper.com), Spectrum Café: DiversiTea and Coffee House for gay teens (URL: http://www.discoveret.org/spectrum), DiscoverET.org (initially KORRNET, a local community network, URL: http://www.discoverET.org), and Knoxville Cares (supportive coalition for LGBTQ and HIV+ people, URL: http://groups.yahoo.com/group/knoxvillecares) to develop allies, networks, intellectual opportunities, tangible programs, and other avenues to represent LGBTQ issues and concerns.	Spring 2005
4. Mehra taught an LIS course entitled "Race, Gender, and Sexuality in the Information Professions" where students were required to identify, assess, and evaluate the campus and community climate and LIS-related information services.	Spring 2005, Spring 2007
5. Mehra and Braquet implement qualitative interview-based research on LGBT issues to evaluate campus climate and LIS-related information services.	Summer and Fall 2005
6. Mehra and Braquet create an e-mail discussion list "LGBTANet" to foster information sharing, communication exchange, and institutional memory building on LGBT issues (URL: http://listserv.utk.edu/archives/lgbtanet.html).	August 2005
7. Mehra collaborates with LGBTQ allies in preparing pro-LGBTQ resolution statements and refining vocabulary constructs representing sexual minorities in a city ordinance nondiscrimination clause that was presented and discussed during focus group and individual meetings with local councilmen Bob Becker and Chris Woodhull.	Fall 2005

8. Mehra and Braquet form part of a contingent from UT libraries and present LGBT promotional display materials during the New Student Welcoming Event hosted by the Lambda Student Union (URL: http://web.utk.edu/~;lambda) at a local club during.   Fall 2005

9. Braquet, Hoemann, and Mehra meet with Chancellor Loren Crabtree and present an initial proposal December 2005 to establish a Commission for People of Diverse Sexual Orientations: Receive an encouraging and supportive response from the Chancellor.   5 December, 2005

10. University of Tennessee president John Petersen authorizes the inclusion of sexual orientation in the University of Tennessee–Knoxville nondiscrimination policy.   December 2005

11. Mehra and Braquet are involved in setting up procedural steps and administrative protocols for an approved Commission for LGBT People.   December 2005–December 2006

12. First meeting of the Commission of LGBT People takes place, and Mehra and Braquet are elected as co-chairs.   12 December, 2006

13. Mehra and Braquet work with faculty/staff/students in the Diversity Experience Workshop Advisory Group to identify appropriate content for diversity experience and training workshops.   2005–2006

14. Braquet developed The Diversity News Channel on the University of Tennessee–Knoxville library server to present current LGBTQ happenings and programs related to LGBTQ themes and events.   Spring 2006

15. Braquet developed a focus on LGBTQ issues in the University of Tennessee–Knoxville library's Cultural Corner (offline and online) (URL: http://www.lib.utk.edu.proxy.lib.utk.edu:90/diversity/culturecorner), a library effort to demarcate a visible physical and virtual space to spotlight issues of contemporary relevance.   Spring 2006

16. Braquet developed the Gay, Lesbian, Bisexual, Transgender Resource Guide (URL: http://libguides.utk.edu/lgbt) that provides online access to local LGBTQ resources and services via the UTK library's website.

17. Mehra and Braquet connect with the grassroots community-based GLBTQ Task Force Against Domestic Violence and contribute to their workshop for community service providers in public agencies (URL: http://www.outandaboutnewspaper.com/article/278#.UNcqqr81ZsQ).   April 2006

18. Commission for LGBT People is involved in: Creating a Web presence, building communication tools and information sharing mechanisms, developing strategies to address equity issues on campus, and conducting research to identify actions to improve campus climate.   2007– ongoing

19.	Braquet and Mehra compile nondiscrimination policies of Peer/AAUP/SEC schools and issue report for UT president Petersen (URL: http://lgbt.utk.edu/commission/ndp.html#peer).	Spring 2007
20.	Braquet and Mehra as part of the Commission for LGBT People's events committee plan programming to raise awareness and visibility of LGBT issues on campus (URL: http://lgbt.utk.edu/commission/pastevents.html).	2007–2009
21.	Sexual Orientation is included in UT's official EEO/AA nondiscrimination policy.	August 2007
22.	Gender Identity is included in UT's official EEO/AA nondiscrimination policy.	January 2008
23.	Braquet works with a library colleague to collect stories of LGBT students, faculty, and staff at UT (URL: http://lgbt.utk.edu/vod).	November 2008
24.	Braquet serves on Safe Zone implementation committee (URL: http://safezone.utk.edu)	Spring 2009
25.	Braquet serves on OUTreach: LGBT & Ally Resource Center implementation committee; Serves as Center Director (URL: http://lgbt.utk.edu/center).	2009; 2010–ongoing

awareness of such issues and advocacy, as well as initiating progressive policies and implementation at all levels.

The authors were both fortunate to gather support from allied students, faculty, staff, adminstrators, and community stakeholders and others, such as members in various committees, their departments and colleges, press contacts, and internal and external agencies and institutions. A discussion topic among allies and LGBT members is how the leadership efforts should acknowledge and represent the specific needs of LGBT employees and expand the marketing and visibility of the campaign to highlight the effects on non-LGBT employees and other stakeholders. The Faculty Senate has indicated it wants to continue the dialogue with and pressure on the university adminstration to pursue and address the benefits equality inequities in its quest to join the ranks of the top 25 universities and colleges in the United States. The authors hope to maintain their spirit, motivation, and energy in this leadership process, furthering human rights efforts to support LGBT rights and equality while continuing to improve conditions at the University of Tennessee–Knoxville and helping it join the ranks of other, more progressive institutions.

NOTES

1. http://www.lib.utk.edu/residents/2003-2005.html.
2. http://www.lib.utk.edu/ius/cards.html.

3. http://www.lib.utk.edu/~share/committees/diversity_html/divers050908.html.

4. The full study, titled "A Website Evaluation of the Top Public Universities in the United States to Assess Their Offering of Domestic Partnership Benefits," is at http://web.utk.edu/~bmehra/domesticpartnershipreport.pdf.

5. Auburn University, Louisiana State University, North Carolina State University, Texas A & M University, University of Florida, University of Georgia, University of Kentucky, University of Maryland–College Park, University of North Carolina–Chapel Hill, University of Texas–Austin, University of Virginia, Virginia Polytechnic Institute.

6. https://web.utk.edu/~bmehra/final.pdf.

7. http://www.utk.edu/volvision-top25/resources/top-25-executive-summary.pdf.

8. http://www.utk.edu/volvision-top25/resources/vol-vision-overview-framework-final.pdf.

9. http://senate.utk.edu/files/2011/09/2-LGBT-benefit-equality-resolution-2_161.pdf.

10. http://senate-utk-edu.wpengine.netdna-cdn.com/files/2011/09/April-2012.min.pdf.

11. http://senate-utk-edu.wpengine.netdna-cdn.com/files/2012/08/2-Ltr-to-Faculty-Senate.pdf.

12. http://senate-utk-edu.wpengine.netdna-cdn.com/files/2012/08/September-2012.min.pdf.

13. http://benefitequalityutk.wordpress.com/2012/10/15/open-letter-to-the-chancellors/.

14. http://www.knoxnews.com/news/2012/oct/22/jimmy-cheek-apologizes-to-ut-faculty-for-partner/?print=1.

15. http://benefitequalityutk.wordpress.com.

16. https://www.facebook.com/pages/The-UT-Knoxville-Domestic-Partnerhip-Benefits-Campaign/189529117839038.

17. http://utdailybeacon.com/news/2012/dec/3/forum-held-discuss-equal-benefits-faculty-domestic/.

18. http://benefitequalityutk.wordpress.com/2012/12/19/look-what-someone-painted-on-the-rock/.

19. http://senate.utk.edu/files/2012/08/Faculty-Senate-01.10.13.pdf.

20. http://senate-utk-edu.wpengine.netdna-cdn.com/files/2012/08/February-2013.min_1.pdf.

21. http://senate-utk-edu.wpengine.netdna-cdn.com/files/2012/08/Draft-Revised-Benefits-and-Profesional-Development-Response-Letter.pdf.

22. http://www.knoxnews.com/news/2013/mar/20/ut-pulls-state-tax-dollars-campus-sex-week/.

REFERENCES

Alvesson, Mats. 2011. "Leadership and Organizational Culture." In *The Sage Handbook of Leadership* , edited by Alan Bryman, David Collinson, Keith Grint, Brad Jackson, and Mary Uhl-Bien, 151–64. Thousand Oaks, CA: Sage.

Anand, Smriti, Jia Hu, Robert Linden, and Prajya Vidyarthi. 2011. "Leader-Member Exchange: Recent Research Findings and Prospects for the Future." In *The Sage Handbook of Leadership*, edited by Alan Bryman, David Collinson, Keith Grint, Brad Jackson, and Mary Uhl-Bien, 311–25. Thousand Oaks, CA: Sage.

Archibald, Jo-Ann. 2008. *Indigenous Storywork: Educating the Heart, Mind, Body and Spirit.* Vancouver: The University of British Columbia.

Bishop, Ann Peterson, Bharat Mehra, Imani Bazzell, and Cynthia Smith. 2003. "Participatory Action Research and Digital Libraries: Reframing Evaluation." In *Digital Library Use: Social Practice in Design and Evaluation*, edited by Anne Peterson Bishop, Nancy van House, and Barbara Buttenfield, 161–90. Cambridge, MA: MIT Press.

Blanchard, Kenneth, Patricia Zigarmi, and Drea Zigarmi. 1985. *Leadership and the One Minute Manager: Increasing Effectiveness through Situational Leadership.* New York: Morrow.

Boehnke, Megan. 2011. "Is UT at Disadvantage over Partner Benefits? Some on Campus Worry Health Insurance Barrier Deters Unmarried Faculty." *Knoxville News Sentinel,*

March 5. http://www.knoxnews.com/news/2011/mar/05/is-ut-at-disadvantage-over-partner-benefits.

———. 2012a. "UT Faculty Senate to Consider Extending Benefits to Employees' Partners." *Knoxville News Sentinel*, March 11. http://www.knoxnews.com/news/2012/mar/11/no-head-line---benefits.

———. 2012b. "UT Faculty Senate to Take Up Domestic Partner Benefits Resolution." *Knox-ville News Sentinel*, March 12. http://www.knoxnews.com/news/2012/mar/12/faculty-sen-ate-committee-approves-resolution-on.

———. 2012c. "UT Faculty Members Unhappy with Response to Same-Sex Benefits Propo-sal." *Knoxville News Sentinel*, September 25. http://www.knoxnews.com/news/2012/sep/25/ut-faculty-members-unhappy-with-response-to-same.

Braquet, Donna, and Bharat Mehra. 2006. "Contextualizing Internet Use Practices of the Cy-ber-Queer: Empowering Information Realities in Everyday Life." *Proceedings of the American Society for Information Science and Technology* 43: 1–10.

Butera, Steve. 2012. "Some University of Tennessee Employees Fight for Domestic Partner-ship Benefits." *WBIR-TV10*, November 29. http://www.wbir.com/news/article/243551/2/Some-UT-employees-fight-for-domestic-partnership-benefits.

Cardona, Nina. 2012. "Chancellors to UT Faculty: No Change in Benefits for the Unmarried." *Nashville Public Radio 90.3 WPLN Nashville*, September 24. http://wpln.org/?p=41446;%20http://chronicle.com/blogs/ticker/u-of-tennessee-faculty-criticize-chancel-lors-views-on-same-sex-benefits/49496?cid=at&utm_source=at&utm_medium=en.

Clapham, Andrew. 2007. *Human Rights: A Short Introduction*. 1st ed. Oxford, U.K.: Oxford University Press.

Clinton, Hillary. 2011. "Hillary Clinton on Gay Rights Abroad: Secretary of State Delivers Historic LGBT Speech in Geneva." Last modified December 6, 2011. http://www.huffingtonpost.com/2011/12/06/hillary-clinton-gay-rights-speech-gene-va_n_1132392.html.

DeSantis, Nick. 2012. "U. of Tennessee Faculty Criticize Chancellor's Views on Same-Sex Benefits." *The Chronicle of Higher Education*, September 25. http://chronicle.com/blogs/ticker/u-of-tennessee-faculty-criticize-chancellors-views-on-same-sex-benefits/49496?cid=at&utm_source=at&utm_medium=en.

Dewey, Barbara I. 2010. *Transforming Research Libraries for the Global Knowledge Society*. 1st ed. Oxford: Chandos.

Evenson, Shelley. 2006. "Directed Storytelling: Interpreting Experience for Design." In *Design Studies: Theory and Research in Graphic Design*, edited by Audrey Bennett and Steven Heller, 231–39. New York: Princeton Architectural Press.

Feak, Christine, and John Swales. 2009. *Telling a Research Story: Writing a Literature Review*. Ann Arbor: University of Michigan Press.

Fiedler, Fred. 1971. "Validation and Extension of the Contingency Model of Leadership Effec-tiveness: A Review of Empirical Findings." *Psychological Bulletin* 76: 128–48.

Greenwood, Davydd, and Morten Levin. 1998. *Introduction to Action Research: Social Re-search for Social Change*. Thousand Oaks, CA: Sage.

Hanna, Kathleen A., Mindy M. Cooper, and Robin A. Crumrin. 2011. *Diversity Programming and Outreach for Academic Libraries (Information Professional)*. Oxford: Chandos.

Hawaii News Now. 2012. "UT Chancellors: Can't Support Same-Sex Benefits." *Hawaii News Now*, September 25. http://www.hawaiinewsnow.com/story/19631857/ut-chancellors-cant-support-same-sex-benefits.

Hersey, Paul. 1985. *The Situational Leader*. New York: Warner Books.

Hersey, Paul, and Kenneth Blanchard. 1971. *Management of Organizational Behavior*. Engle-wood Cliffs, NJ: Prentice Hall.

Hogg, Michael, Robin Martin, and Karen Weeden. 2003. "Leader-Member Relations and So-cial Identity." In *Leadership and Power: Identity Processes in Groups and Organizations*, edited by Daan van Knippenberg and Michael Hogg, 18–33. London: Sage.

House, Robert, and Terence Mitchell. 1974. "Path-Goal Theory of Leadership." *Contemporary Business* 3: 81–97.

Hunt, Lynn. 2008. *Inventing Human Rights: A History*. New York: W. W. Norton.

Jackson, Brad, and Ken Parry. 2008. *A Very Short Fairly Interesting and Reasonably Cheap Book about Studying Leadership.* Thousand Oaks, CA: Sage.

Jones, Andrew. 2005. "The Anthropology of Leadership: Culture and Corporate Leadership in the American South." *Leadership* 1 (3): 259–78.

Kemmis, Stephen, and Robin McTaggart. 1998. *The Action Research Planner.* Victoria, Australia: Deakin University Press.

Lake, Hillary. 2012. "UT Faculty Senate Wants Same-Sex Benefits; Chancellor's Office Rejects Proposal." *WBIR-TV10*, September 25. http://www.wbir.com/news/article/236100/2/UT-Faculty-Senate-wants-same-sex-benefits-Chancellors-office-rejects-proposal.

Larney, Marjorie. 2009. *LGBT Youth Human Rights: Protecting the Human Rights of LGBT American Secondary School Students.* Saarbrücken, Germany: Lambert Academic.

Local8now.com. 2012. "UT Chancellors: Can't Support Same-Sex Benefits." Local8now.com, September 25. http://www.local8now.com/home/headlines/UT-chancellors-cant-support-same-sex-benefits-171205221.html.

McCormick, Joseph Patrick. 2012. "Tennessee: University Says It Cannot Offer Health Insurance Benefits to Unmarried Gay Couples." *Pink News: Europe's Largest Gay News Service*, September 25. http://www.pinknews.co.uk/2012/09/25/tennessee-university-says-it-cannot-offer-health-insurance-benefits-to-unmarried-gay-couples/.

Mehra, Bharat. 2011. "Integrating LGBTIQ Representations across the Library and Information Science Curriculum: A Strategic Framework for Student-Centered Interventions." In *Serving LGBTIQ Library and Archives Users: Essays on Outreach, Service, Collections and Access*, edited by Ellen Greenblatt, 298–309. Jefferson, NC: McFarland.

———. 2009. "A Road Map for Integrating Socially Relevant Research Projects into a Required Library and Information Science Course: From a Service Model to Community Engagement." In *Service Learning: Linking Library Education and Practice*, edited by Loriene Roy, Kelly Jensen, and Alex Hershey Meyers, 142–52. Chicago: ALA Editions.

———. 2006. "An Action Research (AR) Manifesto for Cyberculture Power to 'Marginalized' Cultures of Difference." In *Critical Cyber-Culture Studies*, edited by David Silver and Adrienne Massanari, 205–15. New York: New York University Press.

Mehra, Bharat, Ann Peterson Bishop, Imani Bazzell, and Cynthia Smith. 2002. "Scenarios in the Afya Project as a Participatory Action Research (PAR) Tool for Studying Information Seeking and Use across the "Digital Divide." *Journal of the American Society of Information Science and Technology* 53 (14): 1259–66.

Mehra, Bharat, and Donna Braquet. Under review. "A Website Evaluation of the Top 25 Public Universities in the United States to Assess their Support for Lesbian, Gay, Bisexual, and Transgender People." *Expanding the Circle: Creating an Inclusive Environment in Higher Education for LGBTQ Students and Studies.* Baltimore, MD: Johns Hopkins University Press.

———. 2011. "Progressive LGBTQ Reference: Coming Out in the 21st Century." *Special Issue: Learning Landscapes and the New Reality, Reference Services Review* 39 (3): 401–22.

———. 2007a. "Library and Information Science Professionals as Community Action Researchers in an Academic Setting: Top Ten Directions to Further Institutional Change for People of Diverse Sexual Orientations and Gender Identities." *Library Trends* 56 (2): 542–65.

———. 2007b. "Process of Information Seeking during 'Queer' Youth Coming-Out Experiences." In *Youth Information Seeking Behaviors: Contexts, Theories, Models and Issues*, edited by Mary Chelton and Colleen Cool, 93–131. Toronto: Scarecrow.

———. 2006. "A 'Queer' Manifesto of Interventions for Libraries to 'Come Out' of the Closet!: A Study of 'Queer' Youth Experiences during the Coming Out Process." *Library and Information Science Research Electronic Journal* 16 (1): http://libres.curtin.edu.au/libres16n1.

Mehra, Bharat, Kendra S. Albright, and Kevin Rioux. 2006. "A Practical Framework for Social Justice Research in the Information Professions." *Proceedings of the 69th Annual Meeting of the American Society for Information Science & Technology 2006: Information Realities: Shaping the Digital Future For All.* Austin, TX, November 3–8.

Mehra, Bharat, Kevin Rioux, and Kendra S. Albright. 2009. "Social Justice in Library and Information Science." In *Encyclopedia of Library and Information Sciences*, edited by M. J. Bates and M. N. Maack. New York: Taylor & Francis.

Mehra, Bharat, and William C. Robinson. 2009. "The Community Engagement Model in Library and Information Science Education: A Case Study of a Collection Development and Management Course." *Journal of Education for Library and Information Science* 50 (1): 15–38.

Mehra, Bharat, and Robert J. Sandusky. 2009. "LIS Students as Community Partners in Elective Courses: Applying Community-Based Action Research to Meet the Needs of Underserved Populations." In *Service Learning: Linking Library Education and Practice*, edited by Loriene Roy, Kelly Jensen, and Alex Hershey Meyers, 153–68. Chicago: ALA Editions.

Mehra, Bharat, and Ramesh Srinivasan. 2007. "The Library-Community Convergence Framework for Community Action: Libraries as Catalysts of Social Change." *Libri: International Journal of Libraries and Information Services* 57 (3): 123–39.

Moyn, Samuel. 2012. *The Last Utopia: Human Rights in History*. Cambridge, MA: Belknap Press.

Obama, Barack. 2012. "Presidential Proclamation: Lesbian, Gay, Bisexual, and Transgender Pride Month, 2012." http://www.whitehouse.gov/the-press-office/2012/06/01/presidential-proclamation-lesbian-gay-bisexual-and-transgender-pride-mon.

Papke, Mary. 2005. "Quality Enhancement Plan for SACS Reaccreditation: The International and Intercultural Awareness Initiative." https://my.tennessee.edu/pls/portal/docs/PAGE/WSG/2005QUALITYENHANCEMENTPLAN/docs/qep.pdf.

Parry, Ken. 2011. "Leadership and Organizational Theory." In *The Sage Handbook of Leadership*, edited by Alan Bryman, David Collinson, Keith Grint, Brad Jackson, and Mary Uhl-Bien, 151–64. Thousand Oaks, CA: Sage.

Rahman, Md. A. 2008. "Some Trends in the Praxis of Participatory Action Research." In *The SAGE Handbook of Action Research*, edited by Peter Reason and Hilary Bradbury, 49–62. London: Sage.

Rayward, W. Boyd. 1975. *The Universe of Information: The Work of Paul Otlet for Documentation and International Organization*. FID Publication 520. Moscow: International Federation for Documentation by All-Union Institute for Scientific and Technical Information (VINITI), Academy of Sciences, USSR.

Reason, Peter, and Hilary Bradbury. 2008. *The Sage Handbook of Action Research: Participative Inquiry and Practice*. London: Sage.

Rooke, David, and William Torbert. 2005. "Seven Transformations of Leadership." *Harvard Business Review*. http://hbr.org/product/seven-transformations-of-leadership/an/R0504D-PDF-ENG.

Samek, Toni. 2007. *Librarianship and Human Rights: A 21st Century Guide*. Chandos Information Professional Series. Atlanta: Neal-Schuman.

Shera, Jesse, and Margaret Elizabeth Egan. 1953. "A Review of the Present State of Librarianship and Documentation." In *Documentation*, edited by Samuel C. Bradford, 11–45. London: Crosby, Lockwood.

Stake, Robert E. 1995. *The Art of Case Study Research*. Thousand Oaks, CA: Sage.

Stringer, Ernest. 1999. *Action Research*. Thousand Oaks, CA: Sage.

Thelin, John. 2007. "Expectations and Reality in American Higher Education." *Thoughts & Action* 7: 59–70. http://www.nea.org/assets/img/PubThoughtAndAction/TAA_07_07.pdf.

Thomas, Gary. 2011. "A Typology for the Case Study in Social Science Following a Review of Definition, Discourse and Structure." *Qualitative Inquiry* 17 (6): 511–21.

Uhl-Bien, Mary. 2006. "Relational Leadership Theory: Exploring the Social Process of Leadership and Organizing." *The Leadership Quarterly* 17: 654–76.

Wood, Elizabeth J., Rush Miller, and Amy Knapp. 2006. *Beyond Survival: Managing Academic Libraries in Transition*. Santa Barbara, CA: Libraries Unlimited.

Yin, Robert K. 2008. *Case Study Research: Design and Methods*. 4th ed. Thousand Oaks, CA: Sage.

———. 2011. *Applications of Case Study Research*. 3rd ed. Thousand Oaks, CA: Sage.

Yukl, Gary. 1989. "Managerial Leadership: A Review of Theory and Research." *Journal of Management* 15 (2): 251–89.

———. 1999. "An Evaluation of Conceptual Weaknesses in Transformational and Charismatic Leadership Theories." *The Leadership Quarterly* 10 (2): 285–305.

———. 2011. "Contingency Theories of Effective Leadership." In *The Sage Handbook of Leadership*, edited by Alan Bryman, David Collinson, Keith Grint, Brad Jackson, and Mary Uhl-Bien, 286–98. Thousand Oaks, CA: Sage.

Index

About the Editors and Contributors

Julie Artman is chair of the Collection Management Division of the Leatherby Libraries and part of the teaching faculty in the Department of Theatre at Chapman University. At the Leatherby Libraries she is chair of public services with oversight of the library's information literacy program, and she previously held positions at the University of California, Los Angeles, and the University of Michigan law libraries. Julie holds masters in drama and library and information science. Her background as a theatre director and actor informs her library leadership explorations, and she is developing a text that unites her love of the theatre with the library.

Donna Braquet has been biology librarian at the John C. Hodges Library at the University of Tennessee for nearly ten years. She was recently appointed special assistant to the vice chancellor for diversity and director of the university's OUTreach: LGBT & Ally Resource Center. She was biomedical librarian at the Georgia Institute of Technology, and she received a masters in library and information science from Louisiana State University in 2000 and a bachelors in biology from the University of New Orleans in 1996.

Marta Mestrovic Deyrup is professor/head of technical services at Seton Hall University Libraries and served for six years as the university's co-director of Women and Gender Studies. She is the editor of *The Irish American Experience in New Jersey and Metropolitan New York: Cultural Identity, Hybridity, and Commemoration* (Lexington, 2013) and *Successful Strategies for Teaching Undergraduate Student Research* (Scarecrow, 2013) and author of *The Polish Community of Wallington, NJ* (Arcadia, 2013) and *The Vita Constantini as Literary and Linguistic Construct for the Early Slavs* (VDM Verlag, 2009).

Bradford Lee Eden is dean of library services at Valparaiso University. His previous positions include associate university librarian for technical services and scholarly communication at the University of California, Santa Barbara; head, Web and Digitization Services, and head, Bibliographic and Metadata Services for the University of Nevada, Las Vegas Libraries. He is editor of OCLC Systems & Services: Digital Library Perspectives International and The Bottom Line: Managing Library Finances and is on the editorial boards of *Library Hi Tech* and *Journal of Film Music*. He has recently been named associate editor/editor-designate of *Library Leadership & Management*, the journal of the Library Leadership & Management Association (LLAMA) within ALA. He has masters and PhD degrees in musicology, as well as a masters in library science. He publishes in the areas of metadata, librarianship, medieval music and liturgy, and J.R.R. Tolkien. His two books *Innovative Redesign and Reorganization of Library Technical Services: Paths for the Future and Case Studies* (Libraries Unlimited, 2004) and *More Innovative Redesign and Reorganization of Library Technical Services* (Libraries Unlimited, 2009) are used and cited extensively in the field. He is the author of Metadata and Its Applications (ALA TechSource, 2002), *3D Visualization Techniques* (ALA TechSource, 2005), *Innovative Digital Projects in the Humanities* (ALA TechSource, 2005), *Metadata and Its Applications: New Directions and Updates* (ALA TechSource, 2005), *FRBR: Functional Requirements for Bibliographic Records* (ALA TechSource, 2006), and *Information Organization Future for Libraries* (ALA TechSource, 2007). His recent books include *Middle-earth Minstrel: Essays on Music in Tolkien* (McFarland, 2010) and *The Associate University Librarian Handbook: A Resource Guide* (Scarecrow Press, 2012).

Jody Condit Fagan serves as director of scholarly content systems and associate professor at James Madison University. She is a PhD candidate in JMU's School of Strategic Leadership Studies. She previously worked at Morris Library, Southern Illinois University Carbondale, where she also obtained a master's degree in history; she received her MLS from the College of Information Studies at the University of Maryland, College Park. Jody is currently the editor of the *Journal of Web Librarianship* and has recently published two books, *Comic Book Collections for Libraries* with Bryan D. Fagan (Libraries Unlimited, 2011) and *Web Project Management for Academic Libraries* (Chandos, 2009) with Jennifer A. Keach.

Deborah S. Garson is head of the Research and Instruction Services Department, Monroe C. Gutman Library and instructor in Education at Harvard University Graduate School of Education. She co-teaches the doctoral seminar Researching and Writing a Critical Literature Review (S553). She has responsibility for the research and instruction services of the library and the Gutman Library Writing Services. She is a member of the Research, Teaching and Learning Working Group, served on the Harvard University Library Committee for Public Services, and chaired the Learning Opportunities Advisory Group for the Harvard Libraries. Deborah holds a Masters of Education in Administration, Planning, and Social Policy from the Harvard Graduate School of Education and an MS in Information Science from Simmons College Graduate School of Library and Information Science. She has spent her career in academic libraries, including those of MIT and George Washington University. As a member of the Special Libraries Association (SLA) since 1990, she served as program planner, membership and past chair of the Education Division. She has been a speaker at SLA, the Association of College and Research Libraries (ACRL), and American Educational Research Association (AERA), addressing such topics as embedded librarianship, developing an online tutorial, citation instruction, and the Internet as a resource and research tool. She is also a member of SLA's Boston chapter and has served in a leadership role on various committees. She has reviewed books for HGSE's Usable Knowledge and contributed to other publications. She has been a co-author of "New and Forthcoming in Reference," a regularly featured column in *Education Libraries*, a peer-reviewed publication of the SLA Education Division. Additionally, she is a section contributor to *Magazines for Libraries*. She was awarded the Anne Galler Award for professional excellence by the Education Division and a Chapter Achievement Award by the Boston chapter of the SLA.

Michael Germano is tenured as an associate librarian at California State University, Los Angeles, and publishes and speaks frequently about the importance of strategic innovation in marketing libraries and information resources. He is also an adjunct professor in the Department of Marketing where he teaches courses in sales, community-based social marketing, and social media marketing. Trained as an attorney and librarian (he holds a juris doctorate from Temple University and masters in information science from Simmons College), he is particularly interested in the ways in which leadership and culture influence customer experiences. He holds an undergraduate degree in English with a minor in financial economics from St. Joseph's University. He holds an additional graduate degree in English from New York University. Prior to his appointment at CSULA he worked in a variety of sales and marketing positions at LexisNexis, a subsidiary of Reed Elsevier.

Starr Hoffman is the journalism and digital resources librarian at Columbia University and is also visiting assistant professor at Pratt Institute's School of Information and Library Science. At Columbia, her primary activities include reference, instruction, support for data-intensive research, collection development, and social media outreach. She has a PhD in Higher Education (Library Science minor), a masters in Library Science, and a masters in Art History. Her ongoing research focuses on academic library leadership, higher education mentoring, emerging models of scholarly communication, and online presence among librarians. Publications, experience, and blog can be found on her e-portfolio:http://geekyartistlibrarian.wordpress.com/. She is pleased to connect with others about research, librarianship, or snarky comments on Twitter: @artgeeklibraria.

Jason Martin is the head of public services at the duPont-Ball Library at Stetson University. He also served as an associate librarian at the University of Central Florida and as an assistant librarian at Louisiana State University. Jason received his masters in Library and Information Science from the University of South Florida and his PhD in Education in Educational Leadership, Higher Education Policy Studies from the University of Central Florida.

Bharat Mehra is associate professor in the School of Information Sciences. His research furthers diversity and intercultural communication and addresses social justice and social equity agendas to meet the needs of minority and underserved populations (e.g., lesbian, gay, bisexual, and transgendered people; racial and ethnic minorities; international communities; low-income families; and rural residents). He has applied conceptual frameworks in library and information science (e.g., human information behavior, information seeking and use, social informatics, etc.) in combination with interdisciplinary approaches from critical theory, feminist and cross-cultural studies, postcolonial literature, race and gender research, and community informatics or the use of information and communication technologies to enable and empower disenfranchised communities to bring changes in their sociocultural, sociopolitical, and socioeconomic circumstances. He is the principal investigator of two external grants funded by the Institute of Museum and Library Services entitled "Information Technology Rural Librarian Master's Scholarship Program" (Part 1 and Part 2) that are educating and training information professionals in the southern and central Appalachian region to positively respond to challenges in the 21st century. Dr. Mehra teaches courses on public library management, information organization, collection development, diversity services in libraries, resources for adults (fiction and fiction), and grant development for information professionals.

Susan E. Parker is deputy university librarian at the University Library at UCLA. In addition, she was associate dean of the Library at California State University, Northridge, and has held leadership positions in public and administrative services in the libraries of Tufts University and Harvard Law

School. She holds an MLS from Queens College, City University of New York; an MA in U.S. History from Indiana University; and a BA in History and American Studies with honors from Earlham College. She received her PhD in Industrial and Organizational Psychology from Capella University. Her doctoral dissertation is "Organizational Learning, Innovation, and Employees' Mental Models of Change Following a Disaster: A Case Study of the Morgan Library at Colorado State University." She is a member of the 2003 class of UCLA Senior Fellows in Information Studies and has been selected as an ARL Leadership Fellow for 2013–15. Her expertise is in library leadership, library organizations, and library disaster recovery, as well as budgeting, strategic planning and assessment processes, and buildings and services planning and renovation. Her most recent published works include three chapters in the *The Associate University Librarian Handbook* (Scarecrow Press, 2012) and "Innovation and Change: Influences of Pre-Disaster Leadership in a Post-Disaster Environment" in Volume 31 of *Advances in Library Administration and Organization* (Emerald Group Publishing, 2012).

Dominique Roberts holds JD and MLIS degrees and has experience working in private and public academic libraries. She is an attorney and resides in Los Angeles, California.

Andrew F. Wall is associate professor of higher education and department chair of Education Leadership at the Warner School of Education at the University of Rochester. Andrew also serves at the co-interim director of the Warner Center for Professional Development and Educational Reform and co-chair of the University of Rochester Faculty Senate. He earned his bachelor's from the University of Iowa in Sociology and Political Science, master's in Education from Ball State University, and PhD in Education from the University of Illinois Urbana-Champaign in 2005. His research is in three domains: college student health and learning, assessment and evaluation, and organization, governance, and policy of higher education. His recently published research focuses on college student alcohol use, assessment and evaluation in higher education, and organizational factors related to student success in higher education.

Debra Wallace is executive director, Knowledge and Library Services, Harvard Business School. With a team of over 50 librarians, economists, statisticians, journalists, and information management professionals housed in Baker Library, she oversees a preeminent collection of contemporary and historical business information and a range of custom services for Harvard Business School's diverse community. She is responsible for leveraging the world of business information and the school's priority content to enable high performance in the complex teaching, learning, and research environment at HBS and to further research by scholars from around the world. Her special interest is the role of information in learning—how to find it, use it, package, and present it—to enable effective teaching and promote student learning. She is also a member of the Harvard Library Leadership Team and chair of the Harvard Library Directors' Group. She holds a masters of Education from the University of Manitoba and a PhD from the University of Toronto. She has been at HBS since 2005, and in her current role since 2011.

Kristen E. Willmott earned her PhD in higher education from the University of Rochester. She has a master's in business service management from the Rochester Institute of Technology and a bachelor's in English from Ithaca College. She has a background in higher education administration, admissions, and finance, having worked as an admissions and financial aid officer for the Graduate School of Arts and Sciences at Harvard University from 2005 to 2009. She has also worked as an adjunct instructor for Newbury College, the Harvard University Extension School graduate business program, and Finger Lakes Community College. Willlmott was awarded the Susan B. Anthony Institute for Gender and Women's Studies Annual Dissertation Award in 2013. She is director of Application Boot Camp, a college and graduate school admissions consulting firm based in Concord, MA. Willmott's recently published research has appeared in journals including the *Journal of Cases in Educational Leadership*, *Academic Leadership*, and the *American Association of Behavioral and Social Sciences Journal*. Her research focus centers on tenure, work-life-family management, academic parenting, and underrepresented college student experiences.